Peer Review

Issues in Academic Ethics
Series Editor: Steven M. Cahn

Peer Review

A Critical Inquiry

David Shatz

ROWMAN & LITTLEFIELD PUBLISHERS, INC.
Lanham • Boulder • New York • Toronto • Oxford

ROWMAN & LITTLEFIELD PUBLISHERS, INC.

Published in the United States of America
by Rowman & Littlefield Publishers, Inc.
A wholly owned subsidiary of The Rowman & Littlefield Publishing Group, Inc.
4501 Forbes Boulevard, Suite 200, Lanham, Maryland 20706
www.rowmanlittlefield.com

PO Box 317
Oxford
OX2 9RU, UK

British Library Cataloguing in Publication Information Available

Library of Congress Cataloging-in-Publication Data

Shatz, David.
  Peer review : a critical inquiry / David Shatz.
    p. cm. — (Issues in academic ethics)
  Includes bibliographical references and index.
  ISBN 0-7425-1434-X (hardcover : alk. paper) — ISBN 0-7425-1435-8 (pbk. : alk.
paper)
  1. Scholarly publishing. 2. Peer review. 3. Scholarly electronic publishing. 4.
College teachers—Professional ethics. I. Title. II. Series.
  Z286.S37S53 2004
  070.5—dc22
                                                    2004007919

Printed in the United States of America

To Meira and Raphael, Gedalyah,
and
Daniel, Samuel, Aaron, and Ariella
The best children and grandchildren in the whole wide world, of course

Contents

Acknowledgments

A foundational principle of peer review is that criticism by others can improve a work. That thesis, I think, is amply confirmed by the present book.

Atara Graubard Segal generously read the entire manuscript, including multiple drafts of certain chapters, and wrote comments on almost every page. Her astute questions, criticisms, and suggestions, both stylistic and substantive, led to many a revision; and I have credited her in the text and notes with several important points. I am deeply grateful.

At a later stage, my colleague David Johnson read the entire manuscript with his characteristic care and attention to detail, providing me with another set of penetrating and valuable comments with which to work.

Likewise my profound thanks go to Hilary Kornblith, who graciously read chapters 2–4 and upon receiving each, furnished valuable comments literally within hours. Some of his communications are quoted and discussed in the text. David Berger gave me swift and incisive feedback on the introduction and on chapters 4 and 5. Jonathan Adler provided enjoyable and profitable discussion as well as important detailed comments on chapters 2 and 3. Michael Levin was of enormous help in formulating the original *Monist* article on which chapter 1 is based, and more recently shared some thoughts on chapter 3 as well. I also profited from conversations and correspondence with Margarita Levin, William Kolbrener, and Herbert Leventer about several topics taken up in the book.

Liora Schmelkin kindly shared an excellent paper she wrote on peer review, leading me to literature I had missed and raising important points.

Herbert Leventer and Edward Reichman periodically sent me materials on peer review in medicine, greatly strengthening my bibliography, and also responded to other queries concerning the medical literature. Aaron Levine referred me to an important work on peer review in economics. Pearl Berger pointed me to some crucial articles relevant to chapter 6, assisted me in locating material, and commented valuably on part of the chapter.

My mentor, the late Sidney Morgenbesser was ailing, and I could not burden him with reading the manuscript. But in everything I write, his spirited love of philosophy is an animating force.

I also thank Steven M. Cahn, editor of the series of which this book is a part. Once my teacher, Steve is now a good friend and a collaborator twice over. He has many books to his credit, along with several series editorships, and it is no fluke that he has acquired a reputation as the best editor in the field. His book *Saints and Scamps* pioneered the field of academic ethics, and the existence of Rowman & Littlefield's series on that subject is testament to Steve's creative notions about the directions philosophy can take. His clarity, organization, and efficiency, combined with his understanding, make working with him a pleasure and privilege.

Part of this book was written with the assistance of a summer faculty fellowship from Yeshiva University. I am indebted to Karen Bacon, dean of Yeshiva's Stern College for Women, and Morton Lowengrub, Vice-President for Academic Affairs of the university, for their continuing support of my scholarly work. Yeshiva University, and in particular Rabbi Robert S. Hirt, senior advisor to the president, afforded me the opportunity to edit the *Torah u-Madda Journal* these past five years. The editorial experience I gained from that journal helped me to see firsthand, and to work through, some of the dilemmas and issues with which this book is concerned.

Eve deVaro, Tessa Fallon, and Jason Proetorius of Rowman & Littlefield were a pleasure to work with as they moved the book into and through production.

My wife Chani, ever supportive and understanding, lovingly respected the consuming schedule I had to keep, especially while the book was being completed. She joins me in dedicating this volume, with love, to our precious daughter, son, son-in-law, and grandchildren, the lights of our lives.

Permission to reprint the following articles is gratefully acknowledged.

Chapter 1, "Peer Review and the Marketplace of Ideas," by David Shatz, originally appeared as "Is Peer Review Overrated?" in *The Monist* 79, no. 4 (October 1996): 536–63. Reprinted with permission from Open Court Publishing.

Supplementary Essays

"Ethics and Manuscript Reviewing," by Richard T. De George and Fred Woodward, was originally published in *Scholarly Publishing* 25, no. 3 (April 1994): 133–45. Reprinted with permission from the University of Toronto Press.

"Why Be My Colleague's Keeper? Moral Justifications for Peer Review," by Joe Cain, was originally published in *Science and Engineering Ethics* 5, no. 4 (1999): 531–40. Reprinted with permission from Opragen Publications. Notes have been reformatted.

"Peer-Review Practices of Psychological Journals: The Fate of Published Articles, Submitted Again," by Douglas P. Peters and Stephen J. Ceci, is reprinted from *Peer Commentary on Peer Review*, ed. Stevan J. Harnad (Cambridge: Cambridge University Press, 1982), 3–11, and originally appeared in *Behavioral and Brain Sciences* 5, no. 2 (1982). Reprinted with permission from Cambridge University Press.

"No Bias, No Merit: The Case against Blind Submission," by Stanley Fish, originally appeared in *PMLA* (1988): 739–48. Reprinted with permission from the Modern Language Association of America.

"Fish on Blind Submission," by Jeffrey Skoblow, originally appeared as a letter to the editor in *PMLA* (1989): 216. Reprinted with permission from the Modern Language Association of America.

"Reply to Skoblow," by Stanley Fish, originally appeared as a letter to the editor in *PMLA* (1989): 220. Reprinted with permission from the Modern Language Association of America.

"The Invisible Hand of Peer Review," by Stevan J. Harnad, originally appeared in *Exploit Interactive* 5 (April 2000), www.exploit-lib.org/issue5/peer-review/. Reprinted with permission from the author. Notes have been reformatted.

Introduction

Anyone who labors at academic scholarship knows how dependent that enterprise is on a procedure known as "peer review." A scholar submits a work to a journal, press, or conference committee, or sends a proposal to a foundation; the submission is then evaluated by other professionals who are experts in the area covered by the work. The judgment of these referees determines whether the work is published by the target journal or press, appears on the conference program, or is funded by the desired institution. If rejected by peers at one venue, the work will have to be floated elsewhere—and its ultimate fate may well be oblivion.

The peer review system is often described as a system of certification, and indeed it is, in two senses: acceptance to a journal or publishing house via peer review certifies a body of work, and it also certifies the scholar who produced it. As commonly conceived, to say of a published article or book that it was peer reviewed is to say that it is perceived by experts as a contribution to human knowledge.[1] Much of what people believe at a given time about critical issues, from treatments for liver cancer to what Hume held about time, depends on what has passed peer review. Peer review is a mechanism, then, for quality control; it protects us from contamination by error and poor argument, and affords us truth or contributions to attaining truth.[2]

As I said, the peer review system also certifies the scholar who produced the peer reviewed work. Peer reviewed articles and books are the gold standard as far as hiring, tenure, and promotion committees are concerned. Such committees often look askance at publications that were invited and not peer reviewed. What does not pass peer review, goes the thinking, has no claim to be a valid contribution to human knowledge. Tensions run high since in many fields, particularly the humanities, the overwhelming majority of peer reviewed submissions are rejected.[3] Indeed, careers are often made or destroyed by the process.

Problems with Peer Review

How compelling is this rationale for peer review as a system of quality control or method of certification? Is the system appropriate as is, or should it be reformed or replaced? These questions are acute in light of empirical studies of peer review published during the past quarter century.[4] Such studies, found primarily in the medical and social science literature, raise serious questions about whether peer review is fulfilling its function.

- In one study, investigators deliberately inserted errors into a manuscript, and referees did a poor job of detecting them.
  Conclusion: peer reviewers do a poor job of controlling quality.
- In another study, papers that had been published in journals by authors from prestigious institutions were retyped and resubmitted with a nonprestigious affiliation indicated for the author. Not only did referees mostly fail to recognize these previously published papers in their field, they recommended rejection.
  Conclusion: Referees are biased for authors from prestigious institutions and against authors from nonprestigious ones. They are also not conversant with the published literature.
- Another investigator prepared two versions of a paper describing a certain study. The introduction, description of methodology, and bibliography were identical in both papers, and they differed only in the results the study brought. One version described results that supported a certain view that the referees antecedently believed, and the other had results that negated this antecedently believed position. The referees rated the positive papers high and the negative papers low.
  Conclusion: Referees are biased toward papers that affirm their prior convictions.
- Other researchers have discovered that many heavily cited papers, including some describing work which won a Nobel Prize, were originally rejected by peer review.
  Conclusion: Referees are biased against innovation and/or are poor judges of quality.

Beyond the empirical studies, there are numerous instances of falsehood and fraud that got through the refereeing system. Indeed to call peer reviewed published material "a contribution to human knowledge," as we suggested earlier, is to sound oblivious of the many peer reviewed articles that are subjects of controversy or have turned out to be fraudulent or mistaken.[5]

The cumulative effect of the studies and of experience with peer reviewed articles is to suggest, critics say, that the system does not, in fact, always work. It suffers from widespread bias, subjectivity, and incompetence—and therefore should be reformed or replaced. Falsehoods have been admitted into our belief corpus; truths have been barred from the literature; careers have been ruined or built unjustly.

Some ideas for reform have been implemented as the need for change has become appreciated, but not all problems are solved by those reforms. To solve the problem of bias toward certain institutions and against others, as well as to prevent any other biases such as gender bias, many journals use blind review, in which the reader does not know the author's identity. But apart from problems that can be raised against blind review and that we will explore, we remain with the problem of bias toward certain conclusions and of sheer incompetence vis-à-vis detecting errors and not appreciating truths. And the peer review system is encountering resistance from another quarter as well: the fast pace of modern society and technology. Commenting on medical and perhaps other scientific journals, Robert H. Fletcher and Suzanne W. Fletcher of Harvard Medical School maintain:

> Traditional practices are under threat. The media are clamoring for information faster than traditional peer review and publishing can accommodate. Authors increasingly bypass journals and announce their results directly to the public through the media, even when this is not clearly in the public interest. Advances in electronic information systems are removing technical barriers to access to research results imposed by limits on space and the slow turn-around characteristic of paper-based journals. Western societies are impatient and information hungry and traditional peer review and publishing fit uncomfortably into the culture. Without strong evidence for what is gained by peer review and publishing, we are in danger of abandoning all that might be good about the traditional process in search of more speed and volume of information. We ask as much in other aspects of science and should expect it from our journals.[6]

While the media are not knocking on the doors of philosophers and historians out of hunger for the latest developments in those disciplines, the general quest for speed and the demand for evidence of what is gained affects those fields as well. So far, many feel the required evidence of benefits from peer review is lacking.

A Strange Asymmetry

Peer review, then, has fallen on hard times. The aim of the present volume is to examine critical ethical and epistemological issues that lie at the heart of current scholarly debate about peer review and to evaluate various arguments and proposals for altering the system.

Surprisingly, this is the first book-length study of peer review that utilizes methods and resources of contemporary philosophy. In fact, it is the first wide-ranging treatment of the subject by a scholar in the humanities. I say "surprisingly" because given the ubiquity and importance of evaluation in academia, and the frustrations aroused by the difficulty of publishing in the humanities due to high rejection rates in peer reviewed journals and publishing houses, one would expect that peer review would be existentially crucial and therefore be extensively discussed in print (peer reviewed or otherwise). Furthermore, peer evaluation raises issues about the import and basis of evaluative judgments and the value of free expression, issues of interest to scholars in the humanities. Besides its ethical aspect, the topic also has dimensions of epistemological significance, since it implicates such concepts as truth, bias, relativism, conservatism, consensus, and standards of good argument. Philosophers and other humanities scholars have produced a voluminous literature on these subjects. Yet they have not applied their approaches to these topics to peer review itself, that is, to the very procedures and practices that produced much of the voluminous literature in ethics, epistemology, and so many other fields. Specialists in fields of the humanities have not organized and sparked a systematic and ongoing debate. Why is this?

The paucity of humanities literature on peer review becomes truly striking when we realize that sociologists, psychologists, physical scientists, and medical researchers have produced an immense literature on peer review, one that brings to light both strengths of the system and serious doubts about its reliability, objectivity, and even desirability. Professionals in the natural and social sciences have subjected peer review to both scathing criticism and vigorous defense, with medicine taking the lead, followed by psychology and sociology.[7] The distinguished medical journal *JAMA* (*Journal of the American Medical Association*) has devoted substantial parts of full issues to the pros and cons of peer review, including papers from international congresses held every four years since 1989, and in general major medical journals have published a substantial number of peer review studies. The journal *Behavioral and*

Brain Sciences dedicated issues to the topic in 1982 and 1991. The literature on peer review in the sciences and social sciences can only be described as vast; indeed, there has come into being a field called "journalology," the study of journals and their practices.

The differing amounts of ink spilled on the topic by social scientists and medical practitioners on the one hand and by humanists on the other cries out for explanation. I have no definite explanation to offer for the contrast, but I advance a few speculations to account for it.

The first is economic. To a certain extent scientific researchers live or die by the peer review system, for their ability to carry out research and conduct experiments depends on the availability of grants, to an extent that is not matched in the humanities. This point might at first glance explain only why peer review of *grant applications* would elicit discussion among scientists and social scientists. But the prospects for securing a grant in turn depend on an applicant's track record of publications and previous grants, so peer review of publications is critical; and vice versa, without grants, scientists often cannot publish because they cannot do research. Now obviously these economic implications of peer review are not wholly inapplicable to the humanities—as I said, careers hinge on the peer review process. Still, in the humanities the ability to conduct daily scholarly activities of teaching and research does not as a rule depend on a steady flow of financial resources. Since scientists in both the physical and social sciences have a greater stake in the peer review system than do their counterparts in the humanities, perhaps as a result they devote more explicit attention to the problems it faces.

A second possible explanation has to do with the disparate attitudes of scientists and humanists to the worst-case scenario in which a particular work of theirs is not accepted for publication. The scientist (especially in mathematics and the physical and biological sciences, but also in social science to an extent) sees his or her research to be related to truth in a way that humanists do not. In the scientist's perception, the state of human knowledge will be poorer in concrete ways if there is a wrong decision about publication or funding. Science, in the opinion of many working scientists, grows incrementally, by a steady accumulation of truths. Every experimental result is therefore in the experimenter's mind a small but possibly crucial step forward for humanity, a step that allows others to tread further, a potential addition to the stock of truths or to the evidential base for truths already accepted. It is true that some philosophers deny that science grows by accretion,[8] but this perspective does not necessarily infiltrate the everyday, philosophically and historically unreflective consciousness of a working scientist. And while "the science wars" (the altercation between conservative scientists and adherents of leftist movements such as feminism, multiculturalism, and postmodernism, who see science as a social construction) is a well-known part of academic culture, it may not occur to most scientists to seriously raise unsettling philosophical questions about relativism, historicism, skepticism, and pluralism—and if they raise them, as physicist Alan Sokal did in a celebrated hoax he pulled on a postmodernist journal, they reject these troubling "isms."[9]

The situation in the humanities is different. While philosophical trends and views change, in today's climate many philosophers and professors of literature would not view their conclusions as "the truth." Those in the humanities are likely to be influenced, even if only subtly, by relativism, historicism, skepticism, and pluralism, and thus to have more inhibitions about conceiving their own views as "the truth." If a paper goes unpublished, they may feel, "truth" isn't lost to the world. Now one might have thought that the impact of postmodernism would be to criticize strongly the restrictive effects of peer review and to adopt an "anything goes" approach, because "the journal submission, reviewing and accepting process is predicated on the assumption that there is a singular reality that can be manipulated, conjured, weighed and judged by authors, reviewers, and editors. Gatekeeping . . . implies that that which is kept out can be convincingly demonstrated to be undesirable and vice versa for what is accepted. . . . If there is no totalizing narrative of truth, how can we go on?"[10] If my speculation is right, however, authors in the humanities are willing to accept that their community (i.e., peer reviewers in the discipline) set the standard even if in their view there is no absolute truth that either authors or referees can possess.

Furthermore, propositions in the humanities notoriously will elicit disagreement to an extent far greater than will scientific conclusions. It is no surprise that interreferee agreement (what social scientists call "reliability") is harder to attain in the humanities than in the hard sciences and even social sciences. In the humanities, more than sciences, and certainly more than mathematics, we live in disagreement; dispute is the animating force of the profession. Correlatively, in the sciences you can sometimes *show* that a peer review was wrong, while in the humanities you very rarely can. Thus there is a far more concrete basis for criticizing the review process in the sciences.[11]

In addition, humanities scholars spend much of their professional time in an ivory tower built far above the everyday world—and they know it. When a paper offering a new and correct interpretation of Hume is rejected for publication, the practical loss to the world is far smaller than when a study of alternative treatments for liver cancer is wrongly judged to be invalid. Of course an author writing on Hume could suffer a severe bruise to the ego from rejection, which might precipitate thoughts of writing on peer review, but colleagues may very well shrug off the rejection on the grounds that the world has not suffered a major loss, and therefore not join in the battle. In some areas, such as political philosophy, ethics, and philosophy of religion, the conclusions drawn by authors are often indeed important, but in many areas conclusions will not be perceived as important to the world. And even in the "important" areas, conclusions are hard to deliver with true persuasiveness.

Other considerations come to mind as well to account for the difference between the sciences and the humanities. In science some of the discussion of peer review has been propelled by instances of fabrication, which occur less frequently in the humanities.[12] Again, an assessment of peer review requires empirical studies, which practitioners of the humanities are not trained to undertake; their tenure and promotion committees, moreover, may not regard an empirical study on peer review as a contribution to a humanities scholar's field of expertise. Those in the sciences can afford to write on peer review because their writing consists of scientific studies that will be counted as research in their field.

No matter how many explanations are proffered for the neglect of peer review by those in the humanities, the phenomenon remains surprising. Yet whatever the explanation for the previous near-silence of humanities scholars on the subject, my aim in this book is to begin filling the gap I have described, to initiate an examination of the theoretical underpinnings of the process of peer review and of its value. My objective is to state what assumptions lie behind peer review, what justifies the practice, what its flaws are, how it can be improved, and whether it is overvalued in the scholarly community as a requirement for appointment, tenure, and promotion.

The Multiple Meanings of "Peer Review"

A word about terminology is in order. In contexts outside academia, peer review is simply the evaluation of another's performance by a peer, that is, another professional. In an academic context, this usage of "peer review" refers to an evaluation of all aspects of a professor's performance, including not only scholarship but also teaching and committee service. In academia, though, the term usually conjures up something narrower, namely, the review of articles or books that have been submitted for publication, of articles or books that have already been published, and of proposed research projects. My focus will be this narrow one, that is, the evaluation of scholarship, to the exclusion of such categories as teaching and service to the university. I include in my purview both prepublication peer review of manuscripts by referees and editors and postpublication review by evaluators who decide on hiring, tenure, promotion, and salaries. The relationship between these two kinds of evaluation of scholarship itself needs to be elucidated, and I undertake that as well.

With regard to prepublication review, "peer review" has a narrow and a broad sense. In the narrow sense peer review refers to the process in which a journal editor sends out submitted materials to specialists, experts in the subject of the author's article or book. In this narrow usage, an article is not being peer reviewed when an editor makes decisions about acceptance or rejection without outside consultation. In the broader usage, however, review by any other professional, including the journal's editor, is called peer review, even if the "peer" is not truly a "peer" because he or she is not as great an expert in the field as the author.[13] When people refer to the historical advent of peer review, they sometimes date it by the shift from review by an editor to review by external referees. At least two top philosophy journals, the *Journal of Philosophy* and the *Philosophical Review*, are still generally refereed by the editors (of whom there are many). For purposes of this book it will not matter, except for a few cases I will specify, whether review of an article is conducted by an outside referee or an editor or some other in-house person or persons. But please note that the choice between editor's review and external review is not a matter of indifference. On the one hand, external refereeing causes delays that could be averted when an editor conducts the review, and, furthermore, external referees may consciously or unconsciously wish a journal to take a certain direction and may recommend acceptance or rejection on this basis;[14] on the other hand, an editor may not be as expert as external referees and therefore cannot judge the submission as well.[15] The distinction between editor and external reviewer is simply not germane to my discussion except to the extent that blind review by an editor is unlikely.

I will be confining my discussion to evaluation of journal and book submissions. Peer review of grant proposals is obviously related to journal and book evaluation, but I leave it out of the discussion because of the additional issues it raises.

The Technological Revolution

As hinted earlier, what gives urgency to the topic of peer review is a revolution taking place in scholarly communication. As technology advances it becomes possible to make every work electronically available to all scholars as soon as it is completed, obviating traditional printed volumes and the refereeing process that traditionally dictates their content. E-mail and the World Wide Web have eliminated the practical constraints that until now have made it impossible for journals to publish huge amounts of material and for libraries to acquire and store them. More—much more—can be "published" online, and without the long delays and immense backlogs that previously plagued scholarly production. We therefore confront interesting and formidable choices.

Should this increased capacity for communication be accompanied by an effort to exploit the possibility of instant communication, relax standards of peer review, and present more material quickly for consumption and review by the entire scholarly community? Or is there inherent value in the current high rejection rates? Furthermore, since many electronic journals are unrefereed, how should unrefereed electronic material, such as papers on a website, be evaluated by hiring, tenure, and promotion committees?[16] Should the peer reviewed publication continue to be the gold standard of scholarship in evaluating applicants for job vacancies, tenure, and promotion? Is there value in utilizing selected experts as confidential reviewers, or should we invite input from all those who are interested in a subject? Long before the technological revolution, questions were raised about the need for peer review and the adequacy of the system. Although the revolution has brought some new questions, it has for the most part pushed us to reexamine familiar, well-worn issues.

A physicist formerly at the Los Alamos Lab and now at Cornell University, Paul Ginsparg, has pushed the envelope on these issues by creating an archive of unrefereed physics "e-prints" which is now "the primary means for today's physicists to exchange information."[17] According to Ginsparg, "Traditional peer review has always been an awkward compromise imposed by the inadequacies of the paper medium." It is, he asserts, "organized by multinational commercial publishers." Cosmologist Alan Guth is quoted as saying that "The journals are now playing the role of being historical arbiters of truth rather than real disseminators on a day-to-day basis." Scientists who post papers on Ginsparg's site revise their submissions in response to feedback from others. Worldwide readership discovers errors quickly and reduces duplication. (There is some quality control by which submissions from "random passers-by" are bounced.) Some in the medical community have resisted posting e-prints for fear that the public would rush to unfounded cures. Where different disciplines should go with regard to Web publication and peer review is an intriguing issue.

A Look Ahead

Let me lay out the plan of the book.

In chapter 1, I explore a neglected problem about peer review. Much of Western thinking has displayed a commitment to the "liberal" idea that truth is most likely to emerge when ideas proliferate and come into clash with one another in the "marketplace" of ideas. But peer review, far from seeking to proliferate ideas, seeks to limit the number and range of ideas that reach the public—indeed, the higher a journal's rejection rate, the better the journal is thought to be. The chapter examines a variety of solutions a liberal may offer to this problem, and concludes that none of those responses are truly consistent with liberalism. Peer review therefore makes most sense in a nonliberal framework, or perhaps a modified liberal one. The marketplace conception is false: there is a significant downside to inundation, to too many ideas being in circulation. Experts are charged with controlling—including limiting—the flow of communication.

Chapter 2 explores the most widely discussed issue in the peer review literature, the alleged bias of referees. I distinguish several types of bias—mainly *ad hominem*, affiliational, and ideological—and consider a widely utilized solution to *ad hominem* and affiliational bias, namely blind review, in which the reviewer does not know the author's identity (and often vice versa). I point out that there are serious objections to blind review, and I put forth responses to these objections. The conclusion of this examination is that blind review ought to be adopted but certain exceptions must be admitted.

In chapter 3, I turn to ideological bias, a type of bias in which a referee judges a paper favorably or unfavorably depending upon whether he or she antecedently believes the paper's conclusion. Ideological bias is linked to the charge of conservatism often leveled at peer review: referees and editors, we are told, tend to endorse the paradigm, or generally accepted theory, discouraging innovation. I argue that this stance of conservatism is not as negative as one might think since (a) there is a principle of conservatism recognized by many epistemologists as legitimate; (b) in the nature of the case it is likely that a paradigm will have greater evidential and argumentative support than a new theory. Nonetheless, the chapter develops several responses to these points, that is, various ways to either defuse the principle of conservatism or else to argue that despite the principle of conservatism, innovative papers should be accepted by editors.

In chapter 4, I turn to the subject of book reviews. The reason I cover this topic is twofold. First, book reviews are a form of peer review—they represent a published, unblinded peer review of an author's work. Second, perhaps more significantly, book reviews are an exception to the principle that contributions to scholarly journals require peer review. Generally book reviews are accepted to a journal as is without being revised. This procedure goes against the requirements of peer review. I explain three theories of why book reviews exist and relate these to the problems I identify. The conclusion of the chapter is that book reviews must be improved in specific ways.

Chapter 5 turns to another question: how should hiring, promotion, and tenure committees view works that have not been peer reviewed? The instance I focus on is that of invited articles. I argue that invited articles ought not to be denigrated by hiring, tenure, and promotion committees, for they are subject to postpublication review by experts whom the committees consult. These experts have the benefit of hindsight—they know to what extent the article has influenced the field. This, I maintain, makes the postpublication review potentially more helpful than the knowledge an article was peer reviewed. This point has application to Web publishing, the subject of chapter 6.

In the book's final chapter (6), I discuss the future of peer review. There I explore the question of the Internet's impact, referred to earlier in this introduction. I discuss the advantages and disadvantages of Web publishing—with stress on the advantages—and weigh five strategies for utilizing—or not utilizing—peer review in a Web environment. The chapter brings together several of the issues confronted earlier in the book and in that sense is a fitting capstone.

The chapters I have written are followed by supplementary readings. Many of these readings are referred to in my discussions. They will broaden and enhance the reader's understanding of topics covered in the book, as well as broach a few additional issues.

This book is a study of selected problems and does not enter into every issue that arises with regard to peer review. Topics that are omitted or touched on only lightly in this book include: how to improve peer review vis-à-vis the detection of fraud and plagiarism; the responsibility of referees when fraud and plagiarism are discovered; the obligation of referees not to plagiarize ideas from manuscripts they review and not to share those manuscripts with anyone; the morality of hoaxes used by social scientists in studying peer review; the appropriateness of publishing scientific findings which could undercut the attainment of societal goals like equality; how to allocate credit for multiply authored papers; the propriety of duplication in publication; "double jeopardy" refereeing, in which the same referee who recommended rejection of manuscript X to one journal referees X for another journal; the propriety of submitting the same work to more than one venue, a practice accepted by law reviews and most presses but prohibited by most scholarly journals. One might also be interested in expanded treatments of truth, consensus, and other concepts as they function in a peer review context. The subject of peer review is very rich, and I hope that I or other scholars will eventually undertake discussions of the topics mentioned, thus deepening our understanding of a process we all live with but rarely, in the humanities, stop to contemplate systematically.

This work is concerned with matters of theory but cites empirical studies in the service of theory. I give illustrative examples of certain journals' policies, but by no means do I try to represent the practices of all journals. Certain points apply more to journals in one field than journals in another; for example, the proposal that an author submit a scientific paper with the results section blinded from the referee, in order that the latter not be affected by bias for or against the author's conclusion, does not work for the humanities. At times my presentation shifts rapidly from points applicable to one discipline to points applicable only to another. I hope the reader will not find these shifts hard to follow. In any case, I believe that the approach taken to most of the topics considered is distinctive and that each reader will be able to appropriate it and apply it to his or her own field.

Finally, I intend this book for a wide, cross-disciplinary audience of scholars and researchers. For that reason, I have chosen not to develop the philosophical ideas in a framework that is too technical to hold the interest of the intelligent reader from other disciplines. For example, in chapter 3, I cite various formulations of epistemic conservatism to convey the flavor of the position but do not dwell on the very interesting details that lie behind the formulations. The technical aspects of epistemology might obscure the flow of argument.

A Final Thought

It is intriguing to note that, despite all the criticisms leveled at peer review, the most familiar cliché about peer review (akin to what Churchill said of democracy) is that "it is the worst form of evaluation—except for all the others." Comparing peer review to Los Angeles's freeway system, one author colorfully maintains that "For all the 10-mile tie-ups and occasional shootings, what is astonishing is that it works as well as it does."[18] I join in this assessment, and I trust my reasons will become clear in the course of the book.

Notes

1. A problem in this standard formulation is that technically, p is an item of knowledge only if p is true. But peer reviewed articles frequently contradict each other, so they can't both be items of knowledge. A better formulation is in terms of

"merit"—merit does not require truth. More on the merit of "false" articles may be found in chapter 3, p. 18.

2. See Steve Fuller, "Response to the Japanese Social Epistemologists: Some Ways Forward for the 21st Century," *Social Epistemology* 13 (1999): 287–302.

3. There is one kind of prestigious professional publication that is refereed but not peer refereed, and that is a law review article. Law review articles generally are reviewed by second- and third-year law students. For an interesting analysis of this and other problems with law reviews (as of 1996), along with a proposal that legal scholarship be Web generated, see Bernard J. Hibbitts, "Re-Assessing the Law Review and the Age of Cyberspace," *New York University Law Review* 71 (1996): 615–88, available at www.law.pitt.edu/hibbitts/lastrev.htm (accessed December 1, 2003).

4. The first controlled study relevant to peer review is that of M. J. Mahoney, "Publication Prejudices: An Experimental Study of Confirmatory Bias in the Peer Review System," *Cognitive Therapy and Research* 1 (1977): 161–75. Prior to Mahoney's experiment, investigations of peer review were *post facto*, that is, based on journals' records. Details and bibliography for the other studies described in this paragraph may be found in chapters 2 and 3 of this book.

5. At the most basic level, if one peer reviewed article claims A and another peer-reviewed article claims not-A, one of the articles is mistaken, so both cannot be valid contributions to human knowledge, even if the referees and editor for each of the respective articles thought it was.

6. Robert H. Fletcher and Suzanne W. Fletcher, "Evidence for the Effectiveness of Peer Review," *Science and Engineering Ethics* 3 (1997): 42.

7. For a rich variety of viewpoints on many problems in the review process, see Stevan Harnad, ed., *Peer Commentary on Peer Review: A Case Study in Scientific Quality Control* (Cambridge: Cambridge University Press, 1982), reprinted from *Behavioral and Brain Sciences* 5, no. 2 (1982); see also that journal, 14 (1991): 119–86. A useful survey of studies from 1945 through 1997, with focus on the sciences, is Ann C. Weller, *Editorial Peer Review: Its Strength and Weaknesses* (Medord, N.J.: Information Today, 2001). See also Fiona Godlee and Tom Jefferson, eds., *Peer Review in Health Sciences* (London: BMJ Books, 1999); Anne Hudson Jones and Faith McLellan, eds., *Ethical Issues in Biomedical Publication* (Baltimore, Md.: Johns Hopkins University Press, 2000); Hans-Peter Daniel, *Guardians of Science: Fairness and Reliability of Peer Review*, trans. William E. Russey (New York: Weinheim, 1993); Stephen Lock, *A Difficult Balance: Editorial Peer Review in Medicine* (Philadelphia: ISI, 1985); D. E. Chubin and E. J. Hackett, *Peerless Science: Peer Review and U.S. Science Policy* (Albany, N.Y.: SUNY Press, 1990); Drummond Rennie, ed., "Guarding the Guardians—Research on Editorial Peer Review" (Selected Proceedings from the First International Congress on Peer Review in Biomedical Publication), *Journal of the American Medical Association* (JAMA) 263 (10): 1309–1456; Duncan Lindsey, *The Scientific Publication System in Social Science* (San Francisco: Jossey-Bass, 1978), esp. chap. 7. See also the special issue of *Science and Engineering Ethics* 3 (1997): 1–104. Economists take up peer review in George B. Shepherd, ed., *Rejected: Leading Economists Ponder the Publication Process*

(Sun Lakes, Ariz.: Thomas Horton and Daughters, 1995). Articles by nonscientists appear in the *Journal of Scholarly Publishing* (formerly *Scholarly Publishing*). See in particular: James M. Banner Jr., "Preserving the Integrity of Peer Review," *Scholarly Publishing* 19 (1988): 109–15; Richard T. De George and Fred Woodward, "Ethics and Manuscript Reviewing," *Journal of Scholarly Publishing* 25 (1994): 133–45 [this volume, pp. 165–78]; Michael McGiffert, "Is Justice Blind? An Inquiry into Peer Review," *Scholarly Publishing* 19 (1988): 43–48; Judy Metro, "Is It Publishable?: The Importance of the Editorial Review," *Journal of Scholarly Publishing* 26 (1995): 168–72; Robert Sattelmeyer, "Seven Steps to a Better Review Process," *Scholarly Publishing* 20 (1989): 173–77; Margaret F. Stieg, "Refereeing and the Editorial Process: the *AHR* [American Historical Review] and Webb," *Scholarly Publishing* 14 (1983): 99–122. See also the special issue of *Journal of Information Ethics* 7, no. 2 (fall 1998). Steve Fuller, a philosopher of science, discusses peer review in his book *Science* (Milton Keynes: Open University Press, 1997), chap. 4, and his "Response to the Japanese Social Epistemologists: Some Ways Forward for the 21st Century," 287–302. Finally, see Stanley Fish, "No Bias, No Merit: The Case against Blind Submission," *PMLA* 103 (1988): 739–48, reprinted in Fish, *Doing What Comes Naturally: Change, Rhetoric and the Practice of Theory in Literary and Legal Studies* (Durham, N.C.: Duke University Press, 1989), 163–79 [this volume, pp. 215–30.

8. See for example Thomas Kuhn, *The Structure of Scientific Revolutions*, 2nd ed. (Chicago: University of Chicago Press, 1969).

9. See the Editors of Lingua Franca, eds., *The Sokal Hoax: The Sham That Shook the Academy* (Lincoln: University of Nebraska Press, 2000).

10. Sue P. Ravenscroft and Timothy J. Fogarty, "Social and Ethical Dimensions of the Repeated Journal Reviewer," *Journal of Information Ethics* 7, no. 2 (fall 1998): 42–43.

11. I thank David Berger for this point.

12. This was noted by Atara Graubard Segal.

13. On this point, see Steve Fuller, "Response to the Japanese Social Epistemologists," 287–302.

14. Atara Graubard Segal noted this point.

15. See Ian Douglas-Wilson (former editor of the British medical journal *Lancet*), "Editorial Review: Peerless Pronouncements," *New England Journal of Medicine* 296 (1977): 877.

16. Some of the issues posed by electronic journals are examined in Robin P. Peek and Gregory B. Newby, eds., *Scholarly Publishing: The Electronic Frontier* (Cambridge, Mass.: MIT Press, 1996). See chapter 6 of this book for more detail on the topic.

17. Katie Hafner, "Physics on the Web Is Putting Science Journals on the Line," *New York Times*, April 21, 1998, F3. The Los Alamos site is xxx.lanl.gov. See now the site arXiv.org. The rest of this paragraph quotes from Hafner's reportage; a more rigorous consideration of Ginsparg's view appears in chapter 6.

18. E. Knoll, "The Communities of Scientists and Journal Peer Review," *JAMA* 263 (1990): 1332.

CHAPTER ONE

~~~

Peer Review and the Marketplace of Ideas[1]

When we speak about justifying peer review, we can mean several things.

1. What are the purposes of peer review, and do they justify the practice of allowing only manuscripts that have passed peer review to be published?
2. Do scholars have a duty to submit their work to peer reviewed journals and publishers? Why or why not?
3. Do scholars have a duty to serve as peer reviewers? Why or why not?

In this chapter, I focus on question 1.[2]

Letting Millions of Flowers Bloom

Readers may think it obvious why peer review mechanisms exist: it is to ensure that only quality work is brought before the scholarly community.[3] However, this explanation needs clarification, expansion, and deepening. For a case can be made that much rejected work would be of value.

In an issue of *Behavioral and Brain Sciences* devoted to peer review, one contribution "not entirely facetiously" put forward a radical yet instructive alternative to prevailing practice:

> Let millions of flowers bloom. All one need to do to get published is to write an article, submit it for publication, and pay for its publication. In this way, all

individuals, whether from recognized or unrecognized institutions, would be assured of having their words immortalized. Those articles that catch fire and are cited might come from beggars, thieves, princes, or future Nobel laureates. Let it all hang out: the garbage, mediocrity, and the crown jewels. One could argue that all people are "created equal," endowed with such inalienable rights as the pursuit of truth via totally unrestricted opportunities to publish what they wish.[4]

Essentially, the (partly facetious) proposal is to replace "closed peer review" with "open peer review." Open peer review is review by the scholarly community at large, instead of a few anonymous referees along with an editor or board. As we noted in the introduction, open review could be implemented by means of electronic publishing—some have advocated this sincerely[5]— and without authors necessarily paying for space as the passage (from 1982) suggests. Eventually, there could be one big journal for an entire field, or else journals within a field could be divided according to subject matter rather than standards. Of course scholars could compile and publish lists of works they recommend, but given the proposal *anyone* could publish such a list without *it* passing prepublication review.[6]

It is hard to say who would have the biggest nightmare were open review implemented: readers who have to trek through enormous amounts of junk before finding articles they find rewarding; serious scholars who have to live with the depressing knowledge that flat earth theories now can be said to enjoy "scholarly support"; or a public that finds the medical literature flooded with voodoo and quackery. Let us not forget, either, that editors and sponsoring universities would lose power and prestige even while their workload as judges would be eliminated. All in all, the proposal sounds not only radical but preposterous. And yet like many preposterous proposals, this one challenges us to clarify assumptions and objectives of prevailing custom. Policies that seem to us eternal and necessary in fact may have not always existed— and may well be expendable.[7] At the least it is worth asking whether a procedure less demanding than current peer review—even if less permissive than "letting millions of flowers bloom"—might be better than what we have.

Specifically, one may argue that closed peer review, with its emphasis on selectivity and limitation, conflicts with the pursuit of truth as conceived by liberalism. In his famed argument for free speech, John Stuart Mill asserted that the expression of multiple and diverging viewpoints is more likely to produce truth than would suppressing some viewpoints. Through the proliferation and collision of ideas, truth will emerge; and as for those individuals who already have the truth, they will hold it in a deeper, less dogmatic way by dint of having been challenged.[8] No doubt many philosophers would pay homage to Mill's argument and on that basis sing the virtues of a free exchange of ideas—an ideological marketplace.[9] Indeed, when the topic at hand is, say, diversity within university education, or free speech generally, the marketplace of ideas often takes center stage as a grounds for promoting diversity and free expression without prior review of contributions.[10] Yet prepublication peer review of articles and books *prima facie* runs contrary to Mill's argument. Universities and journals seem to differ sharply in their hospitality to proliferation.

There is also a problem of authority. If one or two of the peer referees do not like an author's ideas, arguments, orientation, methodology, organization, or even writing style, that will often ensure (pending whether revisions are invited) that the ideas will not appear in print where the author wants them and will not reach the hoped-for audience. Mill was concerned that even a majority might be wrong; should we not be all the more concerned, one may ask, that the few—that is, the referees, along with the editor who trusts them—might be mistaken? Why not let others participate in the judgment, putting more reactions in the marketplace? Many heads are better than one, two, or three. There can be vast disagreements among referees as to whether a particular work is of good quality. And even when the work is agreed to be of good—or poor—quality, this does not yet establish a true consensus. One referee may find it well reasoned save in point D, while another will say that point D is particularly telling. Given such discrepancies, why not throw the issue out to a wider net of evaluators—scholarly public opinion? Why not have the issues "settled in the intellectual agora of the whole community rather than by a few referees and an editor working in camera"?[11] Problems of referee competence and bias intensify this concern. Compounding the offense to liberalism, according to some, is the inherent conservativeness of peer review: new and imaginative ideas and methodologies are likely to meet with initial resistance and skepticism and ultimately be aborted.[12]

Referees should be representative of the wider community; they are its proxies. (There are interesting comparisons here to the jury system.) But the wider reception of an article often does not match two referees' recommendation. Replies often point out gaping holes and serious errors in published works. By the same token what if a rejected article contains crown jewels, as happened in the case of Nobel Prize work that was originally rejected?[13] From this point of view, each idea belongs in the marketplace—of print—and the marketplace should be filled with responses to it.[14]

Yet hardly anyone, including liberals, accepts the marketplace objection to peer review. In fact, many academics express the opposite sentiment: that because universities demand that professors produce in quantity, too much gets submitted and too much published. Already in 1973, when the number of journals was significantly smaller than today, a study asserted that "in the view of a significant number of editors and press directors, the philosophy [of publish-or-perish] is in large measure responsible for the proliferation of second-rate material on topics that interest few."[15] Kenneth Eble flatly averred (1983) that "the bulk of what is submitted does not deserve publication anywhere."[16] W. V. O. Quine, one of the most eminent philosophers of the twentieth century, maintained that "quality control is spotty in the burgeoning philosophical press."[17] Drummond Rennie, editor of prominent medical journals, stated:

> There are scarcely any bars to eventual publication. There seems to be no study too fragmented, no hypothesis too trivial, no literature citation too biased or too egotistical, no design too warped, no methodology too bungled, no presentation of results too inaccurate, too obscure, and too contradictory, no analysis too self-serving, no argument too circular, no conclusions too trifling or too unjustified, and no grammar and syntax too offensive for a paper to end up in print.[18]

More recently it has been declared that in published articles in medical journals "poor methodology and reporting are widespread" and that "most medical studies are of low quality and of limited relevance to clinicians."[19] Significantly, one measure of quality in journals is rejection rate. The higher this rate—the more articles a journal refuses to publish—the more likely it is to be regarded as "top" and "prestigious." The best journals, it follows, are not those that proliferate ideas and maximize discussion; they are those that limit the public expression of submitted ideas to perhaps 5–10 percent in some fields. Physics journals have high acceptance rates, but here as elsewhere a higher rejection rate is a mark of quality.[20]

Can this attitude be defended on liberal principles? According to the Millian position, don't even rejected articles contain some interesting and convincing points, often by a rejecting referee's own admission? Don't most works advance the pursuit of truth to some small extent, if only by provoking opponents to sharpen their own positions? Many scholars evince keen interest in reading or hearing unpublished papers, whether in traditional or online form, and they find value even in works that do not win publication; that further feeds the argument for open review. Finally let us not ignore the salutary effects of speed, of getting points into a conversation right after the speaker makes hers, not two to three years later.

In short, the practice of peer review seems to sit uneasily with liberalism's commitment to the proliferation of ideas and to Mill's marketplace conception. It may be added that the publication process limits free expression even for authors whose work has been accepted. Published authors are sometimes not allowed to publish articles or books in the form that they think is best. To satisfy referees and editors, authors may have to delete things they think important, formulate points in a briefer form than they think is feasible (manuscripts often have to be shortened to be accepted), deal with objections they think divert and waste space, or add sections that in their opinion disrupt the flow of their argument. Editors may impose changes that authors do not like but cannot override. The final product in some sense is not the author's work. In this respect, too, the peer review process does not allow for completely free expression. While not raising new issues of principle, this point illustrates the extent to which peer review filters and limits the flow of ideas.[21]

If I am right that peer review and the marketplace conception do not sit well together, we face a choice between abandoning peer review and abandoning the marketplace conception. In my opinion it is the marketplace conception that has to go; peer review stays. In this chapter, however, I am interested primarily in establishing that a champion of the marketplace conception has no way to justify peer review with high rejection rates. Along the way we will encounter good reasons for peer review, reasons which I claim the liberal cannot allow. In the book's final chapter, I will revisit the concept of open review as it emerges in the age of digital technology and electronic publishing.

Understanding the Marketplace Objection

The marketplace objection should not be misunderstood. Liberals typically invoke the marketplace of ideas as an argument against governmental censorship. The difficulty we are considering, however, is not that peer review subjects ideas to *censorship* and *suppression*. Not only is government nowhere in the picture, but a journal or press makes no effort to prevent an author from submitting rejected work elsewhere; for example, journals do not apprise other journals that a work has been rejected, nor do they pass on negative comments. Instead each journal and press begins a refereeing process anew.[22] Even in the extreme case, in which an article eventually is rejected by *every* available journal, the author can disseminate his or her ideas by snail-mailing or e-mailing the paper to colleagues, publishing the piece privately, or communicating via the Web. Thus the process of peer review is a far cry from suppressing or not tolerating ideas. As Alan Goldman points out in discussing free speech on campus, there is a huge difference between *censoring* an idea and *not subsidizing* it.[23] But the marketplace argument against peer review never put forward an equation between peer review and censorship. Rather, the objection was that even if rejection of manuscripts is not a form of censorship or suppression, "burying" a large proportion of them in unread and unprestigious journals or keeping them from circulation altogether frustrates the emergence of truth or at least its pursuit. For truth is best served when discussion and expression are maximized.

It will not do for a liberal defender of peer review to say that, absent suppression, a good article is likely to end up *somewhere* in the marketplace, so all good ideas get expressed eventually. Even apart from whether all good work *does* get published, problems confront this response. To begin with, articles in less prominent journals are multiply jeopardized: because readers will assume (often correctly) that these articles must have been rejected by more prestigious journals, the articles will be read less, cited less frequently, and stand a smaller chance of being communicated widely. Citation indexes, I would think, bear this out. The price of having a few extremely selective and demanding journals is that others are marginalized and in effect never enter the marketplace. Can a liberal justify this?[24] (Sometimes it is even argued that when some groups dominate the channels of communication, governments should step in to guarantee equal access to the marketplace![25])

The attitude of "they can try somewhere else" does not befit a liberal. If an article does contribute something to discussion, why shouldn't the liberal editor want it in *her* journal? If a liberal is willing to see a piece not appear, she must in consistency agree that there is *nothing* valuable in it, and that its being consigned to oblivion is no loss. But if that is her opinion, we are back to the original question: according to the marketplace conception, is it really plausible that *none* of the rejected pieces have *anything* to contribute?

To be sure, a liberal can acquiesce in the exclusion of a few categories of work, but these are limited. One such category is redundant material. If a viewpoint has already been expressed by others in a similar way and in a comparably accessible source, then perhaps it makes no contribution to the marketplace. We should bear in mind, though, that in many contexts—like the classroom and the public forum—expressions of ideas are not unwelcome to liberals just because they are familiar. On the contrary, the best way of settling competition in the market and arriving at truth is allowing one viewpoint to spread and to ultimately win the competition by dominating community opinion.

A second category that liberals can exclude is junk—articles defending the flat earth theory and voodoo. Some hold that Mill's arguments do not cover views that have had their day, lost the competition, and are taken seriously by almost no one.[26] Such weeding, presumably done by an editor in consultation with experts, would make open review sound less outrageous. On the other hand, as Joel Feinberg notes in connection with censorship, truly bizarre views do not even need to be screened since there is no risk in allowing them free circulation.[27]

Third, the utility of free speech is always subject to being outweighed by greater harms. In the applied sciences, for instance medicine, great harm would ensue to the public from eliminating peer review. However, in many areas of the humanities, there is no comparable harm in a relaxation of standards, in allowing scholars to publish papers weaker than those that currently appear.

We can leave it open how the liberal should rule on redundancy, junk, and the applied sciences. For the proposal for open review is but an extreme version of a point that can be stated more moderately and no doubt more plausibly: to wit, that a balance between proliferation and standards—not a top-heavy emphasis on standards—is called for on liberal principles.

Responses to the Marketplace Objection

The most natural justification of closed, demanding peer review would reject the marketplace conception: uninhibited dissemination of ideas is harmful, because the effect of proliferation is inundation, and inundation frustrates the pursuit of truth. Though few ideas are harmful enough to merit censorship, in an open review system the weeds will choke the flowers, leading to the demise of all standards.[28] Furthermore, those specialists who do refereeing *can* know, albeit not infallibly, the difference between the valuable and the worthless, a genuine contribution and wasted words; their judgment is on the whole worthy of credence.

However, anyone prepared to rescue peer review by thus rejecting Mill had better think through the consequences. I cannot embark here on a large-scale examination of these consequences, but free speech is one obvious area which would become limited. I also recognize that free speech can be defended by appeal to liberty rather than the marketplace;[29] and liberty, we have seen, is consistent with peer review, since peer review is not censorship. Still, because a marketplace model has been used to justify a wide range of institutions,[30] one should tread cautiously before rejecting it. For that reason, we should continue to consider whether a Millian framework can support peer review.

The liberal is surprisingly hard pressed to say why quality control is so important. Some of his responses are pragmatic, and I begin with those.

A. Pragmatic Benefits not Related to Truth

1. Constraints on Editors

Peer review is reconciled with Mill's marketplace [says the liberal] by reference to budgetary and manpower constraints. Journals have a limited amount of space *only* because of financial exigencies and limited staff. Otherwise they are fully committed to the marketplace.

I have already dealt with this argument by noting the possibility of journals moving to electronic publishing. But apart from that, if financial considerations are all-important, why aren't authors given the option of vanity publishing—paying for journal space when an article is not recommended by referees? It strains plausibility to claim that vanity publishing is bad only because an author's affluence should not be allowed to determine whether her article gets printed. Suppose that a top journal were given a huge donation, earmarked entirely to publish more articles in the interests of scholarly dialogue and the pursuit of truth. Would not many journals probably reject this loosening of standards?

2. Free Enterprise

Scholarly publications are goods offered to a certain consumer market. Limiting what the public receives is a common practice. Not every TV show, movie, play, op-ed piece, and letter to the editor reaches the public; television networks, movie studios, and newspaper publishers seek to attract consumers. Shoddy goods turn off potential patrons. So it is with scholarly journals: the more selective the journal, the more readers it will attract. Quality control is vital to maintaining the journal's "profits," which include the prestige that redounds to the sponsoring department and university. (Aesthetically attractive, browsable volumes are another reflection of this marketing objective.) A free market allows for the effects of reputation and the marginalizing or failure of inferior products. Peer review is the child of private enterprise.

However, liberals should not be satisfied with this explanation, even if it contains a kernel of empirical truth. In many other marketplace enterprises, there is only one value to be achieved—satisfaction—and satisfaction is defined by success in the market, that is, desirability to consumers. But in the case of the marketplace *of ideas*, the liberal believes, the value ultimately served by proliferation is truth. Sheer market success does not guarantee this independently defined value.[31] There is a possible divergence between market success and truth; and the present reply subordinates possible loss of truth and dialogue to consumerist goals. The consumerist argument seems crass coming from someone supposedly concerned with truth and dialogue.

One might add that the consumerist argument would justify too much, allowing journals to publish inferior material if that would titillate the readership or win benefactors.[32]

3. Credentials-Building

The existence of journals and scholarly presses with high standards for publication makes it easier to judge scholarly performance. If refereeing were eliminated, universities would lose these meaningful measures of scholarly performance.

But credentials can be established without prepublication refereeing; all that is required is postpublication review of a candidate's work and favorable citation by other scholars—as is required for tenure and promotion. With the increased volume of reactions in open review, committees will have plenty to go on (although there will also be more things to respond *to*, which may limit reaction to any particular piece).[33] Furthermore, if scholarship involves the proliferation of knowledge, that goal should not be subordinated to the need to generate a mechanism for fashioning credentials. As sociologist Gordon Fellman complains in another context: "Thus does the academy genuflect to the larger culture's defining the worth of products in terms of *what they can be exchanged for*, rather than their own intrinsic value."[34]

4. Psychological Benefits

Peer review creates pride and self-esteem for those whose work is accepted. When anyone can publish what he or she wants, publications mean less to authors.

But again, pride and self-esteem might be gained from reactions in open review. And what of the anger, depression, frustration, and demoralization that rejected authors feel in the closed review system?

A problem common to proposals 3 and 4 is that the liberal has defended peer review in a seemingly self-defeating way, by subordinating the quest for truth to values that for a liberal should be less important. Liberal defenders of peer review will do better to show how peer review promotes the pursuit of truth and dialogue than to show how, for example, it creates status. Non-liberals are not inhibited from appealing to such benefits of peer review as the building of credentials. For nonliberals, these consequences provide legitimate *additional* reasons for the practice.

We turn now to some other liberal responses.

B. Clarifying the Marketplace Conception

5. Modifying What's Allowed in the Marketplace
The liberal has been misunderstood. The proliferation of *views* per se does not advance the cause of truth. It is rather the proliferation of *well-argued views* that brings this result. Poorly argued views *should* be excluded from the marketplace.[35]

The problem with this suggestion is that what in a referee's opinion is poorly argued may not be poorly argued in the opinion of others. The author's opinion that X is a good argument for *p* will be shut out from the marketplace if referees disagree. According to liberals, the claim that X is a good argument for *p* itself belongs in the marketplace, and is to be evaluated by the wider community.

6. The Proxy Theory
Submitting a paper to a journal *already* places the author's ideas into the marketplace; the referees themselves are among the potential "buyers." If referees expose a problem with an argument, this already is a reaction from the marketplace, and the author must respond or else withdraw. Referees are *proxies* for the wider community of scholars. Since scholars find it immensely difficult to sort through all articles in their fields of interest, they prefer to have the good ones clearly labeled by other experts. Hence scholars tacitly consent to the refereeing system; it's like sending someone to the market to buy you some good fruit when you don't have the time or patience to do it yourself. You don't expect the proxy to pick exactly as you will; but it is not cost effective to do the choosing yourself. So you rely on the judgment of others.

Alas, the proxy idea does not explain why, on liberal principles, you would want *so few* articles as are *actually* published under closed peer review; maybe you would want to see ones a notch or two or three below that, in order to challenge your own views, look at matters from other angles, and promote dialogue. This is especially true when the proxy is not completely reliable. If your proxies have not always chosen wisely in the past, wouldn't you at least want the possibility of glancing at the other wares yourself? It would not make sense for the liberal to say, "Look, all I say is that the proliferation of views will lead to truth. I don't have to claim that I *personally* will benefit from hearing many views." For why *wouldn't* the liberal want to absorb many views, if truth and freedom from dogma are the liberal's aims? And wouldn't the attitude of liberals that they personally need not hear other approaches then justify their ignoring even views that are out there in the literature?

C. Benefits of Peer Review Related to Truth
We come finally to the idea that open review frustrates the emergence of truth while closed review nurtures it.

7. The Effect of Inundation
Letting "millions of flowers bloom" is bound to frustrate truth. Scholars could not sort through all the material available without an enormous wasting of time and energy. It takes too much time to read and evaluate a paper properly. That is why works have to be screened before appearing. Alvin Goldman speaks of the need for "product identification": "the capacity of a communication regime (a way of organizing communication) to ensure that interested readers locate and recognize intellectual products or documents that are evidentially appropriate to their products and inquiries."[36]

In my view, this argument, if cogent—which I believe it is—is not available to a liberal. The marketplace conception did not take into account the problem of inundation and product identification; that is why the notion that proliferation yields truth is *mistaken*. Thus, the inundation and product identification argument may not be consistent with liberalism.[37] If liberals maintain it is consistent, and that they do take inundation into account, then they need to reopen a range of free speech issues. They will, for instance, have to explain why the *government* cannot intervene to limit inundation. I am not saying that liberals have no answer here, only that they owe us one.

8. Improvement in Quality
A peer review system improves the quality of every published work. Knowing that there is intense competition for space motivates scholars to produce the best work of which they are capable. Absent a refereeing

process, one would expect a drop in the quality of even the best papers. In addition, the refereeing process and the often protracted negotiations of points between authors and referees provide authors with valuable feedback, again bolstering quality. Scholars may even be under a professional obligation to submit their ideas for review in the interests of truth.[38] Some scholars will be arrogant enough to think that whatever they say is of quality; peer review forces them to answer to a higher standard, even if many of them do not incorporate referee criticisms when they submit an article to another journal.[39]

Let us first look at the claim that competition spurs quality. The problem with the liberal's use of this point is that even without prepublication peer review, many scholars will wish to produce their best in order to advance their reputations. (Sometimes, scholars back out of invited articles or even withdraw accepted manuscripts because they are dissatisfied with their own products.) Moreover, the liberal has to balance curtailment in quality with frustration of truth. Closed review excludes *so much* material that one has to question whether it strikes a happy balance. If not, the liberal will have difficulty defending closed review.

Regarding feedback: Rare even now is the scholar who does not circulate drafts to other specialists for comments. Since collegial commenting is reciprocally beneficial (people comment on each other's work), such comments are as a rule careful and helpful, possibly more helpful than referees' remarks. But even if comments from outside one's circle are more valuable than comments from acquaintances, we would not need peer review in its current form. Suppose we created a system by which (perhaps paid) referees would continue to provide feedback, but authors were free to do as they wished with that feedback; or a system in which everything would be published —including whatever referees' comments remain after author and referee exchange reactions. Such systems would also spur authors to produce quality, because how their work is received will determine their professional standing. Some authors will make bad decisions. But is it worth excluding so much just to prevent those bad decisions? It is the *exclusion* of too much work that makes peer review problematic on a marketplace conception, and the liberal has not justified that exclusion.

I have argued that the marketplace conception has no way to justify closed peer review with current rejection rates. A payoff of our discussion has been the emergence of several good reasons for adopting peer review. The practice of peer review as it actually exists is sustained by several convictions: that quality control by experts, rather than proliferation, is the avenue to truth; that proliferation leads to inundation, and inundation impedes truth; that scholars are consumers and want preapproved products; that a system of credentials is needed, and this requires refereeing. These considerations, I have suggested, are contrary to the marketplace conception. Hence our system of peer review implies a rejection of the marketplace conception, the very conception on which other features of academic life seem to depend. This result puts a great deal of pressure on liberals to develop nonmarket defenses of their positions or else abandon these positions.

The Nonliberal's Stance

I may have given the impression that once the marketplace conception is rejected, a system of strict, highly exclusionary peer review is easily defended. Actually the nonliberal's position needs clarification.

First, it is not clear that the inundation problem should be solved by high rejection rates. Even now there is inundation in publications, yet scholars keep abreast of unpublished material and sign onto not only screened but also unscreened online services. This suggests tolerance of some degree of inundation; why not tolerance of more articles in journals? As specialization increases, furthermore, readers will need to access mainly those works that pertain to their specialization (using, e.g., key word searches), so the amount of material they will have to sort through may be controlled in this way too. If philosophers worry that more will be out there than they feasibly can read, let them compare the number of philosophy papers that such a system would produce with the quantity of, say, medical articles that are *actually* published.

Also, if universities were to relax the pressure to publish in quantity while a concerted effort were made to eliminate redundancy, a less exclusionary review system would be possible even given inundation problems.

A second area that needs exploration is whether inundation effects require nonliberals to oppose open electronic journals. Evidently the defender of peer review will favor refereed journals and will believe that the scholarly community is worse off when some material is unrefereed. If one defends peer review as a bulwark against inundation, then one must favor limits to what is published. But of course, the nonliberal could also take a live-and-let-live attitude, warning against proliferation but recognizing that some scholars will wallow willingly through unrefereed muck in search of jewels. It remains to be studied whether scholars who defend strict peer review standards in fact disregard unscreened material.

A third issue is: can the nonliberal's insistence on quality allow that some unpublished ideas would contribute something of value to a larger discussion? One way to accommodate rejected papers is to have journals publish abstracts of them. Interested readers could follow up by contacting the author. This proposal would put all ideas into the marketplace even if not all those ideas are published as full-length articles, thereby achieving a balance between quality control and dialogue.

This proposal has a practical drawback, however: authors may not agree to have their abstracts printed, since doing so would advertise the fact that a paper was rejected. As a partial solution, journals could accord "honorable mention" and publish abstracts only of those submissions that earned this status. However, even when publication of the abstract does not damage the author's status, authors might prefer to publish the full article elsewhere rather than steal their own thunder by providing hard copy to interested parties. This would undermine one purpose of printing abstracts. Suppose we do this: only when an article is rejected *everywhere* would its abstract be published. But an article that was rejected everywhere would probably not attract interest, nor would authors want the rejection made obvious. Another problem with the abstracts proposal is that journals may not want to publish papers whose abstracts appear elsewhere, because that will make clear to all that this journal was not the author's first choice. It would also uncomfortably highlight discrepancies between standards of various journals. Some of these problems could be met if the selection of articles for full publication would be made according to their degree of specialization, so that publication of an abstract would carry no negative status.

I leave these as areas for the critic of the marketplace conception (in which I include myself) to contemplate. But we will return to some of these issues in chapter 6, where we study the impact of the Internet on scholarly communication.

A Wider Perspective

The failure of liberalism's marketplace conception to accommodate peer review may reflect a larger problem in that conception. There are significant exceptions or counterexamples to the notion that (in Oliver Wendell Holmes's words), "the ultimate good desired is better reached by free trade in ideas."[40] Alvin Goldman points to a number of instances in which a person or agency properly—or at least arguably properly—limits the flow of information.[41] He objects to the following principle:

> If agent X is going to make a doxastic decision concerning question Q, and agent Y has control over the evidence that is provided to X, then, from a purely epistemic point of view, Y should make available to X all of the evidence relevant to Q which is (at negligible cost) within Y's control.

Contrary to the principle quoted, judges, following the rules of evidence, will withhold from juries certain evidence—hearsay, for example, or information the judges deem irrelevant—that is likely to mislead them or make them judge on the basis of prejudice. This is an instance of "epistemic paternalism": The controller of communication interposes his or her own judgment rather than allow the audience to exercise theirs. Better put, the audience uses its judgment, as the final doxastic choice rests with its members, but they are deprived of some doxastic alternative(s) and the supporting argumentation.[42]

To take another example, in the realm of education, school personnel select curricular materials (textbooks, syllabi, etc.) and leave out certain points of view and their supporting argumentation.

> Mathematics classes do not present alternative (crackpot) mathematics. Science classes do not (often) present the flat-earth viewpoint, Ptolemaic astronomy, or astrology. Schools rarely if ever invite Jeanne Dixon or her ilk to give guest lectures, or recount as serious alternatives the theories of Velikovsky. Classes in health education do not give "equal time" to drug pushers to defend the safety of drug use, or to quacks to present and defend their cures. These omissions probably have veritistically good consequences [consequences conducive to the attainment of truth].[43]

Again, The Federal Trade Commission prohibits false and deceptive advertising. Television and radio news programs simplify material in order to make it digestible and understandable by a wide audience.

At the end of his article, Goldman turns to Mill's marketplace—and peer review.

> The very question of communication control policy is relatively neglected in philosophy, perhaps because the topic has been so thoroughly dominated by the Millian dedication to a free market of ideas. Interestingly, though, organized science and scholarship are very far from laissez-faire marketplaces. On the contrary, professional journals rely heavily on (putatively) expert referees to weed out inferior contributions. Only offerings that are judged methodologically sound, well-informed, and possibly in the direction of truth are accepted for publication (or, in a related arena, given research funding). Thus, even in the intellectual sphere, laissez-faire is not the de facto policy.[44]

More precisely, what Goldman suggests is that whereas governments in free societies pursue a laissez-faire policy of allowing information channels to pro-liferate, "these information channels may themselves be highly restrictive in the messages they transmit." At the highest level (government) is deregula-tion; at lower levels, there is "wise regulation."[45]

At its core, my argument in this chapter has sought to demonstrate that peer review involves a restriction of information flow, just as Goldman notes. However, I would note the following points. (a) The readers of journals may very well want the flow limited, so that they will not have to identify qual-ity themselves and not have to wade through muck. They leave the sorting task to experts. In this sense the policy is not paternalistic in the way that a judge's is or a school's is when they withhold information. There is an ele-ment of "protection" here, but it is a desired protection, as in the case of broadcast news. (b) Nowadays the missing "information" (i.e., rejected pa-per) could be "published" on a professor's website. Goldman sees the case for withholding information as stronger when alternative means of acquiring it are available. Material that is not part of a school curriculum may be read about elsewhere, and people can pick up news that has not been broadcast on one station—they need only to listen to other stations, or read newspa-pers, books, and magazines. This helps justify epistemic paternalism in these cases. So, too, in the case of peer review.[46] With both other journals and Web publication available to the author of a rejected paper, the information "blocked" by peer review can be obtained some other way. Hence epistemic paternalism is justified by Goldman's criteria.

Conclusion

Peer review serves the academic community by controlling the flow of ideas and enhancing the quality of scholarly work. It motivates scholars to produce their best, provides feedback that substantially improves work which is sub-mitted, and enables scholars to identify products they will find worth read-ing. It also facilitates evaluating candidates for appointment, tenure, and promotion. Scholars even may be obligated to submit to peer review as part of their responsibility to contribute well-formed ideas to intellectual dia-logue. But is the cause of intellectual debate and dialogue best served by a system that consigns many works to oblivion or to tiny audiences, based on the judgments of a few? Should we use technology to disseminate far more than we do and to loosen the standards of prepublication peer review? An-swers to these questions depend on how closely one is wedded to liberalism's notion that proliferation promotes truth (and also on how much weight one assigns to the potential interest of future scholars in areas and approaches that our generation marginalizes). I maintain that the liberal stance confronts us with the specter of inundation and is not compatible with the institution of peer review as we know it.

In the next two chapters we will examine some criticisms that have been made of peer review, criticisms which suggest that perhaps a rational scholar will not want to carry out the task of product identification by relying on the judgment of peer reviewers.

Notes

1. The term "marketplace" is not John Stuart Mill's but rather Oliver Wendell Holmes's. See his dissenting opinion in *Abrams v. United States* 250 U.S. 616, 630 (1919).

2. On questions 2 and 3 (and the question of whether there are pragmatic reasons for writing for peer reviewed publications and refereeing for them), see Joe Cain, "Why Be My Colleague's Keeper? Moral Justifications for Peer Review," *Science and Engineering Ethics* 5 (1999): 531–40 [this volume, pp. 179–90].

3. There is a second function often cited, and that is to improve the work on behalf of the author. However, it seems to me that this second function derives from the first: the reason for improving an article is to make it eventually presentable to the rest of the community.

4. Richard M. Perloff and Robert Perloff, "Improving Research on and Policies for Peer Review Practices," in *Peer Commentary on Peer Review*, ed. Stevan Harnad (Cambridge: Cambridge University Press, 1982), 48–49. Hans-Peter Daniel, *Guardians of Science: Fairness and Reliability of Peer Review*, trans. William E. Russey (New York: Weinheim, 1993) refers to scientists who seriously advocate such a position. See also my discussion of Paul Ginsparg's views in chapter 6.

5. See chapter 6.

6. I thank the late Robert Nozick for this last point.

7. *Proceedings of the Royal Society* and *Proceedings of the National Academy of Sciences* went without peer review for a while. See R. Roy and R. Ashburn, "The Perils of Peer Review," *Nature* 414 (2001): 393–94.

8. John Stuart Mill, *On Liberty*, chap. 2.

9. However, many would advocate free speech not because free speech results in truth and removal of dogma but because free speech protects liberty. On the difference between these arguments see, inter alia, C. Edwin Baker, *Human Liberty and Freedom of Speech* (New York: Oxford University Press, 1989). See also Martin P. Golding, *Free Speech on Campus* (Lanham, Md.: Rowman & Littlefield, 2000).

10. Alvin Goldman distinguishes literal and metaphorical meanings of the "marketplace." See *Knowledge in a Social World* (New York: Oxford University Press,

1999), 192–217. In its literal meaning, the competitive market mechanism promotes the discovery of truth. In its metaphorical meaning, the marketplace of ideas is marketlike, in that debates are "wide open and robust," but this result is not necessarily achieved by the mechanism of the market. Government regulation might even be necessary to achieve the good result. I thank Martin Golding, the late Robert Nozick, and Ross Zucker for valuable discussion of the marketplace conception.

11. Robert K. Adair, "A Physics Editor Comments on Peters and Ceci's Peer-review Study," in Peer Commentary on Peer Review, ed. Harnad, 12. Adair is speaking only of controversial submissions, but I've taken the liberty of recruiting his formulation for my own purposes.

12. See, for example, Harnad, introduction to Peer Commentary on Peer Review, 1–2. On conservatism, see chapter 4.

13. See chapter 3, pp. 89–92.

14. In a print environment, a published idea that is discredited remains available. In the context of the Internet, posted papers may be withdrawn once the marketplace quashes them. This brings us to the idea I discuss in chapter 6, viz. that papers be refereed by the whole community. Actually, my response to the argument just raised for having the public serve as referee is found in chapter 6 rather than here.

15. W. Pell, "Facts of Scholarly Publishing," PMLA 88 (1973): 639–44.

16. Kenneth Eble, "Conflicts between Scholarship and Teaching," in A Professor's Duties, ed. Peter Markie (Lanham, Md.: Rowman & Littlefield, 1994), 216.

17. W. V. O. Quine, Theories and Things (Cambridge, Mass.: Harvard University Press, 1981), 192.

18. Drummond Rennie, "Guarding the Guardians," JAMA 256 (1986): 2391.

19. The first quote is from D. G. Altmann, "Poor-quality Medical Research: What Can Journals Do?" JAMA 287 (2002): 2765; the second is from K. Abbasi et al., "Four Futures for Scientific and Medical Publishing," British Medical Journal 325 (2002): 1472.

20. The Guidebook for Publishing Philosophy, ed. Eric Hoffman (Newark, Del.: American Philosophical Association), publishes data on acceptance rates by different journals. The journal Ethics publishes data each year on the fate of submissions. Certain physics journals accept nearly 80 percent of submissions, the prestigious ones 45 percent (my source, though, is from 1982: Robert K. Adair, "A Physics Editor Comments on Peters and Ceci's Peer-review Study," in Peer Commentary on Peer Review, ed. Harnad, 12). See also L. L. Hargens, "Variation in Journal Peer Review Systems: Possible Causes and Consequences," JAMA 263 (1990): 1348–52. A 1971 study gives high acceptance rates for geology and linguistics as well; see Harriet Zuckerman and Robert K. Merton, "Patterns of Evaluation in Science: Institutionalization, Structure, and Function of the Referee System," Minerva 9 (1971): 77.

21. It seems unfair that readers might hold an author accountable for a change he or she did not want but was necessitated by another's judgment, regardless of whether the change was for the better or for the worse. Likewise it seems not right for an author to get credit for a well-written article when it is a skilled copy editor who has cre-

ated that smooth flow in the prose. Those who evaluate candidates for tenure and promotion have only the hard, cold printed word to go by when they form their opinion.

22. That the earlier report is not solicited is odd if we try to build a consensus; the explanation seems to be that editors wish not to doom the rejected article. Gerald Dworkin, then editor of *Ethics*, inquires whether it is proper to retain as a referee for an article someone who has already refereed the article for another journal. See *Ethics* 103 (January 1993): 219–20.

23. See Alan Goldman, "Diversity within University Faculties," in *Morality, Responsibility, and the University*, ed. Cahn, 219–23.

24. Some have suggested that journals should allow multiple submissions—submission of an article to several journals at once—in order to make more journals competitive. For arguments both for and against this proposal, see D. V. Cicchetti, "The Reliability of Peer Review for Manuscript and Grant Submissions: A Cross-Disciplinary Investigation," *Behavioral and Brain Sciences* 14 (1991): 132; and Duncan Lindsey, *The Scientific Publication System in Social Science* (San Francisco: Jossey-Bass, 1978), 104–5.

25. See, for example, Baker, *Human Liberty and Freedom of Speech*, 5, 15; Golding, *Free Speech on Campus*, 20.

26. Something like this is suggested by Goldman, *Knowledge in a Social World*, 221.

27. Joel Feinberg, "Limits to the Free Expression of Opinion," in *Philosophy of Law*, ed. Joel Feinberg and Jules Coleman, 7th ed. (Belmont, Calif.: Wadsworth, 2004), 263.

28. This way of putting things was suggested by Margarita Levin.

29. See Baker, *Human Liberty and Freedom of Speech*.

30. Besides figuring in voluminous ethical and legal discussions of free speech (see, e.g., Baker, *Human Liberty and Freedom of Speech*, chap. 1), marketplace models have been used to defend democracy, free trade, and even pop culture. Common to these justifications is the notion that proliferation maximizes well-being.

31. I thank Michael Levin for clarifying this distinction and helping formulate this paragraph.

32. Interestingly, many journals would publish articles by famous philosophers because of who wrote them; the articles would not be published if written by someone else. One could argue that such articles are published out of a desire to give scholars (present and future) a more comprehensive view of this individual's thought, which is certainly a contribution to scholarship. But one might also view this practice as simply getting attention and earning status. On the whole I think the practice is defensible, but will not press that claim here. See chapter 2, pp. 56–58.

33. The high acceptance rates in some fields (see note 20) suggest that a field can do evaluations of personnel even when acceptance rates are high.

34. Gordon Fellman, "On the Fetishism of Publications and the Secrets Thereof," *Academe* 81 (Jan.-Feb. 1995): 27. (Liberals might substitute the word "instrumental" for "intrinsic," since ideas have value as contributions to a larger quest.) Describing scholarly publishing today, one observer writes: "Forget about advancing the intellect; for the academic, what scholarly publishing is for is to advance the intellectual."

(Judith Shulevitz, "Keepers of the Tenure Track," *New York Times Book Review*, [October 28, 1995], 46.)

35. Alan Gewirth has advanced a similar argument in denying academic freedom to professors who ignore accepted criteria of academic argument. See his "Human Rights and Academic Freedom," in *Morality, Responsibility, and the University*, ed. Steven M. Cahn (Philadelphia: Temple University Press, 1990), 8–31.

36. Goldman, *Knowledge in a Social World*, 175.

37. Michael Levin pointed out to me that articles are often rejected not because referees think they contain false or redundant theses, but because they are so poorly "packaged" that they could not contribute to the pursuit of truth. This is a cogent point, but it points up a weakness in the marketplace conception akin to the failure to consider the effects of inundation. Liberals have not proposed to exclude views from the marketplace on the grounds that they are poorly expressed, let alone advocate prior screening for this defect.

38. See Theodore Benditt, "The Research Demands of Teaching in Modern Higher Education," in *Morality, Responsibility, and the University*, ed. Cahn, 93–108, esp. 105ff.; Markie, *A Professor's Duties*, 79–80. Benditt and Markie both ground this obligation in the teacher's responsibility to teach: if teachers are to present their own ideas to students, those ideas must first undergo testing. I find this particular argument problematic, but there may be other arguments for demanding that scholars submit to review. See chapter 5, pp. 136–38, note 22.

39. For statistics on the failure of authors to revise in accordance with criticism when they submit to another journal, see S. Lock and J. Smith, "Peer Review at Work," *Scholarly Publishing* 17 (1986): 303–16; L. L. Hargens, "Variation in Journal Peer Review Systems: Possible Causes and Consequences," *JAMA* 263 (1990): 1348–52; A. Yankauer, "Peering at Peer Review," *CBE Views* 8 (1985): 7–10; S. C. Patterson and S. K. Smithers, "Monitoring Scholarly Journal Publication in Political Science: The Role of the APSR," *Political Science and Politics* 23 (1990): 647–56. J. V. Bradley, "Pernicious Publication Practices," *Bulletin of the Psychonomic Society* 18 (1981): 31–34, reports that 21 percent of respondents said they would be more careful if they knew it would not be refereed, 6 percent said they would be less careful, and the rest (73 percent) said they would be equally careful.

40. See note 1.

41. Alvin Goldman, "Epistemic Paternalism," *Journal of Philosophy* 88, no. 3 (1991): 113–31.

42. For this clarification, see Goldman, "Epistemic Paternalism," 126.

43. Goldman, "Epistemic Paternalism," 121.

44. Goldman, "Epistemic Paternalism," 131.

45. See also Goldman, *Knowledge in a Social World*, 211.

46. State censorship is different, then, because it leaves no alternative channels available.

CHAPTER TWO

~~~~~

Bias and Anonymity
in the Peer Review Process

In a valuable examination of issues in peer review, psychology professor Liora Schmelkin lists the complaints leveled at peer review as follows:

(a) being prone to bias, including reviewer bias, editor bias, various forms of publication bias; (b) unscientific and lacking in evidence for its benefits; (c) having no measurable outcome, and when research is conducted, it is typically on the quality of the review, rather than the quality of the manuscript; (d) conservative, tending to accept for publication articles that are less controversial and less innovative; (e) slow and expensive; (f) yielding papers that are often grossly flawed [Schmelkin brings evidence of low-quality publications]; (g) unable to detect fraud; (h) sloppy; (i) subjective; (j) secretive; (k) having many reviewers who are incompetent; (l) having relatively low agreement among reviewers of the same manuscript; (m) having difficulty in handling dissent; (n) unnecessary; (o) leading to potential dishonesty among the reviewers, who sometimes steal ideas from the manuscripts they review; (p) stifling scientific communication and hence slowing the advancement of knowledge; (q) subject to various forms of political pressure; (r) incestuous, with a small group of reviewers reviewing each other's work, particularly in small narrowly defined specialty areas; and (s) having reviewers who are caustic, nasty, overcritical, arbitrary, self-serving, savage, uncivil, irresponsible, arrogant, inappropriate "and there are probably a few other choice adjectives out there in the literature."[1]

A formidable list indeed! No book can take on all these criticisms adequately. My focus in this chapter is complaint (a), and in the next chapter complaint (d). At various points in the course of the book, we will touch on (albeit often very lightly) nearly all of the other charges.

The Bias Problem: Background

Probably the most frequently voiced concern about the peer review system is the potential for bias and lack of objectivity on the part of reviewers. Referees are expected to provide objective evaluations of the works they review, evaluations that consider only a quality called *merit*. Bias is any feature of an evaluator's cognitive or attitudinal mind-set that could interfere with an objective evaluation.[2] A bias could introduce extraneous considerations—considerations unrelated to merit—into the assessment. (I say "*could* interfere" and "*could* introduce" because a bias might be suppressed by the evaluator, with the result that his or her evaluation will be objective though the bias remains.)

By the very nature of a review, it has been argued,[3] reviewers tend to focus on negatives, magnifying flaws that they would not be sensitive to were they reading the article in print. Some authors even deliberately include flaws that are easily fixable in order that referees walk away satisfied having noted those.[4] Nevertheless, referee bias can be either negative or positive: that is, a bias may lead to a more negative evaluation of an article than the referee would give were it not for the biasing factor, or it may lead to a more positive evaluation, in which case we may speak of a "halo effect," whereby the quality of a work is exaggerated upward by the appraiser.[5] Or the bias may make no difference: a biased evaluation might be identical with what an unbiased evaluation would yield.

Of horror stories about biased referees there is an abundant supply. In response, defenders of the maligned referees charge that complaints by rejected authors often result from psychodynamic mechanisms such as denial and frustration-aggression.[6] One psychologist colorfully frames the competing allegations this way:

> Given two or three drinks, almost any researcher who does not publish in American Psychological Association journals can produce shocking tales of the unjust treatment accorded his, or his friend's, publication efforts. APA defenders, of course, realize that these are just the sour grapes of a second-rate researcher.[7]

In light, however, of the extensive researches of Daniel Kahneman, Richard Nisbett, Lee Ross, Amos Tversky, and others that document the role of bias in judgment,[8] it is difficult to imagine that referees are immune to bias. Furthermore, while rejected authors are likewise subject to bias about the peer review process, the fact their complaints about referees are personally motivated does not entail that they are false. Indeed, empirical studies purport to show that biased refereeing is widespread.[9]

The existence of referee bias should not dictate abandoning the peer review system entirely. As we saw when reflecting on why marketplace conceptions of truth should not be invoked to dispense with peer review, we always confront the question, "What is the alternative?" At the same time, biased evaluations arouse profound concern, and it is no wonder that most of the energy that has gone into reforming peer review has been directed toward eliminating, or at least reducing, the problem.[10]

To decry biased refereeing is platitudinous; and like most platitudes, the one that says bias is bad has a large and valuable core of truth. But the topic of bias is substantially more complex, both empirically and philosophically, than is usually supposed; furthermore, the usual remedy for bias of certain types—blind review—is not a panacea and is not appropriate for all cases. Before getting to my main arguments, I need to describe some types of bias and some ways in which bias can arise.

Types of Bias

The three categories of bias that are most pertinent to issues surrounding peer review are *ad hominem* bias, affiliational bias, and ideological bias. I will also comment briefly on aesthetic bias.[11] Awareness of bias can itself produce bias. By being wary of succumbing to bias, one might stimulate bias of another sort—"bend over backwards" bias. A referee—either out of a desire to look fair or out of a genuine commitment to fairness—might be so concerned with rooting out his or her bias (whether *ad hominem*, affiliational, or ideological) that the referee will rate the paper too positively or too negatively. For my purposes this is just another variant of the type of bias which the referee is trying to eliminate.

Ad Hominem Bias

Ad hominem bias is bias for or against a particular person. Examples of *ad hominem* bias include negative bias against an author because of personal jealousy and positive bias for the author because of friendship or sympathy for the author's personal situation (e.g., she's up for tenure and this decision will make or break her career). *Ad hominem* bias is also possible when a referee is competing with a given author for a certain position or a certain honor. The referee and the author generally will be in the same specialty, and sometimes it is in the referee's interest that the author's submission be rejected—a straightforward conflict of interest. Or, to take an opposite sort of conflict of interest, both may belong to an old boys' network, and follow an unwritten code by which each promotes the other's efforts. A referee may favor his or her advisors' or students' submissions, or may have negative feelings toward authors who seem overproductive. Some referees may be offended that a submitted paper does not cite work of theirs, or may feel their own tenure prospects are threatened by author criticism; others may be enticed to recommend acceptance of a submission because the paper does cite their work. This is a kind of self-interested bias, an *ad hominem* positive attitude toward anything that will promote oneself, and a negative attitude toward anything that slights oneself. (Editors are subject to this bias too, but I will frame the arguments in terms of referees.)

These are especially crude forms of *ad hominem* bias. In them the referee is not evaluating the submission on the merit of the work at all, but is merely giving expression to his feelings toward the author or his occupation with self. When the referee is affected by jealousy, friendship, or sympathy, the referee's judgment is not looking to the merits of the author's scholarship at all, though he or she may mistakenly deny this. There is another form of *ad hominem* bias, however, in which, because of prior exposure to an author's work, with which the reviewer has been impressed favorably or unfavorably, the reviewer does not evaluate the submission based on the work's merits but rather on the merits he or she assigns, in biased or unbiased fashion, to the author's overall scholarship. In cases where the author is not a known commodity, reviewers assess work more critically. One experimenter retyped Jerzy Kozinski's novel *Steps*—which won a National Book Award for fiction in 1969—and submitted it, untitled and under an assumed name, to fourteen major publishing houses and thirteen literary agents. The result? No one recognized the work, and no one thought it should be published.[12]

If a reviewer knows something about the author's work, then he or she may extrapolate from previous impressions to the work being considered now. Besides assuming that his or her evaluations of the earlier work were sound, when in truth they may have been formed without scrutiny and prolonged attention, this referee is essentially ignoring the possibility that the present work differs in quality from those he or she has seen already because the author has (in one type of case) improved dramatically through experience or (in another type of case) is resting on laurels or is waxing overconfident. Sociologist Robert Merton has referred to referees' favoring accomplished authors as an example of "the Matthew effect" known to sociologists: "For whosoever hath, to him shall be given and he shall have more abundance; but whosoever hath not, from him shall be taken away even that he hath."[13] The Matthew effect entrenches the powerful and weakens the powerless.

Affiliational Bias

In some cases a referee might think that *as a class*, members of a particular group do work that is inferior or superior to members of other groups. Even though the referee thus biased knows that not every member of the class is inferior or superior in that way, a bias is manifested by the referee's assuming that what holds of most members of the class (in the referee's opinion) holds of the particular member whose work he or she is now judging. Biases based on gender or race are the most egregious examples of this pattern of bias.[14] Affiliational bias is another form.

Affiliational bias is bias for or against an author because the author's institution is regarded by the referee as prestigious or not prestigious, which in turn leads the referee to say of the author, "Wow, he must be good!" or alternatively, "He can't be too good." The referee thinks that researchers at Harvard or Stanford do excellent work, while researchers at institution X do mediocre work. A study by M. Gordon offers the following conclusion: that referees from major universities favor papers by researchers at major universities, while researchers at minor universities have no preference for either major or minor universities.[15] This does not mean that the major-school reviewers view authors from similar schools as buddies or members of their fraternity. Instead, the bias might arise from the fact that reviewers from major schools are likely to have similar training and to use similar methods (assuming that professors at major schools are likely to have trained at major schools and that the major schools provide similar training), or to have the same sense of what is important and what is not. In this last case affiliational bias shades over into ideological bias, or, more accurately, the other way around.

Such biases can affect not only referees but editors. Indeed editors may have an interest in publishing work by authors from high-prestige institutions; it adds to the journal's status.

Dana Crane showed that as the number of referees from a certain kind of institution increases so do the chances of a more successful submission from an institution of that type.[16] And in a notorious study, probably the best known of its kind, psychologists Douglas P. Peters and Stephen J. Ceci selected twelve already published research articles by investigators from prestigious and productive psychology departments—one article from each of twelve highly regarded journals. These journals all had high rejection rates (around 80 percent), were regarded as impact journals (based on citation rates) and used a nonblind refereeing process. The investigators altered the names of the authors and their institutions to make them sound nonprestigious—for example, the "Tri-Valley Center for Human Potential"; then they resubmitted the articles to the very journals that eighteen to thirty-two months earlier had published them. Only three of thirty-eight editors and reviewers detected the resubmissions; and eight of the nine undetected articles were rejected.[17] The fact so few resubmissions were detected suggests that referees are somewhat less than fully *au courant* with the state of their field, an assertion that is surely disturbing—plagiarism was going by undetected and referees were showing their ignorance. This finding, however, is peripheral to our present concerns.[18] More important is the finding that referees reacted differently to the original submissions and to the doctored resubmission. It is difficult to say whether this shows bias for famous institutions or bias against unknown ones (rejected articles were not resubmitted with prestigious affiliations attached to them), but the conclusion is surely disturbing in either case.[19] Agreement between reviewers, furthermore, cannot be very significant if all or many are biased by the same factor.

The journal *Behavioral and Brain Sciences* published some fifty-six responses to the Peters-Ceci study. Putting to one side criticisms of the deceptive procedure used, the most common criticism of the study was that the sample size was too small. Differences, it was alleged, could be random and traced to chance; referees were likely to be critical anyway since the journals in question had high rejection rates. Alternatively, results might be explained by the general tendencies of the respective referees to recommend or reject; discrepancies are due to the fact these were different referees, who may have differing personalities, differing ages, and differing levels of experience and competence from the original ones. There is no control group of previous rejected authors, and a controlled study is not possible when you cannot assume the variables are matched.[20] Other critics of Peters and Ceci pointed out that two years had lapsed between the original submission and the resubmission, making it only logical that referees would be less impressed by the resubmissions—the papers seemed that much out of date.[21] Still other critics noted that the study used names like "Tri-Valley Center for Human Potential" rather than a university name. Perhaps an obscure *university* address would have fared better. The most interesting response in my opinion was that it is reasonable to import knowledge of an author's affiliation into an evaluation, because there really *is* a correlation between institutional prestige and quality of work. This response raises fascinating issues and I will return to it later in this chapter.

Peters and Ceci's paper is a celebrated study and is routinely quoted in the peer review literature. Often it is taken as the last word, if not the only word. But apart from criticisms that were published in *Behavioral and Brain Science* together with the study, over two decades have elapsed since the paper's publication, and certain more recent studies have failed to confirm bias of the sort that study identified, or have found that such bias appears in modified form. One 1994 study of work submitted to the *Journal of Pediatrics* showed no affiliational bias with regard to major manuscripts, though it did show affiliational bias in the case of brief reports.[22] The authors of that study hypothesized that the difference in responses to brief reports resulted from genuine differences in quality. Investigators at minor institutions lack research facilities, have limited opportunity to work with established investigators, and therefore are more likely to submit brief reports of lesser quality. I don't see, however, why this would not result in a difference in major manuscripts too. Moreover, the explanation provides fodder for those who would justify treating authors from different institutions differently, on the grounds that the quality of work coming from one school and the quality of work coming from another really are different. As I mentioned I shall return to this issue and its implications.

Interestingly, in another study published that same year (1994), blinded reviewers at the *Journal of Developmental and Behavioral Pediatrics* tended to give higher scores to manuscripts by authors with more previous articles, while unblinded reviewers did not. The authors describe this part of their results as showing "unbiased" judgment by the blinded reviewers and bias on the part of the unblinded ones. That the blinded reviewers are said to lack bias only points up the fact that an author who is experienced at publishing and has done good enough work to be published in the past is more likely to submit a quality manuscript. But this raises the question: if so, is it really bias to favor a more heavily published author when you are an *unblinded* referee? Can't you appeal to statistical correlation? This issue, referred to twice already, will be a crucial one that anyone who insists on blind review must face. Turning next to the results for unblinded referees, editorial board members suggested to the researchers that in not favoring well-published authors unblinded reviewers were showing jealousy toward more accomplished authors.[23] Another observer suggests that the reviewers expected more of authors with good publication records.[24] I would suggest that there may be a "bend over backwards bias" operative here. The study's authors themselves, who did not examine the causes of the bias, invoke affiliational and gender bias as possible factors, but it is not clear exactly which way these biases would tilt.

It is quite possible that by the time the 1994 studies were carried out, the Peters-Ceci study, or general awareness of biases among referees (and editors), had sensitized reviewers (and editors) to the problem of negative bias toward low-prestige institutions, leading to reduction in affiliational bias. Perhaps the study awoke the refereeing community to other sources of bias, such as previous publishing record. Also, in a tight job market, top-notch scholars may wind up at mediocre institutions, undermining the presumed empirical basis of the bias that referees may show against authors from low-prestige institutions (though by this logic bias for authors from high-prestige institutions would remain intact). Finally, changes in the social climate in the direction of egalitarian thinking may have helped diminish bias in refereeing.[25] Whatever changes have taken place, however, since the Peters-Ceci study, it is difficult to believe that today no referees display affiliational or *ad hominem* bias. These remain categories of bias for which we must be on the lookout.

Ideological Bias

Ideological bias is exemplified by a referee (or editor) who antecedently holds strong views for or against an author's position. Psychologists refer to "confirmatory bias," a bias in favor of ideas that confirm one's own position— more technically, "the tendency to be attentive to and supportive of what confirms one's view and to ignore or discredit what contradicts one's view."[26] In studies of belief-perseverance, subjects were told that they were being tested for their ability to discriminate between genuine suicide notes and inauthentic ones. They were then given false feedback by the experimenters as to whether their ability was average, much above average, or much below average. Afterwards the subjects were debriefed and told that the feedback was in fact random. Yet they persevered in their earlier assessment of their abilities, the assessment based on the feedback they now were told was random. Various interpretations of these results are possible, but one, endorsed by the study's authors, is that the subjects were exhibiting confirmatory bias.[27] A confirmatory bias may result in a referee assigning greater/lesser weight to a particular strength or weakness of an author's position than he would otherwise, or a referee bending over backwards either to look tolerant or to truly be tolerant of a position different from his or her own.

Critics of peer review charge that ideological bias often is a bias of the times—that is, that papers challenging widely accepted views are likely to meet with rejection, while those supporting prevailing theories are likely to be accepted.[28] Since the empowered are more likely to be engaged as referees than the powerless, the cycle continues: those who share the prevailing view recommend rejection of papers by those who do not. But ideological bias is not always bias toward a current paradigm: clearly a reviewer may be biased on an issue that has not enjoyed a consensus. He or she may have published on the topic, or may simply harbor preconceptions.

In recent years the problem of ideological bias was brought forcefully to the public when physicist Alan Sokal published a paper in the journal *Social Text* that included intentional nonsense. It was accepted, Sokal averred, because it spoke the lingo of the postmodern school at whom his hoax was directed and "flattered the editors' ideological preconceptions."[29]

In a 1977 study—described by the investigator as the first controlled experiment in peer review—psychologist Michael J. Mahoney divided seventy-five reviewers into five groups and asked them to react to a (manufactured) paper on a controversial issue in psychology, the influence of behavioral reinforcers on intrinsic motivation. Each of the five groups was sent the identical introduction and methodology and bibliography sections, but the sections on reported results and on interpretation were made different from group to group. When evaluating methodology and presentation of data, the reviewers rated these categories high when the paper reported confirmatory results (results that conformed with the reviewers' presumed theoretical perspective) and lower when the results were disconfirmatory ones (negative or mixed). Also, the likelihood of a referee discovering a certain technical error in the manuscript was found to be contingent on the bias of the reviewer in favor of positive results. Of those who read a confirmatory paper, 25 percent detected the error; of those who read a disconfirmatory paper, 71 percent did.[30]

In another investigation, two versions of a case study were submitted to a journal of social work. One version stated that a social work intervention had a positive outcome, the other that it did not. Social work journals were more likely to accept the former version while rejecting the latter.[31]

One type of bias toward a particular conclusion is bias in favor of studies with positive results (results that confirm a positively framed hypothesis under examination). So widespread in science is bias in favor of positive results thought to be that one author facetiously suggested establishing a journal of negative results. However recent studies suggest that this bias does not exist—in submitted papers, there is no difference in acceptance rates between positive and negative papers; rather, authors tend not to submit negative papers.[32]

Ideological bias sometimes shades over into *ad hominem* bias of the "self-interest bias" sort. As Harry Redner observes, since referees are the authorities in a field, *ex hypothesi* they would lose their long-standing social status if they endorsed revolutionary ideas.[33] This point was made colorfully in a letter by Thomas Huxley:

> I know that the paper I have just sent in [to the Royal Society] is very original and of some importance, and I am equally sure that if it is referred to the judgment of my particular friend. . . that it will not be published. He won't be able to say a word against it, but he will pooh-pooh it to a dead certainty.
> You will ask with some wonderment, Why? Because for the last twenty years . . . [he] has been regarded as the great authority on these matters, and has no one to read on his heels, until at last, I think, he has come to look upon the Natural World as his special preserve, and no poachers allowed. So I must manouevre a little to get my poor memoir out of his hands.[34]

R. L. Meile reports that a manuscript of his that was rejected twice had both times been refereed by the very author whose research he had put into question.[35] Another author states: "the process asks a referee to suppress humans' natural tendency to self-preservation. The referee must evaluate fairly a paper that may eviscerate the referee's life work."[36]

It is important to realize that not every instance of a referee viewing a work as inferior because it conflicts with her antecedent view is a case of ideological bias. To begin with, in some cases the evidence may support the referee's prior view better than it supports the view taken in the submission, and the referee may be influenced only by the evidence. More importantly, according to many philosophers, there is a legitimate principle called "epistemic conservatism" or "methodological conservatism" that permits or mandates a person to prefer his or her prior view in certain circumstances even when the evidence may not seem to provide adequate support for that prior view. The line between ideological bias and epistemic conservatism is not easy to draw. The next chapter will be devoted to clarifying the scope and limits of epistemic conservatism.

Aesthetic Bias

Does an article strike readers as intellectually more sound when it comes out in print than when it was in mere typescript? Does the substance of an article typed on a messy manuscript look better when it's retyped in a pleasing font? If the answer is yes, then aesthetic bias exists. Looks affect assessment of content; people judge books by their cover. I have often heard people say, "his article seemed better in print than in typescript."

Aesthetic bias is assumed to exist in employment. People applying for a job are advised to make their resumes and cover letters neat, and to put them on nice paper, because doing so will impress their prospective employers favorably.[37] However, assuming that a neat resume is correlated with good job performance—I don't know whether the hypothesis has been tested—this fact has no bearing on the case of articles. The argument for taking appearance into account in the case of job seekers is that if aesthetics influence judgments about a job candidate, this reflects not a bias but an objective judgment: a sloppy c.v. points to sloppy work habits. But referees couldn't care less whether an author is sloppy in his typing. They care only about whether he is sloppy in his thinking. I have met many distinguished academicians whose offices always look like a hurricane just hit them. Their work's quality is still high. Hence there is no good argument for allowing aesthetic considerations to enter into an objective assessment of a submission's worth.[38]

This completes my inventory of biases. It is not a complete list, but it does cover the most salient ones. A paradox with published studies that provide evidence of bias is that if the study is valid, the bias identified may have been operative in the acceptance of the study itself. Furthermore, whenever a researcher does work drawing on previous studies, the affiliation or personal identity of the researchers behind those studies would be playing a role in whether the author takes the study seriously. The possibilities for applying the study's results to itself are many. I will content myself just to note this point, without removing the complexities and perhaps paradoxes it creates.[39]

Particular charges of biased refereeing, we should note, vary in plausibility, based on several factors. Thus, one might cry "bias!" if her paper has been rejected by one journal using two referees; but if her paper has been rejected by several journals, the allegation of bias diminishes in cogency—which is not to say, let me add, that being accepted by one journal is evidence of bias at another one that earlier decided on rejection. (For one thing, the accepting journal may have a lower rejection rate.) Also, disagreement on an issue in the humanities is different from disagreement on an issue in the sciences or mathematics: the more disagreement characterizes the field in general, the more difficult it is to prove bias. Next, the lower the rejection rate of a journal or publisher, the more a charge of bias is likely to arise when a paper is rejected. Finally, the more editors and referees are sensitive to the literature on bias and know that psychologists might be studying their journal, the more they will do to curtail bias.[40]

How Bias Operates

Before we turn to evaluate the most common remedy for biases—more exactly, for *ad hominem* and affiliational bias—let me add a few points about how bias operates.

1. Bias may affect an assessment either by affecting the action the referee takes, or by affecting the referee's judgment of merit. Someone biased against women may recommend rejection of a woman's article either because, though he thinks well of the submission, he does not want women to gain power, or because he has a biased perception of the quality of women's work that adversely affects his assessment of merit. In the first case merit is bypassed altogether; no judgment of merit is relevant to the decision. In the second case a judgment is made about merit but is affected by extraneous considerations.

2. Robert Nozick notes (in another context) that biases can enter an evaluation in two ways.[41] In one case, a bias can influence an evaluator to apply a given set of standards differentially. This may be termed first-level bias. In another case, an evaluator might exhibit second-level bias, which is bias in the selection of standards:

> [W]hen the explanation of why *these* standards rather than others are given, or why these weights rather than others are given, in part involves the belief by some that these very standards and weights would work to the exclusion of certain groups [for our purposes we may add: "or individuals"—D. S.] and this motivated them to put forward these particular standards.[42]

Presumably an evaluator can place greater or lesser emphasis on a particular strength or weakness of a submission, depending on his or her bias, and come to a conclusion that is based on personal attitudes rather than merit. Thus, a bias against an author does not manifest itself in a referee recommending rejection without giving supporting reasons; rather, referees who are influenced by bias against a submission point to flaws but assign them greater importance than they would were the biasing factor absent. (In scientific papers, the rubric "methodological flaws" is a convenient one for biased referees to invoke.) Likewise, a referee who is biased in favor of a particular submission will notice flaws but will assign them minor significance.

This leads us to a puzzle about bias. In some fields there is general agreement over what counts as sound research methodology, what constitutes an important problem, and other foundational questions; but in other fields there is much disagreement about such matters.[43] Suppose that in a particular field some experts hold that M is a good method while other experts think it is not. Suppose that referee R believes M is a good method, but because R is biased, R faults an author for using M. The position R takes about the manuscript surely is justi*fiable* given that other experts reject M. But R's evaluation is biased. Suppose the journal editor realizes that R's report is biased. Can't one argue that the editor should give weight to the report because after all the position the report takes is a defensible one and one that other experts may have on the same grounds? My inclination is that the editor should treat the use of M as a serious problem and to judge the manuscript exactly as he or she would were there to be no issue of bias. To do otherwise is to commit the genetic fallacy, the fallacy of assuming that because a view has its origins in irrational processes (such as bias) therefore it is false. Biases can help the referees and editors who hold the biases to identify real problems in a manuscript.

3. If person S has a bias, then S can come to an impartial judgment only if the bias is eliminated. When I speak of "eliminating" the bias, I mean that S either (i) eradicates the attitude in question, or else (ii) prevents it from playing a causal role in judgment. The difference between (i) and (ii) is illustrated by procedures for jury selection. Prospective jurors who admit, in *voir dire*, to harboring prejudices are not necessarily dismissed from the jury pool for a given case. They are not required, as a condition of serving, to have feelings different from the ones they do. Instead, they are asked to prevent those feelings from playing a causal role in judgment. The person is asked, as it were, to weigh the relationship between a certain body of evidence and the conclusion "the defendant is guilty beyond a reasonable doubt." If we entrust people's lives to juries and juries depend on this sort of elimination of bias, the existence of bias does not automatically spell a biased conclusion in a professional judgment. A referee who is asked to prevent a particular attitude of hers from influencing her evaluation of a project resembles the famous Kantian moral agent, who conquers natural feelings in order to comply with duty, in this case the duty to judge impartially. No one should require someone who referees a paper to be neutral as to the position taken in the paper (ensuring no positive or negative ideological bias), nor is it reasonable that a referee should have no opinion about the author or the author's institution before refereeing a paper. All that is required is that the referee put these opinions aside in judging the work, except perhaps for extreme cases (e.g., a physicist judging an astrology paper).[44]

4. In some cases, the operation of a bias leads to the same bottom-line result that an unbiased evaluation would yield. You may like Joe's book because Joe is a friend of yours, but it could very well be that you would judge it to be good even were he not a friend of yours. In fact, in some

cases, an unbiased evaluation would not be as close to the truth as the biased one is. Suppose, again, that you like Joe's book because Joe is a friend of yours, but were you to judge the book without the bias operating you would misunderstand Joe's arguments and reason poorly about them, leading to a negative evaluation. If the book really is good, your bias has brought you closer to the truth than an unbiased evaluation would have. This hardly seems like a good reason to allow referees to be influenced by their biases, but the possibility of the case arising deserves to be noted.

Blind Review: For and Against

The antidote usually proposed for *ad hominem* and affiliational bias is "blind" or anonymous review, a procedure whereby referees are not apprised of a manuscript's author or the author's affiliation. Use of blind review suggests that reviewers, as a group, cannot be relied upon to eradicate their biases or cannot be relied upon to prevent the biases from playing a causal role. Because some of the factors that might lead to biased judgments by referees may also lead to biased judgments by editors who must interpret and assign weight to referees' reports, it is not illogical to propose not only that referees be kept in the dark, but also that if possible an author's identity be withheld even from editors until they have made a decision on the manuscript. Predecision correspondence with the author in such cases can be carried on by a staff member—for example, an editorial assistant or managing editor.[45] Advocates of blind review do not as a rule carry the argument this far, but the issue is worth raising in light of Edmund Byrne's charge that "since the prestige of a journal is in part based on the percentage of papers that are rejected as initially submitted, there is a built-in incentive not to 'waste time' on papers whose authors are at low-echelon institutions. Then, too, even if an editor opts to send a paper out for review, he can influence its fate by a judicious choice of reviewer(s)."[46] A 1971 study showed that prestigious authors were more likely to have their papers accepted by editors without peer review.[47] (Editors may have ideological biases too which play themselves out in choice of manuscripts to publish, but blind review does not help with regard to ideological bias.) In most of what follows, nothing hinges on whether the blinding process extends to editors, but in a few instances my recommendations exploit the notion that an editor will know the author's identity.[48]

The arguments for blind review are simple to state. They reflect a standard distinction in ethics between considerations of fairness and considerations of utility. First, proponents claim, blind review is *fair*, as opposed to unblinded review, which is *unfair* because it allows for evaluations to be infected by bias and therefore not be judged on their merits. Second, blind review promotes utility: it is more likely to lead to truth, since it prevents the operation of biases that may block a reviewer from perceiving truth. In cases where the biased evaluation leads to the same outcome that an unbiased one would have, there is no loss of utility; but the element of unfairness remains. It is unfair to give a biased evaluation even in that case, even though the author cannot claim he or she was harmed. One other consideration in favor of blind review is that according to at least one study, blinded reviewers produce reports of better quality than unblinded ones. (Other studies found no difference, however.)[49] Finally, authors would probably prefer anonymity to be spared the embarrassment of a highly critical referee knowing their identity.

Surprisingly, there are several arguments that may be leveled against blind review. I do not think that overall these are persuasive, but they are thought-provoking, and some, I think, may make us skeptical about the necessity for blind review in all cases.

1. Community

Some argue that a blinded system is perforce impersonal, and as such "erode[s] the humanistic values that are supposedly at the heart of [the academic] enterprise."[50] This criticism takes on importance in light of such books as David Damrosch's *We Scholars*,[51] which argues that current academic research is excessively individualistic and frustrates the goal of creating an academic community. When scholars become aware not only of what topics are being mined by others in their discipline, but also who is mining them, a sense of community is fostered. As Stanley Fish (a critic of blind review) notes, proponents of blind review are likely to concede that "impersonality brings its dangers."[52] Preposting of publications on websites for the purpose of eliciting comments from all subscribers violates the canons of blind review, but it is an accepted practice. With Web postings, reviewers know the names of the authors of the papers they are judging. This, arguably, is a concession to the need to maintain community, and it underscores the validity of the aim of community as opposed to the aims of blind review.

Blinding the names of authors is only half the story of blind review. It is common practice for journals to "double blind," that is, to hide the identity of referees from authors just like the other way around.[53] Quite apart from the danger, often expressed, that suppressing referees' identities increases the likelihood of irresponsible evaluations because some referees write careless reports when they know they will remain anonymous, the practice of blinding referees' identities diminishes the potential for further personal communication between two individuals who are working in the same specialty. In sum, one may argue against both author anonymity and referee anonymity on the grounds that whether singly or in tandem they nurture an impersonal atmosphere that is detrimental to academic life. Obviously there is no algorithm for weighing the disvalue of blinded review as against its value, but a consuming emphasis on merit overlooks the concern about impersonality.

To counter this argument, a proponent of blind review must show that unblinded review brings with it not just *some* deviations from the principle that publications should be judged on merit, but *significant* deviations, that is, significant enough to warrant sacrificing the good of "scholarly community." Conceivably a defender of blind review will point to the fact that his is a concern about fairness, while the objector's is a concern about utility, and that considerations of fairness are weightier than considerations of utility. This argument depends on a particular weighing of fairness versus utility coupled with an assumption about the extent of unfairness entailed by unblinded review. In my opinion fairness ought to trump utility in this case, and the loss with regard to community is not so great as to outweigh the problems of bias. In carrying out this weighing, we might press the questions: Is community a value all by itself, or is community valued because community enables the pursuit of certain aims shared by its members? If the latter, and among the community's aims is to bring truth to light and to be fair to members, wouldn't these aims better be realized by blind review? Also, are we speaking about a community of all professors, or only those who submit work for publication? If the aim is a community of all professors, and reviewing only creates a community of authors who submit and authors who publish, isn't that deleterious to the larger aims? Without answers to these questions the "community" argument is too rough to be cogent.[54]

Furthermore, the argument from community could be used in the opposite direction. Unblinding enables a biased referee to exclude an unknown author or authors at low-prestige institutions from the bounds of the community. A larger community is created by including people from universities that are not prominent and authors who are not well known. As Edmund Byrne notes, on one conception of the academic profession, members of the profession have a responsibility to help others "enter, master and advance the profession." Blind review promotes this aim, bringing scholars into the community of the published who otherwise would find entry too difficult.[55]

Finally, the community argument is glib. Perhaps authors and referees will come to hate each other. Perhaps most referees will do too little refereeing for that to make a difference vis-à-vis the aim of community. Perhaps community can be fostered perfectly well by postpublication connections. All these factors have to be weighed in constructing the argument from community.[56]

2. The Ubiquity of Bias Thesis (UBT)

Some thinkers believe that every evaluation that anyone makes is infected by bias—that it is impossible for human beings to make bias-free judgments. If so, blind review capitulates "to the spurious notions about objectivity and absolute value that . . . scientists and social scientists banter about."[57] On the thesis that bias is ubiquitous—UBT—there ostensibly is no need to discuss further the problems of biased refereeing. For, as Nozick inquires: "If it is held to be impossible to eliminate bias, then in what sense does charging bias constitute a criticism?"[58] Because bias is ineliminable and infects even judgments that we like to classify as rational and objective, therefore, the argument goes, bias is no evil at all. If merit cannot be identified, there is no point in trying to identify it any more than there is a point in trying to jump out of our own skins. (Of course, if UBT is true, then those who believe UBT have a bias toward it, an irony and paradox I wish to note but will not explore further.)

As stated, this is a poor argument against blind review. Blind review does not purport to eliminate all biases. But it does purport to eliminate some—*ad hominem* and affiliational bias, along with biases based on gender or race. The aim of placing constraints on a refereeing system is not to achieve perfection; for instance ideological bias (regrettably) would remain, as blind review does not touch that. Bias may be ubiquitous, but some biases are eliminable by blinding, and it is desirable to eliminate those biases which can be eliminated. A system in which biases are eliminated to the extent possible is fairer than one in which no such effort is made.

Still, it is worth pressing on a bit to assess UBT itself, because blind review will not eliminate all biases. Consider two explanations, proposed by Nozick, of why bias is ubiquitous (if indeed it is). One is that there is some particular bias or biases that are intrinsically resistant to elimination. The other is that not all biases can be eliminated simultaneously.[59] If we pay heed to this distinction, then the conclusion that bias need not be eliminated does not follow from the affirmation that bias is ineliminable. For suppose that the reason bias is ubiquitous is not that some particular bias or biases are intrinsically resistant to elimination but that not all biases can be eliminated simultaneously. One cannot then criticize a referee for having bias *simpliciter* (that, after all, is inevitable and ineliminable), but one can charge a referee with not eliminating all *eliminable* biases—in other words, with not doing the best that he or she can. So, even if some degree of bias is sure to operate, ostensibly referees ought to minimize bias, by eliminating those of their biases that are eliminable. The strong conclusion that bias is not bad does not follow from the ubiquity of bias, so long as that ubiquity is due to the impossibility of eliminating all biases simultaneously and not to the existence of some particular bias or biases that are ineliminable.

And it does seem implausible that no biases are eliminable without blinding. Hence referees would seem to have some obligation to eliminate those biases that are eliminable without blinding. If a referee feels that a particular bias is ineliminable, the referee ought to apprise the editor of this fact and withdraw if the editor deems it appropriate.

The moral to draw is that even if having some bias or other is inevitable, a good deal can be done to bring bias within tolerable bounds. It is within that domain that referees bear responsibility to eliminate bias even if UBT is true.[60]

Interestingly, though, in some cases *not* eliminating a bias leads to a fairer result overall. Consider a case of an unblinded submission. Suppose that a referee has conflicting biases—one positive and one negative. For example (a particularly crude one!): he has negative feelings toward the author because the two of them bickered at a conference, but he is positively biased because the author is ailing and he has sympathy for him. Our first instinct of course is that the referee either withdraw or seek to suppress the biases. But in this case the two biases could mitigate each other, if not cancel each other out, and their simultaneous existence creates a fairer result on the whole than the elimination of one of them. (If the referee eliminates one of the biases, the other bias will prevail.) So the truth of UBT does not automatically preclude a fair evaluation—or an evaluation with a fair result—in all cases.

Imagine a jury in which two members have a strong bias, one holding a bias for the defendant and the other against. If the juror with a bias for the defendant leaves the jury, the jury is now less biased—but less fair as well.[61] Given this analogy, we may say that a referee does a fairer job if he follows not the directive, "eliminate all eliminable biases," but rather the more qualified principle, "eliminate biases according to a pattern that will lead to a fairer result overall." In this vein Stephen Lock, editor of a British medical journal, mentions a view that referees ought to be chosen so as to have opposite attributes.[62] Carefully chosen biased judging (and biased refereeing) could actually produce a fairer result overall.

I think it must be conceded that biases might mitigate or cancel each other in the way just described. But given (as Atara Graubard Segal noted to me) the difficulties in calculating and determining when one is dealing with this phenomenon, one achieves a still fairer result by picking referees with few known biases, and by referees trying to eliminate their biases to the extent possible. Judges in the American court system are expected to withdraw from cases when they are biased—independently of whether they or others have countervailing biases, and even independently of whether they can overcome the bias. It is assumed that there are enough prospective judges all of whose biases can be eliminated. (Of course if UBT is accepted, the elimination of *all* bias is a pipe dream. But even given UBT, we can find judges with *few* biases.) In addition, a referee should not withdraw if other referees are likely to be even more biased, and the referee arguably need not withdraw if they will be *as* biased.

In sum, the ubiquity of bias thesis does not make blind review pointless. Blinding eliminates some biases, in particular *ad hominem* and affiliational, as well as biases based on gender or race. Further, even given UBT, referees can work to eliminate other biases they have. The referee's remaining biases may have a small effect on the evaluation. Or, the remaining ones might mitigate or cancel each other. The point is this: we do the best we can, and elimination of some biases is a worthy step even if other biases remain.

3. Fish's "No Intrinsic Merit" Argument

Stanley Fish has constructed a provocative argument in his essay, "No Bias, No Merit: The Case against Blind Submission."[63] The principle behind blind review is to ensure that in making their evaluations readers are not influenced by extraneous factors, that is, factors other than the intrinsic merits of the article.[64] Extraneous factors supposedly include "rank, affiliation, professional status, past achievements, ideological identification, sex, or anything that might be known about the author."[65] Now, the problem Fish sees is that "merit is not in fact identifiable apart from the 'extraneous considerations' that blind submission would supposedly eliminate." "There is no set of standards that operates independently of the institutional circumstances that have been labelled extraneous." Age, gender, rank, professional status, previous achievements, ideology—all these are "essential to the process by which intrinsic considerations are identified and put into place." The identity of an author and various facts about the author go into the assessment of merit. "I want to argue, in short, that there is no such thing as intrinsic merit, and indeed, if I may paraphrase James I, 'no bias, no merit.'"[66]

What is the basis for this strange-sounding claim? Much of Fish's case rests on a single sort of example, where a work is written by a prominent author. The identity of the person who says that *p*, is relevant to whether *p* has merit. When C. S. Lewis declared (this is Fish's own example) that the concluding books of *Paradise Lost* are an "untransmuted lump of futurity,"

> Lewis' status as an authority on Renaissance literature was such that he could offer readings without courting the risk facing others who might go against the professional grain, the risk of not being listened to, of remaining unpublished, of being unattended to, the risk of producing something that was by definition—a definition derived from prevailing institutional conditions—without merit.[67]

Because of Lewis's outlook, it would be over fifteen years before a group of scholars could begin rehabilitating the concluding books of *Paradise Lost* by demonstrating their subtlety and complexity. And it would be another fifteen years before Raymond Waddington could pronounce their efforts successful. Nowadays, as Waddington argued, "few of us . . . could risk echoing Lewis' condemnation." Similarly, "if Northrop Frye should write an essay attacking archetypal criticism, the article would be of much greater significance than an article by another scholar attacking the same approach."[68]

Fish's position is taken by a star author (Fish). But let us evaluate it on its merits.

Fish is clearly right, I believe, about three points. First, in the absence of blind review, a pronouncement by a prominent author—a "star" (this is not Fish's word here)[69]—is more likely to be published than is the same pronouncement written by someone who is not established in the profession. This is usually because the work will be perceived as important (Fish would say constitutive of the field) and perhaps as likely to be true, though sometimes it may be published because of its interest to future historians of a field. Second—a corollary of the first point—a position may achieve the status "is thought to have merit" because so-and-so holds it. Third, Fish is right that standards change in a profession and that individuals help shape what counts as an interesting issue, a correct assumption, or a sound methodology. To a definite extent judgments of merit depend on time and place. Hence I can agree that "merit, rather than being a quality that can be identified independently of professional or institutional conditions, is a product of those conditions; and moreover, since those conditions are not stable but change continually, the shape of what will be recognized as meritorious is always in the process of changing too."[70] But it is a leap from these facts to conclude that blind review is objectionable, for the following reasons.

Regarding the relativity of standards in a profession, in a given time and a given place a referee would have no trouble determining merit in the non-Fishian sense—scholars do that all the time. Notice that ethical standards, too, change with time and society, but this does not render the work of ethicists pointless. Relativity is not anarchy.

Regarding the fact that "stars" can publish things that others cannot, and that their doing so can confer upon a view the status, "is perceived to have merit," a few points need to be made. First, Fish's argument could in principle be extended from star authors to scholars at star institutions to scholars in a certain age group to scholars of a certain gender or race, depending on the degree to which a profession's members are biased in favor of certain institutions, genders, or races. After all, at a given time the voices of one group may be taken more seriously than the voices of another. But this means that Fish's argument could license prejudice of the worst sort, maintaining that at a given time a person's race or gender is part of or what constitutes the merit of his or her work. It is precisely to prevent outlandish positions from achieving the status of "merit" just because someone important, or someone who belongs to a group that is perceived as important, holds them, that we ought to adopt blind review. Contrary to some indications by Fish, one ordinarily is not able to infer from a blinded work the identity of an author, the school he or she belongs to, or the author's gender.[71] What the reviewer does evaluate is merit—using criteria of the profession at that time, but not the criterion "who says it?" It is true that, with blind review, what Fish believes to be one aspect of merit—the author's identity—will not be taken into account. But on his view, it seems, this omission will be a deficiency only when the author is a star, and in most cases blinding will be unproblematic. Fish should not confuse the fact that once a star author's identity is known a work of hers will be taken seriously and be influential, with the notion that being written by a star is a necessary condition of merit. I also believe that Fish has conflated being influential with having merit, but I will not press this distinction beyond calling attention to it.[72]

Another response to Fish may be that in fact exceptions should be made for star authors; their manuscripts should not be reviewed blindly. I proceed shortly to take up this question. One other question to raise about Fish's proposal to unblind is whether it would fare as well as blind review if the test of time is applied.[73]

There is a final wrinkle to consider. Despite the title of his article, Fish denies, in a response to critics, that he was arguing against blind submission. He insists that he was arguing only "against a certain *characterization* of blind submission as a policy that will eliminate politics from the process of selection"; he was "point[ing] out that inevitably that policy will have its own politics."[74] I have dealt with his argument concerning merit as an argument against blind review because that argument makes sense of part of the original text and has intrinsic interest. But if Fish does not oppose blind review but only wishes to say it has its own politics, there is no objection to blind review here, and we need not consider his work in this section.

Or perhaps there is an objection here, not to blind review, but to *preferring* blind review. The objection will be that, while blind submission is an acceptable policy, if one favors blind review on the grounds that it avoids politics, one has flimsy grounds for *preferring* or *agitating for* blind review. Blind review has its own politics. Defenders of blind review might concede this but argue that a politics of fairness and equality, and a politics that seeks to prevent the Matthew effect, is superior to a politics that entrenches the powerful. Fish argues, however, that "one argument I won't listen to . . . claims moral and intellectual purity for a practice that is informed no less than any other by the interests and hopes of particular groups."[75] Thus might he repel arguments from fairness and equality and the Matthew effect. To this I can say only that the genetic fallacy is operating in his reply. That those who want a fairer system have political objectives does not invalidate the merits (!) of the (fair) system they espouse.[76]

4. Star Authors

Editors face an interesting challenge to blind review when a famous or "star" author submits an article.[77] In these cases a journal may not be interested in the article on account of its merits (putting aside Fish's definition of merit) but on entirely different grounds. The journal's audience will probably be interested in the piece even if it is not argued as well as normally is needed for acceptance.

A long-range view of the profession requires referees to understand that some pieces are historically important because they shed light on a famous person's development as a thinker. Also, publishing an article by a star enhances a journal's prestige. Book publishers have economic reasons to favor star authors—their books will sell well, besides attracting attention and enhancing the press's prestige; and in fact once an author has proven himself, he often is offered a contract without having written a word of his next book, and without the eventual manuscript going to referees. Sending the article or book to referees unblinded invites *ad hominem* bias; not sending it for external refereeing at all displays such a bias too. But there is some logic in allowing bias for star authors while not allowing bias for unknown authors— and therefore in unblinding star submissions while blinding others' submissions. Admittedly, if a referee knows that a journal sends submissions by star authors unblinded, and the rest blinded, the referee may infer of a blinded submission that he or she receives that it is not written by a star, and this may itself create an *ad hominem* bias. But if the pool of stars is known to be very small, referees will realize that very good scholars are in the "nonstar" category, and will not be influenced negatively by their bias.

A counter to this permissive attitude about lifting the veil in the case of a star author is that it produces the Matthew effect. The rich get richer, and the poor become poorer since the rich take up the available print space. If lifting the veil means that the rich get richer and the poor poorer, then, the argument goes, the veil ought not be lifted even when there is justification for the rich getting richer.

Here I reply, first, that the rich getting richer is not as bad a result as the argument would have it. If it were, much else in academic life would have to be changed. Do we require anthology editors to invite unknown authors lest we produce the Matthew effect? Do we blind promotion committees to where a candidate has published articles, whether his or her works have appeared in prestigious and potentially bias-inducing places? Second, it is not as if referees were constitutionally incapable of recognizing merit in papers by unknown authors or flaws in papers by known authors: compare once again the jury system where people are asked to set aside their prejudices. (But then you will ask: what was the point of unblinding? Answer: To let the referee take the author's identity into account in the final recommendation.) Third, one can distinguish between bias for already famous authors and bias against unknown authors. The former could be justified even if the latter is not, for the scholarly community will have an interest in further work by a famous author even when it is qualitatively not up to the standard met by work of unknown authors. To be sure, allotting space to a famous author means taking away space from an unknown author, but the number of articles affected by this is small (and in electronic journals may not exist at all). Fourth, a publication by a star author may raise a journal's or publisher's profile, thereby benefiting all other contributors, including unknown authors.[78]

Despite the plausibility of the case I outlined for unblinding submissions by star authors, I think a compromise between the two sides of this question is possible. Send all manuscripts blinded; but have the editor make the judgment about what weight to assign to the author's stardom. This way if the referee's report is strongly negative, the editor may include that as factor.

It is possible to argue for unblinding stars' manuscripts by adopting a certain view about the responsibilities of editors and publishers. Richard T. De George and Fred Woodward maintain that

> No author has any right to have his or her manuscript accepted or published by any press or journal, no matter how good it is or good the author thinks it is. No press or journal has any obligation to publish any particular manuscript, again no matter how good it is. . . . [E]ditors have no ethical obligation to publish the best manuscripts. . . . [P]ublishers have many considerations to balance in deciding to publish a manuscript—quality being only one of them.[79]

The authors call this "the doctrine of publishing-at-will," which is comparable in some ways to "employment-at-will," that is, "the doctrine that employers have the right to hire whomever they wish, and to fire for any reason or no reason; and that employees may work for whomever they choose who offers them work, and to quit whenever they want or for no reason."[80] If one endorses De George and Woodward's argument, the appropriateness of preferring stars' manuscripts—or anyone else's—is a simple corollary. In truth, their analysis strikes me as too permissive, and they themselves do not want to justify discrimination based on gender, race, or national origin; this leads to the question of whether other sorts of discrimination—other forms of bias—might be disallowed as "inappropriate to the press and to the work being considered," thereby constraining editors and limiting the application of the "publishing-at-will" doctrine.[81] Furthermore one might want to insist that editors have *professional* obligations that preclude favoring certain authors over others, even if they do not have straight ethical obligations. All this can be debated. But at the bottom line De George and Woodward are correct, I think, that quality is but one of the considerations that book publishers have to ponder. After all, they have a professional obligation to help their publishing houses' finances and good reputation.

5. Bias Improves Work

An author could actually profit from "negative" referee bias, for a negatively biased referee may spot weaknesses in an argument that a less antagonistic one would overlook, weaknesses that the author will try to repair. Indeed the referee's interest in spotting weaknesses and the author's penchant to defend him- or herself are products of similar biases, and both lead to the author's sharpening his position and to enhanced dialogue. At some point, to be sure, we want the referee to retreat from criticism (if the author convincingly answers the criticism), and bias stands in the way of that. But the process can be productive for the author.[82]

The question to be asked is whether this consideration justifies doing away with blind review. I think not. First, the phenomenon described occurs too infrequently to generate an argument against blind review. Second, it seems to me that biased referee criticism will be most valuable when the bias in question is ideological. An editor may even prefer to send a submission to a referee he knows has opinions contrary to the submission's author. But in the case of *ad hominem* and affiliational bias it is unlikely that a referee will furnish as productive a critique. (To be sure, he or she might.) Third, rejection of the paper seems a high price for the author—and, where the paper is good, the journal's readers—to pay for the improvements stimulated by a sharp critique, though the revised submission might be accepted by another journal. Fourth, there is a consideration of fairness: it seems unfair that a paper is rejected because the referee has a bias, independently of whether the bias results in improvement of the paper. Fifth, the overall, all-things-considered calculation of costs vs. benefits of unblinding will be on the side of cost. (As I conceded, a bias might lead to a more fair evaluation, not merely a more helpful one; an unbiased referee might be lazy with regard to assessing crucial dimensions. But these cases are in a small minority.)

So far we have been assuming that bias improves work when the bias is negative. What about positive bias, though? What are its effects? A referee's positive bias could lead to the referee strengthening the paper considerably. Because of a bias toward the author or the author's affiliation, the referee could feel the need to be especially helpful, either because he or she likes the author or because he or she wants to impress the author—the latter is famous and teaches at a famous school. The referee may then put more work into the paper than he or she would otherwise, and will construct arguments and locate evidence that significantly buttress the author's case. It is situations of this sort that lead some scholars to refer to referees as sometimes "coauthors." Blind review would prevent this sort of situation. Now, the kind of improvement brought about by the bias seems quite beneficial. Can it be argued that submissions should be unblinded because they allow for improvements of this sort?

Here I suggest weighing the benefit against the cost. The described benefit of unblinding is not likely to occur often, and the cost of unblinding is the failure of good papers to be published along with a general unfairness. So, there is a real cost here to blind review, but not enough to outweigh the benefits.

6. Consistency

A sixth argument against blinded review is that insisting on blind review creates a deep inconsistency within academic practice. In many other situations, academicians display no troubled feelings toward unblinded evaluations. Decisions about hiring and promotion must be made knowing at what universities a candidate has taught previously. Decisions about what books to buy are based on knowing an author's previous work and knowing (in the case of anthologies) which authors are contributing to the volume that one is contemplating purchasing. Academic evaluation depends upon the possibility of referees (here extended to include potential employers) offering unbiased evaluations of an author's work postpublication, knowing full well who the author is, his or her university affiliation, and where the candidate's work has been published. No one objects to an evaluator, in a tenure or promotion decision, looking with special favor on pieces published in particular journals.

On the contrary, that's what committees are asked to look for. But this is based on an inductive argument whose conclusion is that work published in journal X is good. Why not then allow prepublication referees to use other sorts of inductive arguments based on what university has hired this person or how this person's other writings have been received? If blind review is needed in the case of publication, why is there no agitation for it in other areas of academic life? Indeed even in the area of refereeing books, which seems so analogous to refereeing journal articles, common practice is to allow unblinded review.[83]

This argument is as challenging as it is intriguing. One problem with it, however, is that some of the inductive judgments it points to are used only when it is unfeasible to evaluate a work on its merits. Consider job applications. No search committee can afford to read every candidate's every article; they can and should read a sample by every short-listed candidate. The fact that this is typically done suggests that on the contrary the prestige of the journal is not taken to guarantee high quality. As for the fact that book manuscripts, as distinct from journal submissions, are usually refereed unblinded, this practice strikes me as wrong and hence as no counter to the claims of blind review. Still I think it undeniable that many academic judgments are quite properly rendered in unblinded fashion, using inductive arguments. What follows is not that journal reviews should be unblinded, but that blind review is not as critical as often asserted. I will have more to say on this topic later.

7. An Author's Program

Knowing an author's identity may legitimately aid a referee. A paper under submission may be closely linked to other papers an author has published; both may be part of the same general program. In this case the quality of the submission cannot be assessed properly without seeing it in the wider context of the program. The more promising the program is, the more appropriate the paper may be to publish. In such cases lifting the veil and explaining the role that the submission plays in a larger program may lead to a more just result. As conceded earlier the inference isn't foolproof, since an author's work is frequently uneven. But it seems to deliver a conclusion with reasonably high probability. "On most topics, it is actually important and appropriate to know the author's identity and past role in the series of ongoing debates."[84]

It is true that, in most cases of this sort, the author is likely to have cited his or her other papers in footnotes, so the cover will have been blown anyway if the referee is up on work in the field (as ought to be the case). However, a blind review policy dictates that the author use a "third-person" rather than first-person reference in footnotes, so in some cases the referee may not know that the present author is the one who wrote those other works.

There is a way of handling the case just described that allows some preservation of anonymity for referees, and that is for authors of papers to communicate separately with the editor that their paper is part of a larger program and to request that the importance of the paper be judged in the context of this larger project. The *editor* can then make a judgment as to whether this requires lifting the veil of anonymity, so that the referee can judge the paper in the context of the author's larger program. Or the editor may make that judgment herself once the referee's report is on hand. Using the larger program as a context for judgment is especially important if the journal audience is likely to be interested in the program. With so many papers and work-in-progress indications posted on professors' websites, papers can be easily identified as part of a larger program. (However, editors generally will not have a good enough command of the field to know the significance of the larger program and it makes more sense to ask a referee, who is a specialist in the area.)

8. Spotting Duplication

Unblinding helps a referee or editor spot outright duplication of the author's own work. Authors nowadays sometimes recycle earlier work to puff up their curriculum vitae.[85] This is a lamentable practice, notwithstanding the fact that it brings an author's ideas to a wider audience; redundant articles crowd out other worthy contributions. It is easier for a referee to notice and/or check for duplication when the referee knows who the author is. (Again, theoretically an editor could perform this task, but the editor may not be enough of a specialist to carry it out.)[86]

Once again, it must be conceded that in some instances lifting the veil of anonymity gives a referee a better context for evaluation than keeping the veil on. But is lifting the veil really necessary? The editor could ask authors to declare whether any of their publications resemble the one under submission and perhaps even to enclose a copy of those publications. An independent party could then check the paper out for the sole purpose of spotting duplication, even before the referee judges the paper strictly on its merits. The delay caused by this procedure need not be more than a few days.

9. Futility

Blinding does not always accomplish what it aims to do. Blinding does not make it impossible for a referee to figure out who a manuscript's author is, especially when the author has published significant material previously and the referee works in the same field. Studies estimate the rate of successful blinding in science to be 50 to 76 percent, but this includes conclusions drawn from self-reference in works cited in the text or notes.[87] An editor of an economics journal states, however: "Yet, rare is the reader who cannot guess the author's name, and so the supposed protection and value of the formal anonymity are often hollow."[88]

My initial reply is that while in many cases, blinding is futile, the statistics have to be adjusted once self-references are eliminated; and even if blinding is futile in the remaining cases, that is not sufficient to justify unblinding the rest. Better put: faced with a choice between blinding all and unblinding all, we are best off with blinding all. There is, however, another point to make here. What affects the outcome of an evaluation is not the *knowledge* of who wrote the manuscript, but the belief; even when a referee guesses incorrectly, the belief that person S wrote the piece may generate a bias. This sort of problem is well known to scientists who have conducted randomized clinical trials. In a randomized trial, patients are not apprised whether they are receiving an experimental drug or a placebo. Patients sometimes take a guess about what they are receiving, and their belief in turn affects how they feel. In large randomized clinical trials, the validity of the study is preserved by randomizing the patients to the two drugs; since patients on both sides of the study will take guesses, the differences between the two groups of patients will still be informative. No comparable remedy exists to nullify the effects of guessing by referees. (Compounding the problem, an author could load his manuscript with "see my" references that, without imparting false information, convey an inflated sense of the author's publication record and importance. I presume a good editor will have these eliminated before sending the paper to referees.)

The argument is, in short, that blinding does not eliminate *ad hominem* bias completely. The point is well taken, but it should be borne in mind that in many or most cases the referee will not venture a guess once all clues are suppressed by the editor (or an assistant, if blinding extends to the editor). Furthermore, as has been remarked more than once in this book, and many times elsewhere, blind peer review is the worst system except for all the others. It is still better to blind than to unblind, even though referees may take guesses.

10. Empirical Studies Suggesting Blinding Makes No Difference
Recent empirical studies suggest that whether a paper is given to a referee blinded or unblinded makes no difference to the reviewer's recommendation.[89] In some of these studies the identical papers were sent to referees, one referee's copy being blinded and the other referee's copy left unblinded. Con-

sidering the other studies we have seen on bias, the finding of no difference is truly surprising, albeit welcome. As I indicated earlier, times may have changed due to increased sensitivity toward problems of bias. Clearly the matter deserves more empirical study. It will suffice, I think, to note two points.

First, as Frank Davidoff points out, the reviewers in the studies frequently were able to identify the authors or take a guess, so we were not really dealing with true blind review.[90] Second, in one study done of abstracts submitted to a program on urology, blinded and unblinded abstracts were sent to different sets of referees. Abstracts were graded by combining scores of the two methods. The investigators found that changing which method was used would have had "a substantial impact" on the same actual roster of the program. Only 60 percent of the abstracts accepted would have been chosen by either method. Furthermore, 20 percent of the five abstracts in each subject category graded most highly by one method would not have been accepted for inclusion by the other method.[91] One expects some differences between reviewers both of whom judge objectively, and the study does not say whether bias was involved in any of the cases; but the discrepancies suggest that the choice of method is not a matter of indifference. At the same time, we do not know which method was "better." One can only await the results of further studies (and metastudies) of whether blinding matters to specific decisions and whether blinding improves reviews.

11. Inductive Arguments vs. Bias: Wherein the Difference?

The quality of an author's previous work and the quality of work produced by authors at this author's institution can ground an inductive argument concerning a piece under submission. This pattern of inductive reasoning is hardly foreign to academic judgments. It is used by editors of journals or books when they invite particular contributors to participate in a volume based on their track record, and by readers who buy a particular anthology of essays because they're excited by who's in it.

An inductive argument concerning affiliational bias is made by several commentaries in reply to the paper by Peters and Ceci cited earlier, which sought to show the existence of affilational bias:

> If we assume that the study shows mainly positive bias for prestigious schools and researchers, I would wonder whether such bias is *always* inimical to the interests of good reviewing. Individuals reporting a study from Stanford, for instance, hold their appointments at that school because in all probability they have demonstrable ability and a record of good research. A reviewer may be justified in assuming at the outset that such people know what

they are doing. . . . It is not always possible to make the same assumption in the case of unknown colleagues, and hence the latter are apt to be judged more closely on what they actually describe.[92]

I am in full sympathy with rejecting papers from unknown authors working in unknown institutions. How does one know that data are not fabricated? Those of us who publish establish some kind of track record.[93]

[B]ut science is not democratic, and it is neither unnatural nor wrong that the work of scientists who have achieved eminence through a long record of important and successful research is accepted with fewer reservations than the work of less scientists.[94]

Also, "on the average, the work of established investigators in good institutions is more likely to have had prior review from competent peers and associates even before reaching the journal."[95]

The claim at hand is that researchers from prestigious departments can be assumed to have followed certain research design protocols that researchers from other departments cannot be assumed to have followed; that they have more colleagues and have gotten better feedback; that they are under more pressure to produce quality work, and thus have more to lose if a paper is rejected. These considerations either apply straightforwardly in the humanities as well (better feedback from colleagues, more pressure to produce quality work) or have analogues (sound method being the analogue of good research design). In general, it has been argued that a central factor in science is trust in the testimony of others. "Scientific propositions often must be accepted on the basis of evidence that only others have. Consequently, much scientific knowledge rests on the moral and epistemic character of scientists."[96] The author of this quotation is concerned with the problem of fraudulent research, which, he argues, often cannot be detected by peer review;[97] our issue is not fraud but reliability of investigators in the more general sense. Nevertheless it seems to me one could argue more generally that track records of individual authors are relevant to accepting the sincerity and reliability of their testimony as to what went on in a laboratory and what conditions prevailed there. And in a field like history, where one could detect fraud more easily by reexamining the documents cited as evidence, it is generally far too laborious to do that, so the historian must be trusted.[98] Here again inductive judgments have to be used based on the track records of the researchers involved. Finally, one can extend this point to make the case that an author's track record of good publications or the high quality of his or her school's research can ground an inductive argument for or against publication.

If the inductive correlation holds, blind review seems to blind the referee not only to the author's identity, but to important facts that need to enter a judgment of quality. Clearly if the piece is given to the referee unblinded, the referee must read the article and decide on its merits, instead of relying on an inductive judgment. That doesn't seem much to ask. Furthermore, reading it is necessary even if the piece is given to the referee unblinded. To see why, consider the following two instances of inductive argument, where we might not require further examination beyond the induction, and contrast them with a third case:

- A law school has to choose the best candidates from among 10,000 applicants. The school is well aware that some people who had only average scores on the LSAT would, if admitted, have excellent records in law schools and fine legal careers thereafter. Extensive inspection of letters of recommendation might help identify those students. But the admissions committee decides that it just isn't cost-efficient; better to let a few good ones slip through the cracks than invest the time and manpower to come up with a better result.
- A university advertises for a faculty position. Three hundred resumes pour in. To make the initial cuts, the search committee looks for people who have published. This leaves 200 candidates viable. They then decide to look for people who've published in specific top-tier journals. They know that further investigation into the rejected candidates might show that their work, published in lesser journals, was of the same or better quality as those left in the running. But it isn't cost-efficient to investigate.

Now consider this case:

- A scholar is asked to referee a paper he knows has been rejected before, by several journals. Inductively it is unlikely that he will recommend acceptance. Can he skip reading the paper?

The first two examples bring out a crucial point: using inductive evaluative judgments rather than examining specimens individually can be justified on a basis of cost-effectiveness. It is not the case, however, that referees who have agreed to review a paper can excuse themselves from doing a careful reading on grounds of cost-effectiveness. So they must read the paper, quite apart from the fact that they incur a responsibility to do so by agreeing to the editor's request to review it.[99]

But assuming the reader must read the paper, knowing who wrote a paper can be helpful in the evaluation, for the process of making judgments about quality often is complicated. Referees often need to think long and hard about any argument they are asked to evaluate, and a responsible referee has to take into account the possibility that his or her objection is flawed. Conscientious referees therefore sometimes have the experience of wondering, when they find a problem with a paper, "Is it him or me?" "Did I miss something or did the author really make this mistake?" Haven't many of us objected strenuously to certain positions, only to find our criticisms rebutted and shown to rest on a misunderstanding? If the paper's author is someone who is known to be a formidable arguer, the referee is perfectly justified in being more careful about trusting her own objections than if the paper's author is a slouch. Knowing the author's affiliation sometimes helps one pick the most credible hypothesis to explain why the referee sees a difficulty. Blind review, of course, eradicates all such inductive arguments. As such, it might be criticized as forcing referees to make judgments . . . well, blindfolded.

Let us distinguish three theses, one descriptive, the other two prescriptive. (1) The descriptive thesis is that when referees favor authors from major universities over authors from minor universities, they do so because they use an inductive argument whose conclusion is that this paper by a major-university author is probably a good one. Nothing in the empirical research informs us as to whether referees consciously use such an argument, but research like the Peters-Ceci study suggests that such an argument could be attributed at least at the unconscious level. (2) The first prescriptive thesis is that author affiliations should be disclosed to referees *ab initio* because knowledge of affiliations helps reviewers make good judgments about papers. (3) The second prescriptive thesis is that a reviewer who used the inductive argument would be justified in doing so but reviews should be blinded anyway.

Many of us are probably drawn to (3), but why? What sense does (3) make? Why shouldn't affiliations be disclosed *ab initio*, as per (2)? Why prevent the use of inductive arguments? I proceed now to lay out four answers.

A. Inductive arguments of the sort we are dealing with are dangerous. They might be used to justify bias of race or gender, not because one race or gender is inferior to another, but because a referee may *perceive* one to be inferior to another and may justify a negative judgment on the basis of what that referee considers a good inductive argument.

B. Any inductive generalization based on the correlation between high-quality work and being a member of a certain institution is subject to many exceptions. Poor work may be done by professors in prestigious schools and excellent work by professors in mediocre institutions, even though a randomly chosen paper by a professor at a top university is more likely to be superior to a randomly chosen paper from a weak institution. As we noted earlier, in a tight job market, top-notch scholars may wind up at mediocre institutions, diminishing the reasonableness of an inductive argument in support of favoring prestigious institutions.

C. There are subtle epistemological points to be made based on work by Jonathan Adler.[100] A conclusion based on *ad hominem* or affiliational induction yields a *judgment with high probability* that the paper is good/bad, but not *knowledge* that a paper is good/bad. That high probability does not suffice for knowledge is evident from the well-known lottery problem, in which no matter how many tickets have been sold in a lottery, no one can know of any particular ticket that it will lose, assuming a fair lottery. Thus belief with high probability is to be distinguished from knowledge.[101] Adler gives other examples to illustrate the point. Consider a factory that manufactures widgets. Of every 1,000 widgets, 999 are good and 1 is defective. In an effort to upgrade detection of defective widgets, the company installs a device to check each widget. The device has an error rate of .003. Now compare two workers, Smith and Jones. Smith puts the device aside and simply stamps each widget "OK." He will be right in 999 out of 1,000 cases. Jones uses the detector scrupulously, and stamps each widget according to the device's determination. Because Jones uses the device, he as a result has a lower rate of correct stampings than does Smith. But, Adler claims, Smith can merely be justified to a high probability in believing that a widget is OK, but only Jones can *know* the widget is OK. Also, only Jones, but not Smith, can detach his judgment from a probability assignment and accept it as true. In like manner, an inductive judgment "so and so is from school X, so this paper is good" is a probability judgment, but a judgment of merit based on reading a paper yields an all-out judgment.

Would knowing who the author is, or the author's affiliation, constitute *additional* evidence that one's judgment based on reading the paper is right, and improve the referee's judgment? Not necessarily. Taking a cue from Adler (this is not his precise position), one might want to distinguish between evidence that a submission is good/bad and evidence that the reviewer is a good/bad reviewer. The best evidence that a submission is good/bad is the reviewer's judgment of the quality of the argument. If the reviewer later learns that the author is person X or is from institution Y, this is evidence not that the paper is good/bad, but that the reviewer did a good/bad job. The evaluation *of the paper* should proceed from the best possible grounds, in this case the qualities of the paper.[102]

D. Possibly the distinction just made will be rejected—after all, there is a strong intuition that knowing the author's identity does affect one's evaluation of a paper, and not only one's evaluation of one's own ability as a judge. Hilary Kornblith portrayed this to me nicely in correspondence:

> Suppose I read a paper carefully, twice, and didn't think much of it. I read it carefully and gave it my undivided attention. But now, I'm given additional information about the paper. It was written by someone whose work I think very well of and whom I know to be extremely responsible in the work he does: he doesn't just toss off stuff to meet deadlines and so on. So if this person wrote the paper, the epistemic likelihood that there was something in it I just missed is surely higher than it would be if it were, say, written by one of my first-year students. That would give me reason, I would think, to read it again. In an extreme case, it might even give me reason to think that if I still can't find anything good in it, I probably missed something. I don't see any good reason to deny this.

However, Kornblith continues:

> But I also think that it has no bearing on the review process, because the potential benefits of providing this information are small by comparison with the likely costs, even when one considers only epistemic matters.

The "costs" of unblinded review are that a bias is unfair, and that it obstructs a referee's ability to perceive the truth more than it helps it.

Kornblith's judgment that the benefits of unblinded review are outweighed by the costs might be debated. I suggest that this is where proponents and opponents of blind review will part company. Opponents will see the inductive correlations as having the potential to enhance referee judgment; proponents will see the correlation as having the potential to pervert it. If you find it difficult to say who is right, I am with you; it is difficult. But on the whole I think the proponents of blind review are correct.

12. Another Inconsistency?

I spoke earlier (pp. 59–60 in this chapter) about a seeming inconsistency between the use of inductive judgments in other academic contexts and their banishment from peer review. Here is one more inconsistency in the blind review process—an irony, if you wish. On what basis does an editor act? What influences his or her decision? Surely, the main influence is the opinion of the experts who refereed the paper. The editor knows the referees' identity, their affiliation, their gender, their race. Now, if we were to follow principles of blind review with thorough consistency, we would have to blind referees' reports to editors, lest information about the referees bias the editor. (The editor may favor the judgments of referees from school X, he or she might want to play up to certain referees, etc.) Perhaps you will say that we ought to conceal the referee's identities from the editor by having an assistant editor assign referees. This, it can be retorted, will make it very difficult for the editor to know the quality of the report. The inductive argument based on who the referee is, is genuinely helpful. The system that exists, then, is a strange amalgam of blind review (by referees) and inductive arguments (by editors who view referees' reports). Perhaps we are being inconsistent by insisting on blind review by referees.

A defender of blind review can retort that the inductive argument is not really of much help to the editor, and blinding of the editor to these data is indeed not an obstacle to editorial judgment. Being a prestigious author from a prestigious school does not mean that one is a good referee. Prestige does not protect against the intrusion of bias against an author or against careless reading of a manuscript. The referee's sense of responsibility is as important as the referee's ability in the relevant field. Still, there are other bases for the induction by the editor. The editor may know the referee to be a responsible reviewer and careful reader. In that case knowing the referee's identity is of help to the editor. And for that reason we should not blind the referee's report to the editor.

Once again we see how criticism of blind peer review can be generated by referring to the use of inductive arguments in other contexts. The proponent of blind review remains with the weighing of the benefits of unblinded review against its costs.

Where We Are

Our consideration of objections to blind review has been lengthy and not every point has been settled. Nevertheless we are in roughly the following position. Certain arguments against blind review have essentially failed: the argument from community; the argument from UBT; Fish's argument, the argument that bias improves work; and the argument from the futility of blinding (though the latter is stronger than the others that fail). Certain arguments bring out reasonable exceptions to a policy of blind review and suggest cases where unmasking makes sense. The argument for unblinding the papers of star authors is the best example of an exception, but I have sought alternatives to unmasking in the case where a submission is part of a larger program and where unblinding could help a referee spot duplication.

Certainly the most challenging arguments against blind review policies are those that bring out the fact that we utilize inductive correlations in so many other areas of academe, like deciding what books to buy and whom to hire, tenure, or promote. There we allow positive conclusions to be drawn from who an author is (the book-buying case) and where an author published (the hiring-tenure-promotion case). In like fashion, information about who wrote a particular paper and what institution they belong to could provide valuable information to a referee. Again, an editor knows best how to evaluate a referee's report when the editor knows the referee's identity; why can't a referee for a paper use knowledge about the author to evaluate the paper? At the same time, there are high costs in unblinding all submissions, costs in fairness and utility, and that is why I favor blind review despite all the objections to it.

Referee Anonymity

Until now, we have been discussing blinding the names of manuscript authors from reviewers. As noted earlier, however, there is another issue about blinding—namely, blinding the names of reviewers from authors. The only argument we considered that is relevant to that issue is the argument from community. It is time to take a closer look at the question.

Society, it has been said, is less tolerant today than it used to be of what it sees as power without responsibility.[103] It may be that for this reason many believe that referees, insofar as they exercise power, should be "accountable" for their comments. "Accountability" may refer to several things. It may refer to the fact that a journal will not use a referee whose previous reports have been shoddy and out of sync with other reviewers'. It may imply that authors should review the referee's report, evaluating their own evaluators (despite the bias entailed in such a procedure). Or it could imply that the referee must sign the report and disclose his or her identity to authors. The referee who signs a report is said to be more "accountable" than an anonymous one, presumably in the sense that the author knows whom to hold responsible for the comments. I maintain that the term "publicly accountable" is more accurate, since a referee is accountable to the editor in any case, in the event he or she submits a poorly done report. To be publicly accountable is to be accountable to, among others, the author. Even here it isn't clear why an anonymous referee can't be accountable, but I will not press the point.

There are prices to pay for this more public accountability. In the case of a negative review, the disadvantages of signing are potentially great, especially for younger faculty. And even senior faculty may be reluctant to express their views candidly, just as is the case with regard to letters of recommendation for other scholars. Also, it may be too difficult to recruit reviewers willing to reveal their identity, and acceptance rates might increase if reports have to be signed.[104] Yet, studies show that reviewers are willing to sign. In a particularly thoughtful analysis in *Cardiovascular Research*, Alexandre Fabiato analyzes the pros and cons of open (signed) review and concludes in support of the practice. His paper is the subject of open commentary in the same journal issue.[105] Here is a summary of the arguments pro and con, in which I have expanded on one developed by Richard Smith:[106] I will comment on a few of the arguments. The arguments Fabiato compiles are based on responses to questionnaires developed by the journal. Eighty-three percent of the reviewers and 70 percent of the authors favored reviewer anonymity.

Pro:

1. Open (signed) reviewing helps reviewers maintain an appropriate balance between their judgmental role and their role in helping authors. Signed reviews help the authors, and "it is more natural to achieve this constructive role of the reviewer in signed rather than in anonymous reviews, and signing the reviews helps the reviewers to remember their commitment to be auxiliaries rather than adversaries to the authors."[107] I do not find this formulation persuasive, because I do not associate signing with being an auxiliary; but it is certainly easier to carry out the helping role when one can use the phone and send e-mails or letters with return addresses to an author. Revealing the referees' identity also spares the editor time; the editor need not act as an intermediary.[108]
2. "The credentials of the reviewers will add credibility to their comments." Fabiato notes studies that show that authors often do not revise their rejected papers before submitting them to another journal. Oddly, the suggestion that knowing the reviewer's credentials adds credibility sounds like an endorsement of *ad hominem* bias in favor of certain referees. Anonymous reports have the advantage of being judged on their merits.
3. Open reviewing renders reviewers more accountable. Their reputation will be at stake.
4. Open reviewing helps reduce the intolerable abuses of the system, such as delays or unfair dealings.

5. Open reviewing may help resolve problems in controversial areas of research.
6. In a respectable scientific community there seems to be little justification for secrecy. (This argument strikes me as question-begging: we are trying to determine whether there is justification for secrecy.)
7. Open reviewing will render the peer review process less disagreeable and more polite. Studies show that signed reviews are more courteous.
8. New technology may render open reviewing a necessity. (We will touch on this argument more in chapter 6.)
9. This is a point of my own: a signed report allows a referee to get credit where credit is due, as an author can now include the referee in the acknowledgments by name.

Con:

1. Junior reviewers fear reprisal by established authors.
2. Creation of an "old boy/girl" network favoring established scientists. Established scientists might accept leniently the papers of people in their group, expecting reciprocity. Established authors could take advantage of former students who review their papers.
3. Creation of resentment and animosity.
4. Open reviewing will cause a higher acceptance rate, since reviewers will not wish to write critically. (Controlled studies have shown that blinded reviews are more critical.) Fabiato points out that editors may still interpret the reviewer's tactful wording in a way that will detect a criticism. But it seems to me that authors will point to the nice wording to hassle the editor over a decision to reject.
5. Open reviewing will cause more work and problems for editors. They will have a hard time finding reviewers for bad papers and will lose potential reviewers who wish to remain anonymous. Also, they will have a harder time explaining rejections to authors since negative referees' reports will be less strongly worded.
6. One should not change a system that generally works.

All that having been said, medical journals published several studies on whether unmasking reviewers affects the quality of their reports. Some of the studies suggest there is no difference.[109] Hence, while open review increases public accountability of referees, leads to more polite discourse, and carries other advantages, the actual quality of reports may be unaffected. The question is the subject of ongoing empirical inquiry and ethical debate, but the tendency in medical journals is toward unmasking reviewers.[110]

One last point. Some of the "pro" arguments Fabiato lists would support not only unmasking of reviewers but also unmasking of authors. (Arguments 6–8 seem to me to fall into this category.) It is not clear to me whether advocates of signed reviews also advocate nonblind refereeing. Fabiato, without arguing exactly this way, approves of nonblind reviewing in the biological sciences while allowing that in psychology, where "the interpretation of the data is more subjective," reviewing should be blind. However, our earlier discussion of the inductive argument brought out the fact that knowing an author's identity or affiliation could be helpful in evaluating a manuscript. The problem with advocating nonblind review on this basis is that the argument overlooks the risks of making all refereeing nonblind. On the whole, blind review is better. And that point could apply to the biological sciences as well as to other fields.

Notes

1. Liora Schmelkin, "Peer Review: Standard or Delusion," Division 5 Presidential Address to the American Psychological Association, August 9, 2003. I thank Dr. Schmelkin for permitting me to cite her manuscript.

2. If younger referees are tougher on submissions than older referees, or if men and women as a class react differently to the same work, we speak of a bias even though it is hard to find a specific belief or attitude that constitutes the bias.

3. See H. L. Roediger III, "The Role of Journal Editors in the Scientific Process," in *Scientific Excellence: Origins and Assessment*, ed. D. N. Jackson and J. P. Rushton (Newbury Park, Calif.: Sage, 1987), 222–52; R. Crandall, "What Should Be Done to Improve Reviewing?" *Behavioral and Brain Sciences* 14 (1991): 143; P. Bacchetti, "The Peer Review of Statistics in Medical Research: The Other Problem," *British Medical Journal* 324 (2002): 1271–73.

4. "The Publication Game: Beyond Quality in the Search for a Lengthy Vitae," *Journal of Social Behavior and Personality* 2 (1987): 3–12; R. A. Finke, "Recommendations for Contemporary Editorial Practices," *American Psychologist* 45 (1990): 669–70. I thank Liora Schmelkin for these references.

5. See R. E. Nisbett and T. D. Wilson, "The Halo Effect: Evidence for Unconscious Alterations of Judgments," *Journal of Personality and Social Psychology* 35 (1977): 250–56.

6. H. L. Roediger III, "The Role of Journal Editors in the Scientific Process," in *Scientific Excellence*, ed. D. N. Jackson and J. P. Rushton (Newbury Park, Calif.: Sage, 1987), 222–52.

7. D. L. Schaeffer, "Do APA Journals Play Professional Favorites?" *American Psychologist* 25 (1970): 362–65.

8. See Richard Nisbett and Lee Ross, *Human Inference: Strategies and Shortcomings of Social Judgment* (Englewood Cliffs, N.J.: Prentice-Hall, 1980); Daniel Kahneman, Paul Slovic, and Amos Tversky, eds., *Judgments under Uncertainty: Heuristics and Biases* (Cambridge: Cambridge University Press, 1982); Thomas Gilovich, Dale Griffin, and Daniel Kahneman, eds., *Heuristics and Biases: The Psychology of Intuitive Judgment* (Cambridge: Cambridge University Press, 2002).

9. See the studies cited later in this chapter.

10. Even when there is no bias operative, the competence of referees is a genuine issue. In one study, editors deliberately inserted eight errors into a paper they had accepted and sent the paper to 400 referees. A few reviewers commented on some of the errors, but only some, and some reviewers failed to detect the errors at all. See F. Godlee, C. R. Gale, and C. N. Martyn, "The Effect on the Quality of Peer Review of Blinding Reviewers and Asking Them to Sign Their Reports: A Randomized Clinical Trial," *JAMA* 280 (1998): 237–40.

11. David W. Sharp, "What Can and Should Be Done to Reduce Publication Bias?" *Journal of the American Medical Association* 263, no. 10 (1990): 1390–91, lists eighteen kinds of bias. Most of his categories fall under one of mine.

12. C. Ross, "Rejected," *New West* 4 (1979): 39–41. See also Harry Redner, "Pathologies of Science," *Social Epistemology* 1 (1987): 225.

13. See Robert Merton, "The Matthew Effect in Science," *Science* 159 (1968): 56–63; *The Sociology of Science* (Chicago: University of Chicago Press, 1973), 437–59. The verse is Matthew 25:29.

14. See the study by M. E. Lloyd, "Gender Factors in Reviewer Recommendation for Manuscript Publication," *Journal of Applied Behavior and Analysis* 23 (1990): 539–43, where manuscripts authored by females were accepted significantly more by female reviewers (62 percent) than by male reviewers (21 percent). The Modern Language Association's move toward blind review was brought about after complaints of bias against females. After blind review was instituted there was a dramatic rise in acceptance of papers by females. See David Horrobin, "Peer Review: A Philosophically Faulty Concept Which Is Proving Disastrous for Science," in *Peer Commentary on Peer Review*, ed. Stevan J. Harnad (Cambridge: Cambridge University Press, 1982), 33.

15. M. Gordon, *A Study of the Evaluation of Research Papers by Primary Journals in the UK* (Leicester: Primary Communications Research Centre, 1978).

16. Dana Crane, "The Gatekeepers of Science: Some Factors Affecting the Selection of Articles for Scientific Journals," *American Sociologist* 32 (1967): 195–201.

17. Douglas P. Peters and Stephen J. Ceci, "Peer-review Practices of Psychological Journals: The Fate of Published Articles, Submitted Again," *Behavioral and Brain Sciences* 5, no. 2 (1982): 3–11 [this volume, pp. 191–214]. This issue of the journal was reproduced as *Peer Commentary on Peer Review*, ed. Stevan J. Harnad (Cambridge: Cambridge University Press, 1982). More literature may be found in *Behavioral and Brain Sciences* (1991): 128. Also see M. J. Mahoney, Douglas P. Peters, and Stephen J. Ceci, "A Manuscript Masquerade: How Well Does the Peer Review Process Work?" *Sciences*

20 (Sept. 1980): 16–19; "Publication Prejudices: An Experimental Study of Confirmatory Bias in the Peer Review System," *Cognitive Therapy and Research* 1 (1977): 161–75.

18. Stephen Lock, *A Difficult Balance: Editorial Peer Review in Medicine* (Philadelphia: ISI Press, 1986), 46–47, points out some factors that might make the reviewers' failure to recognize articles more understandable.

19. In their "Authors' Response" (Harnad, *Peer Commentary on Peer Review*, 63) Peters and Ceci admit that, as some of their critics said, the bias may be only against authors from low-prestige institutions and not toward authors from high-prestige institutions. But they express uncertainty on this point.

20. See D. V. Chiccetti, "The Reliability of Peer Review for Manuscript and Grant Submissions," *Behavioral and Brain Sciences* 14 (1991): 128.

21. Ceci and Peters deny this based on referees' actual comments, which did not give outdatedness as a reason for rejection. But cf. Rick Crandall, "Editorial Responsibilities in Manuscript Review," in *Peer Commentary on Peer Review*, ed. Harnad, 23–24.

22. J. M. Garfunkel, M. H. Ulshen, H. J. Mamrick, and E. E. Lawson, "Effects of Institutional Prestige on Reviewers' Recommendations and Editorial Decisions," *JAMA* 272 (1994): 137–38.

23. M. Fisher, S. B. Friedman, and B. Strauss, "The Effects of Blinding on Acceptance of Research Papers by Peer Review," *JAMA* 272 (1994): 143–46.

24. See Fiona Godlee, "The Ethics of Peer Review," in *Ethical Issues in Biomedical Publication*, ed. Anne Hudson Jones and Faith McLellan (Baltimore, Md.: Johns Hopkins University Press, 2000), 73.

25. See Godlee, "The Ethics of Peer Review," 73–74.

26. See Duncan Lindsey, *The Scientific Publication System in Social Science* (San Francisco: Jossey-Bass, 1978), 98; J. M. Mahoney, "Publication Prejudices: An Experimental Study of Confirmatory Bias in the Peer Review System," *Cognitive Therapy and Research* 1 (1977): 161–75.

27. For the perseverance studies and their explanation in terms of confirmatory bias, see Nisbett and Ross, *Human Inference*, 181; the original study is L. Ross, M. R. Lepper, and M. Hubbard, "Perseverance in Self-Perception and Social Perception: Biased Attributional Processes in the Debriefing Paradigm," *Journal of Personality and Social Psychology* 32 (1975): 880–92. For explanations of perseverance in terms other than confirmatory bias, see Alvin I. Goldman, *Epistemology and Cognition* (Cambridge, Mass.: Harvard University Press, 1986), 214–21; Jonathan E. Adler, *Belief's Own Ethics* (Cambridge, Mass.: MIT Press, 2002), 288–90.

28. See for example, Brian Martin, *Suppression Stories* (Wollongong: Fund for Intellectual Dissent, 1997), chap. 5; Gordan Moran, *Silencing Scientists and Scholars in Other Fields: Power, Paradigm Controls, Peer Review, and Scholarly Communication* (Greenwich, Conn.: Ablex Publishing Corporation, 1998); Russell Eisenman, "Peer Review of Scholarly Work: The Good, the Bad, and the Ugly," *Journal of Information Ethics* 7, no. 2 (fall 1998): 7–8.

29. See the Editors of Lingua Franca, eds., *The Sokal Hoax: The Sham that Shook the Academy* (Lincoln: University of Nebraska Press, 2000), and especially Sokal,

"Revelation: A Physicist Experiments with Cultural Studies," 49–53. The quoted material is on page 49. Many people assume as well that *ad hominem* and affiliational biases were operating—here he was, a physics professor at New York University, championing the postmodern cause. Surely that would add luster to the viewpoint.

30. See Mahoney, "Publication Prejudices: An Experimental Study of Confirmatory Bias in the Peer Review System," *Cognitive Therapy and Research* 1 (1977): 161–75. Also see L. Goodstein and K. Brazis, "Credibility of Psychologists: An Empirical Study," *Psychological Reports* 27 (1970): 835–38.

31. W. M. Epstein, "Confirmation and Response Bias among Social Work Journals," *Science, Human Values, and Technology* 15 (1990): 9–38.

32. On whether the bias exists, see: C. Maxwell, "Clinical Trials, Reviews, and the Journal of Negative Results," *British Journal of Clinical Pharmacology* 1 (1981): 15–18; K. Dickersin, "The Existence of Publication Bias and Risk Factors for Its Occurrence," *JAMA* 263 (1990): 1385–89; Carlin Olson et al., "Publication Bias in Editorial Decisionmaking," *JAMA* 287, no. 21 (2002): 2825–28.

33. Redner, "Pathologies of Science," 225–26.

34. Quoted by H. Zuckerman and Robert K. Merton, "Patterns of evaluation in science: institutionalization, structure, and functions of the referee system," *Minerva* 9 (1971): 66–100.

35. R. L. Meile, "The Case against Double Jeopardy," letter, *American Sociologist* 12 (1977): 52.

36. George B. Shepherd, ed., *Rejected: Leading Economists Ponder the Publication Process* (Sun Lakes, Ariz.: Thomas Horton and Daughters, 1995), 127.

37. Nowadays, with resumes submitted over the Web, there is less emphasis on matters like fancy paper.

38. Will standardizing the fonts, spacing, and margin settings of submitted manuscripts eliminate the problem? Only when a given referee is looking at various submissions; standardization guards against a referee's viewing one paper as better than another due to extraneous aesthetic effects. But this is of no help because referees will be evaluating only a small number of submissions to the journal.

An author's writing style may also predispose a reviewer to think well of a manuscript. This point brings us to a basic question: should good writing be a criterion for evaluation? If so, is this an allowable form of bias?

39. Cf. David Shatz, "Skepticism and Naturalized Epistemology," in *Naturalism: A Critical Appraisal*, ed. Steven J. Wagner and Richard Warner (Notre Dame, Ind.: Notre Dame University Press, 1993), sect. 4.

40. I thank Jonathan Adler for suggesting these points.

41. Robert Nozick, *The Nature of Rationality* (Princeton, N.J.: Princeton University Press, 1993), 103–7 (he is not specifically speaking of biased refereeing).

42. Nozick, *Nature of Rationality*, 103.

43. See also Sue P. Ravenscroft and Timothy J. Fogarty, "Social and Ethical Dimensions of the Repeated Journal Reviewer," *Journal of Information Ethics* 7, no. 2 (fall 1998): 33–36. They speak of "high consensus" and "low consensus" fields.

44. I thank Jonathan Adler for noting this sort of exception.

45. See Duncan Lindsey, *The Scientific Publication System in Social Science* (San Francisco: Jossey-Bass, 1978), 114. Stringent blind review systems sometimes yield unintended comic results. I know a professor who received a paper to referee from a journal that had developed an array of blinding procedures. He read the paper and then composed his written evaluation: "I think this is a brilliant, creative paper worthy of publication in the very best of journals. I should mention, however, that I may be biased in my assessment, since I myself wrote the piece."

46. Edmund F. Byrne, "Reviewing Academic Books: Are There Ethical Issues," *Journal of Information Ethics* 11, no. 1 (spring 2002): 57.

47. Zuckerman and Merton, "Patterns of Evaluation in Science."

48. There is evidence of an unconscious bias on the part of editors. When editors sent manuscripts to reviewers in an area that was not their specialty, they tended to get one review in favor, one against, and one recommending to revise and resubmit. By contrast, when they sent out manuscripts in their own specialty, there was more consensus among reviewers. This suggests that the editors were more familiar with the social network in their own specialty. What gets published seems to be affected by an editorial bias. See J. Miller and R. Perrucci, "Editor's Note," *Contemporary Sociology* 31 (2002): ix–x. I thank Liora Schmelkin for the reference; I have also borrowed from her formulation of the point in "Peer Review: Standard or Delusion."

In a study in the *Journal of Economic Perspectives* 8 (1994): 153–63, Daniel S. Hamermash tested whether editors send manuscripts by known authors to better referees on whom they are likely to rely, and manuscripts by unknown authors to referees on whom they were unlikely to rely. His results suggest that there is no such correlation.

49. See R. A. McNutt, A. T. Evans, R. H. E. Fletcher, and S. W. Fletcher, "The Effects of Blinding on the Quality of Peer Reviews: A Randomized Trial," *JAMA* 63 (1990): 1371–76; R. H. Fletcher and S. W. Fletcher, "Evidence for the Effectiveness of Peer Review," *Science and Engineering Ethics* 3 (1997): 35–50. Cf. Fiona Godlee, Catharine Gale, and Christopher N. Martyn, "Effect on the Quality of Peer Review of Blinding Reviewers and Asking Them to Sign Their Reports," *JAMA* 280 (1998): 237–40 (this study showed that neither blinding reviewers nor making them sign their reports had any effect on detection of errors); Amy C. Justice, Mildred K. Cho, Margaret A. Winker, Jesse A. Berlin, and Drummond Rennie, "Does Masking Author Identity Improve Review Quality? A Randomized Controlled Trial," *JAMA* 280 (1998): 240–42; Susan van Rooyen, Fiona Godlee, Stephen Evans, Richard Smith, and Nick Black, "Effect of Blinding and Unmasking on the Quality of Peer Review," *JAMA* 280 (1998): 234–37 (blinding or unmasking reviewers' identities from each other made no significant difference to review quality, reviewers' recommendations, or time taken to review); S. van Rooyen, F. Godlee, S. Evans, N. Black, R. Smith, "The Effect of Open Peer Review on the Quality of Review and the Reviewers' Recommendations: A Randomized Clinical Trial," *BMJ* 318 (1999): 23–27 (no difference in critical level of the report).

50. See William Schaefer, "Anonymous Review: A Report from the Executive Director," *MLA Newsletter* 10, no. 2 (1978): 4; the wording here is that of Stanley Fish, "No Bias, No Merit: The Case against Blind Submission," in *Doing What Comes Naturally: Change, Rhetoric, and the Practice of Theory in Literacy and Legal Studies* (Durham, N.C.: Duke University Press, 1989), 163.

51. David Damrosch, *We Scholars* (Cambridge, Mass.: Harvard University Press, 1995), 199.

52. Fish, "No Bias, No Merit," 163.

53. Some journals (for example, *Noûs* and *Philosophy and Phenomenological Research*) list all the referees they used the previous year.

54. Atara Graubard Segal brought out to me the importance of these questions.

55. Byrne, "Reviewing Academic Books," 63.

56. For a consideration of differing types of academic "communities," see Robert J. Silverman, "The Impact of Electronic Publishing on the Academic Community," in *Scholarly Publishing: The Electronic Frontier*, ed. Robin B. Peek and Gregory B. Newby (Cambridge, Mass.: MIT Press, 1996), 55–69.

57. "Correspondence," *MLA Newsletter* 10, no. 3 (1978): 4.

58. Nozick, *Nature of Rationality*, xii.

59. Here I follow the wording of Nozick, *Nature of Rationality*, xii, except that I consider the possibility that several biases may be intrinsically resistant to elimination.

60. This formulation was suggested by Hilary Kornblith.

61. I heard this example proposed by Robert Nozick in another context.

62. Lock, 69.

63. Fish, "No Bias, No Merit," in *Doing What Comes Naturally*, 163–79; originally in *PMLA* (1988): 739–48 [this volume, pp. 215–30].

64. Fish is quoting William Schaefer, "Anonymous Review: A Report from the Executive Director," in the *MLA Newsletter* 10, no. 2 (1978): 4; my citation is slightly short of verbatim.

65. See Fish, *Doing What Comes Naturally*, 164.

66. Fish, *Doing What Comes Naturally*, 164.

67. Fish, *Doing What Comes Naturally*, 166.

68. Schaefer, "Anonymous Review," 5, cited by Fish, *Doing What Comes Naturally*, 167.

69. The word is also used by Louise Z. Smith in her critique of Fish, "Anonymous Review and the Boundaries of 'Intrinsic Merit,'" *Journal of Information Ethics* 7, no. 2 (fall 1998): 54–67.

70. Fish, *Doing What Comes Naturally*, 166.

71. See also Smith, "Anonymous Review and the Boundaries of 'Intrinsic Merit,'" 56–57.

72. Atara Graubard Segal asked whether Fish would allow that Lewis's statements were detrimental to the field. I'm not sure how he would answer this, given that Lewis's pronouncements automatically have "merit."

73. That is, would blinded articles be viewed more positively over time. Jonathan Adler suggested this question.

74. Stanley Fish, *PMLA* 104, no. 2 (1989): 220; also "No Bias, No Merit."

75. Fish, *PMLA* 104, no. 2 (1989): 220.

76. See also Smith, "Anonymous Review and the Boundaries of 'Intrinsic Merit,'" 58.

77. Fish's argument, considered earlier, figures here.

78. Atara Graubard Segal raised this last point.

79. Richard T. De George and Fred Woodward, "Ethics and Manuscript Reviewing," *Journal of Scholarly Publishing* 25, no. 3 (1994): 134, 142.

80. De George and Woodward, 143, note 3.

81. De George and Woodward, 142.

82. In fact, psychologist Robert Bornstein has proposed that the role of referees should be adversarial. That is, referees should not be asked to assess the paper's merits but rather to "make every effort to challenge and rebut [the manuscript]." In Bornstein's scheme, the author in turn would be asked to rebut the review, and an associate editor will evaluate the critique and rebuttal and arrive at a decision. "Because the role of reviewer is shifted to that of 'prosecuting attorney,' the author can no longer expect an objective assessment of his or her work, but merely a rigorous and thorough critique." See Robert Bornstein, "Manuscript Review in Psychology: An Alternative Model," *American Psychologist* (May 1990): 672–73.

83. For criticism of this practice, see Byrne, "Reviewing Academic Books."

84. William L. Shepherd, in *Rejected*, ed. George B. Shepherd, 120.

85. For an interesting variant of this point, see Damrosch, *We Scholars*, 182.

86. For arguments allowing duplication, however, see Joseph S. Fulda, "Multiple Publication Reconsidered," *Journal of Information Ethics* 7, no. 2 (fall 1998): 47–53; cf. Edward J. Huth, "Repetitive and Divided Publication," in *Ethical Issues in Biomedical Publication*, ed. Jones and McLellan, 112–36.

87. Godlee, "The Ethics of Peer Review," 74. See also R. A. McNutt, A. T. Evans, R. H. Fletcher, and S. W. Fletcher, "The Effects of Blinding on Peer Review: A Randomized Trial," *JAMA* 263 (1990): 1371–76; T. Jefferson, P. Alderson, E. Wager, and F. Davidoff, "Effects of Editorial Peer Review: A Systematic Review," *JAMA* 287 (2002): 2784–86, and the literature cited there.

88. William L. Shepherd, in *Rejected*, ed. George B. Shepherd, 120.

89. See van Rooyen et al., "Effect of Open Peer Review," and Justice et al., "Masking Author Identity," cited in note 49.

90. Frank Davidoff, "Masking, Blinding and Peer Review: The Blind Leading the Blinded," *Annals of Internal Medicine* 128 (1998): 66–68.

91. See J. Smith Jr., R. Nixon, A. J. Bueschen, D. D. Venable, and H. H. Henry II, "Impact of Blinded versus Unblinded Abstract Review on Scientific Program Content," *Journal of Urology* 68 (2002): 2123–25.

92. Russell G. Geen, "Review Bias: Positive or Negative, Good or Bad?" in *Peer Commentary on Peer Review*, ed. Harnad, 27.

93. Rosalyn S. Yalow, "Competency Testing for Reviewers and Editors," in *Peer Commentary on Peer Review*, ed. Harnad, 60.

94. Robert K. Adair, "A Physics Editor Comments on Peters and Ceci's Peer-review Study," in *Peer Commentary on Peer Review*, ed. Harnad, 12.

95. Yalow, "Competency Testing," 60. The author's expertise as we have noted elsewhere is not important in this context.

96. John Hardwig, "The Role of Trust in Knowledge," *Journal of Philosophy* 88 (December 1991): 706. For an extension of Hardwig's point, see Mark Owen Webb, "Why I Know about as Much as You: A Reply to Hardwig," *Journal of Philosophy* 90 (May 1993): 260–70. See also Hardwig, "Epistemic Dependence," *Journal of Philosophy* 82 (1985): 335–49.

97. See also S. Lock and F. Wells, eds., *Fraud and Misconduct in Medical Research* (London: BMJ, 1993).

98. An award-winning study which argued, to the delight of gun-control advocates, that probate records show limited gun use in early America, was recently contested—successfully, in the eyes of many—with considerable fanfare, by trying to retrace the author's claimed sources. For recent material on this, see the author Michael Bellesiles's defense at hnn.us/articles/1869.html and his critics' reply at hnn.us/articles/1870.html (accessed December 1, 2003). I thank Robert David Johnson for the references.

99. Jonathan Adler pointed out to me, however, that when a journal has a huge number of submissions and a high rejection rate, it could use inductive arguments to filter and reduce the original pool. At the next stage referees would judge papers for the quality of their arguments.

100. Jonathan Adler, *Belief's Own Ethics* (Cambridge, Mass.: MIT Press, 2002), chap. 10.

101. But cf. David Johnson, *Truth without Paradox* (Lanham, Md.: Rowman & Littlefield, 2004), chap. 5.

102. My use of the distinction between believing that *p* and believing that one is a good judge of whether *p* is not as subtle as Adler's distinction. Adler would see arguments based on affiliation as affecting level of confidence but not the belief itself.

103. Noted by Godlee, "Ethics of Peer Review," 76.

104. See Godlee, "Ethics of Peer Review," 75.

105. Alexandre Fabiato, "Anonymity of Reviewers," *Cardiovascular Research* 28 (1994): 1134–39. See also Seymour Epstein, "What Can Be Done to Enhance the Journal Review Process?" *American Psychologist* 50 (1995): 883–85, and reactions by Beth Rabinovich, "A Perspective on the Journal Review Process," *American Psychologist* 51 (1996): 1190; and Mark A. Fine, "Reflections on Enhancing Accountability in the Peer Review Process," *American Psychologist* 51 (1996): 1190–91. Gordon Moran asks the critical question of whether, if a referee's comments were to be published under his or her name alongside of the paper being evaluated, or as a book review in the case of a book he or she has evaluated, the referee would or would not

modify them. If the referee would modify them, this is disturbing; if not, there was no need for secrecy in the first place. See Moran, *Silencing Scientists and Scholars*, 25.

106. Richard Smith, "The Future of Peer Review," in *Peer Review in Health Sciences*, ed. Fiona Godlee and Tom Jefferson (London: BMJ Books, 1999), 248.

107. Fabiato, "Anonymity of Reviewers," 1135.

108. While Fabiato says that the editor should forbid any direct interaction between author and reviewer during the review process, he goes on to say that continuation of discussion outside the channels provided by the journal "cannot be prevented and may have healthy results." See "Anonymity of Reviewers."

109. See yet again: Godlee, Gail, and Martyn, "Effect on the Quality of Peer Review" (cited in note 10); van Rooyen et al., "Effect of Blinding and Unmasking" and "The Effect of Open Peer Review" (cited in note 49).

110. Recent works include H. M. Brown, "Peer Review Should Not Be Anonymous," *British Medical Journal* 326 (2003): 824; F. Godlee, "Making Reviewers Visible: Openness, Accountability, and Credit," *JAMA* 287 (2002): 2762–65.

CHAPTER THREE

Is Peer Review Inherently Conservative? Should It Be?

The Charge of Conservatism

In the preceding chapter, we encountered the allegation that referees and editors display ideological bias in favor of prevailing theories. To frame this allegation in different words, the peer review process is marked by an undue or improper[1] conservatism, by the wrongful rejection of submissions that go against the conventional. While it is difficult to define "innovation"[2]—not many theories fall as evidently into this category as, say, relativity or the uncertainty principle—scholars across several fields have the perception that old ideas fare well and new ideas fare badly in the publishing game.

Conservatism is thought to hamper the growth of knowledge, as well as to make books and journals less interesting to readers than they would be otherwise. Medical journal editor Stephen Lock alleges that peer review tends to "favor unadventurous nibblings at the margin of truth rather than quantum leaps."[3] Harry Redner, a political scientist who has written on the history and philosophy of science, states that "one of the roles of journals almost appears to be to sift out and reject really original contributions."[4] Economist Graciella Chichilnisky writes:

> In my experience, the more innovative and interesting the paper, the more likely it is to be rejected. . . . At a certain point one feels one would become more acceptable socially if one stopped producing new, and perhaps unsettling, ideas. Rewriting or extending the best work of others, or one's best pieces, in more accessible or polished ways could be easier, more rewarding, and more acceptable.[5]

No less eminent a figure than economics Nobel laureate Kenneth Arrow reports, "If I may venture an observation based solely on cases that have come to my attention (a clearly nonrandom sample), I think the publication selection procedure at the major [economics] journals has become methodologically more conservative, more given to preferring small wrinkles in existing analysis to genuinely new ideas."[6] David F. Horrobin, a former medical journal editor, maintains: "most scientists follow the crowd when it comes to recognition of brilliance . . . ordinary scientists consistently fight against or ignore the truly innovative."[7] J. Scott Armstrong, once editor of the *Journal of Forecasting*, sets down an "author's formula" that reads as follows: in order to get published, authors should (1) not pick an important problem, (2) not challenge existing beliefs, (3) not obtain surprising results, (4) not use simple methods, (5) not use full disclosure, (6) not write clearly.[8] Notice: referee forms often ask for a comment on innovativeness. The writers I have quoted are implying that the journal does not really want that quality.

Some observers think that conservatism affects the political structure of the profession. Because innovative articles are difficult to publish, published authors tend to be adherents of the prevailing paradigm; but they are the ones who become referees and editors, further entrenching the paradigm. Sue P. Ravenscroft and Timothy J. Fogarty assert: "Papers within accepted paradigms are more likely to be accepted than papers offering new theories, approaches or methodologies. This further concentrates power within a smaller, elite group, who are the only ones privileged or permitted to extend theoretical or research boundaries."[9] Richard Whitley alleges that even something so taken for granted as the scholarly requirement to note other literature keeps the dominant view in power.[10] It has even been said: "When we come across things we don't like . . . we cut them off, we referee them to death."[11]

Gordon Moran, an independent scholar, has sought to document the charge of conservatism and manuscript-killing with stories of silencing and suppression, in various disciplines, of theories that bucked the trend.[12] The attempts Moran identifies to "kill" innovative articles and ruin their authors give rise to Moran's question: "How can science be self-correcting if peer review authorities do not allow corrections [of existing publications] to be published?"[13] The strangeness of the situation is intensified if we recall the view of science held by Karl Popper. For Popper, the very activity of science is falsification; and the more content-ful a theory, the more open it is to falsification. Falsification is exactly what we expect of a theory.[14] While few philosophers of science are straightforward Popperians, the falsifiability of scientific theories and the self-correcting nature of science is often taken to be what demarcates science from psuedoscience. What Moran is asking, in effect, is:

Why, then, is it so hard to accept a falsification when it emerges?

Moran contrasts academic rhetoric with academic reality. The rhetoric says that:

> Scholars are committed and devoted to seeking the truth; scholars enjoy academic freedom in their pursuit of truth; scholarly research and communication are characterized by openness, free exchange of ideas, and open debate that involves critical inquiry, analysis, and evaluation; science is self-correcting; peer review fosters quality control and integrity in research grants and publications; science and scholarly research and communication are based on trust; and so forth.[15]

In sharp contrast, the academic reality Moran sees, in fields from art history to genetics to astronomy to politics, is the suppression, silencing, harassment, and ostracism of scholars whose approaches are "paradigm-busters." Senior faculty intimidate junior, and double standards are applied. The ugly price one pays for bucking a trend deters scholars, particularly untenured ones, from submitting grant proposals or manuscripts that express what they really think. Why commit academic suicide?[16]

While the authors I quoted vary in the extent to which they allege aggressive attempts to "kill" articles and silence scholars, their tone is uniformly critical of conservatism. Various suggestions have been advanced as a corrective that will encourage innovation. For example, in scientific journals there can be "results-blind" peer review, in which the reviewer evaluates only the research design and is not told the results; indeed the author could submit the design before the experiment has been conducted. Once the results can be added to it, the paper, if accepted, is published.[17] It has also been suggested that people who are not experts in the area the paper focuses on be called upon to render a judgment, since they are less likely to be taken in by the prevailing paradigm.[18]

But is conservatism as objectionable as the writers I quoted imply? Just as reflection enabled us to see that bias in some instances is justifiable, so too, before we condemn the perceived conservatism of peer review, we need to inquire whether conservatism really deserves to be condemned. Let there be no mistake: the stories Moran and others tell about suppression involve morally odious tactics. The conduct of the perpetrators undermines academic values like free speech, open debate, and integrity, and cannot be condoned. Nevertheless, we can distinguish between, on the one hand, the propriety of the tactics and, on the other hand, the propriety of the academic community, and in particular referees and editors, being skeptical of paradigm-busters. Maybe they *should* be reluctant to publish submissions putting forward such theories. Perhaps the critics are wrong to think of all conservative decisions as instances of ideological bias.

The Epistemological Basis for Conservatism

The Principle of Epistemic Conservatism

I take it as agreed on all hands that often an innovative approach is simply not well argued and not appropriately backed up by evidence. No issue of ideological bias arises here. Rejection of innovative papers that are truly bad is entirely proper, and surely some papers put forth wild, unsupported speculations unworthy of publication. The interesting issue is this: if a paper is good but goes against the prevailing trend, is it wrong for a referee to recommend rejection (or an editor to decide on rejection) on the grounds that the paper goes against the trend?

Not necessarily, one might reply. An accepted principle of scientific inquiry is epistemic conservatism (EC, also known as methodological conservatism). EC sometimes is presented as a description of epistemic practice, and sometimes as a normative principle. I will assume for the moment it is normative as well as descriptive.

The principle can be formulated in distinct ways, each with its distinct implications. Let me just convey the flavor of the principle by offering samples of it, without entering for now into the differences in import among the samples.

- The mere fact you believe that p provides a reason—some measure of justification—for you to continue to believe that p.
- Theory T1 may be preferred to theory T2 if T1 fits better with what we already believe. If you are confronted with a new theory T2 and already believe T1, and the theories are equal in evidential support, explanatory power, simplicity, and so on, continue to believe T1 because it was the first.[19]
- In adjusting our belief system to new evidence we seek to maximize coherence and minimize change.[20] On this view, one aim in responding to new evidence is "minimum mutilation" of one's extant belief system. We do have to tinker with the system in the face of contrary evidence, but the tinkering involves surrendering peripheral background beliefs rather than central ones.
- We may rationally reject a view because of its conflict with our present views even though there is nothing we can point to at present to show that the (new) view is false.[21]

When data or arguments arise that cut against an accepted theory, conservatism, in certain formulations, allows us to bracket objections to what we believe. Thomas Kuhn made famous the idea that scientists hold on to a "paradigm" theory even when new data has begun to undermine it.[22] Suppose that B. F. Skinner were to have given up his long-standing commitment to behaviorism just because of some objection someone raised at a conference, to which he has no reply. This would not only be strange psychologically[23] (how could he just give it up?), but also would be unwarranted epistemologically (is he right to give it up just because of one objection?). We fully expect our theories to encounter objections along the way that we cannot easily answer, and we are not expected to crumble in the face of a problem.

Charles Willard, a communications professor, states: "I submit that community conservatism is a defensible epistemic posture. When new ideas challenge prevailing consensus, it *ought to be* tough sledding."[24] Given EC, Willard's position seems highly defensible.

The reason behind the principle of EC is not easy to discern; the principle is not immediately intuitive.[25] To critics, conservatism seems to be a polite word for dogmatism. Defenders may say that the principle of EC is warranted because it is accepted in practice. This seems circular, however—the fact we already believe that previously held beliefs are rational is taken as a reason to hold that previously held beliefs are rational. Perhaps, alternatively, the basis for EC is pragmatic: EC is a form of self-preservation. It rescues our belief systems from instability and frequent changes of view that are cognitively inefficient and could be disruptive to our existence. The principle has survival value—it is evolutionarily advantageous. It is not that beliefs maintained in accordance with EC are more likely to be true, just that pragmatically it is better to hold on to the antecedently held theory.

Some philosophers relate EC to an idea made famous by W. V. O. Quine, that all epistemic justification is relative to an assumed background of believed theory. If so, these background beliefs must be justified.[26] A further consideration in defense of EC is that, according to some philosophers, it is only EC that rescues us from the jaws of skepticism about our commonsense beliefs. The skeptic says that our representations of the world could be caused by our being manipulated by nefarious demons or scientists. But EC thankfully permits us to discard this explanation.[27]

In any event, EC is respectable according to many philosophers. It underlies such major approaches as Quine's theory of belief revision, Bayesian conditionalization, and John Rawls's notion of reflective equilibrium.[28] Rather than reflexively condemn the conservatism of peer reviewers outright, a defender of EC would say, we must seek to harmonize criticism of peer review's conservatism with an appreciation of the rationality of holding on to a prevailing view. We need to demarcate cases of ideological bias from cases of legitimate conservatism.[29]

Evidential Asymmetry

Let us turn to a second argument, one that could both explain and justify conservative outcomes at journals and publishers. It stands to reason that a thesis that has not yet been examined by the wider scholarly community will not enjoy the kind of support that the incumbent thesis enjoys. Science, especially, is a communal endeavor, and when a community works on developing a particular claim, the claim's support often grows far beyond what it had originally, leaving newcomers at a disadvantage. An innovative thesis often results from a creative intuitive insight that does not have the empirical and other kinds of argumentative support enjoyed by longer-standing theses. It also often reflects the labors of a lone or relatively isolated individual or team. The manpower is lacking to gather more evidence or generate new arguments. Consequently, it is to be expected that the case for an innovative thesis is less cogent than the case for a conventional one. Often when an innovative paper is published, it could be aptly titled, and sometimes is, "Toward a Theory of X." It does not present a full-blown theory, but merely points in a new direction, with some initial evidence and arguments.

Appealing to the paucity of data and new arguments supporting new theories not only explains why conservatism would operate. It seeks to *justify* conservatism. Referees who recommend rejection of innovative papers do so in good faith. They are merely comparing epistemic merits. From this standpoint, it is not referee bias that accounts for the problems that innovative papers encounter in winning acceptance to journals. Rather, it is the inferior state of support for the papers' assertions when those assertions are first being advanced. The papers are not rejected even though they have merit; rather they are rejected because they automatically have less merit than a less innovative paper is likely to have. This point does not amount to an expression of the *principle* we have called EC. For it does not claim that the fact a view is antecedently believed per se yields adequate reason for denying a view that goes against that antecedently held view. Rather, the claim is only that if we compare the evidence and other reasons enjoyed by the paradigm with the evidence and other reasons enjoyed by the new approach, the paradigm generally will win. A conservative *outcome* need not flow only from the *principle* of EC. It can arise by straightforward comparison of the evidence and argumentation for the competing theories. I assume that in such cases rejection of the innovation is defensible, and the burden is on those who would seek to justify accepting the paper despite the *relative* lack of support for its innovative thesis.

Let me frame the matter this way. Consider three possible recommendations to make about innovative papers:

B1: EC is true, and/or paradigms have greater support than innovative theories, so innovative papers should be rejected.

B2: Because referees are biased against innovative papers, referees ought to be careful to eliminate this bias when they evaluate submissions. This proposal necessitates rejecting EC and treating all approaches equally, whether they have been held to previously or instead are new.

B3: Standards of cogency for accepting innovative papers should be lower than the standards of cogency for accepting papers that are not as innovative. One cannot reasonably expect an innovative paper to have the evidence and supporting argument enjoyed by a prevailing theory. But innovation must take place or the discipline in question will be stultified. It is therefore permissible, within limits, for referees to favor a growth area.[30]

Each of these policies is problematic. B1 would make the growth of knowledge and the self-correctiveness of a discipline very unlikely. B2 ignores an epistemic principle that has widespread support and does not address the fact that paradigms tend to be better supported than new theories. B3 likewise invites an objection: If innovative papers are not as well supported as noninnovative ones, why should they be accepted? Hence the question, what should be done with innovative papers?

In the rest of this chapter, I want to do two things. First, I want to say just a bit more about whether the charge that peer review is conservative is borne out empirically. Next, I want to suggest ways in which the publication of innovative papers can be justified in the face of a principle of EC and even in the face of the fact that entrenched theories have more support than new ones.

Evidence of Conservatism

To back up allegations that peer review militates against innovation, researchers not only have cited anecdotal evidence of horror stories (à la

Moran) but have shown that the percentage of important papers is decreasing over time. (The study was done in an economics journal.)[31] More commonly (here I revert back to hard science), they have systematically identified important scientific papers that initially had been rejected by journals—importance being measured by citations and prizes. Often these papers were rejected more than once, and in some cases rejection came swiftly. Now, the fact that innovative papers were originally rejected and therefore enjoyed only later recognition does not by itself prove that they had a difficult time winning acceptance *because* they were innovative. But there are considerations that suggest that in some cases their innovativeness was the cause of rejection.

Examples commonly cited of innovative works that received delayed recognition are papers presenting the discovery of blood typing, Jenner's 1796 paper describing vaccinations against smallpox, Krebs's paper describing the citric acid cycles, Glick et al.'s paper on the separate activity of B-lymphocytes, and Murray Gell-Mann's work on quarks. Juan Miguel Campanario cites many instances of highly cited, even Nobel-class work being initially rejected in two provocatively titled papers, "On Influential Books and Journal Articles Initially Rejected because of Negative Referee's Evaluations" and "Have Referees Rejected Some of the Most-Cited Articles of All Times?"[32] Building on a considerable body of previous work by Eugene Garfield, Campanario developed his study on resistance to innovation using the "Citation Classics" section of the journal *Cross Currents*. "Citation Classics" publishes commentaries by authors of highly cited articles in which the authors explain their work and sometimes describe the obstacles they encountered in both research and publication. Not all authors provide commentaries, and Campanario admits that authors who encountered unfair refereeing practices or difficulties may have a stronger motivation to write commentaries that reveal these obstacles. Even so, his results are interesting.

In "On Influential Books" Campanario compiled a formidable list, mostly in science but some in economics, but was unable to determine the relative frequency of rejections of highly cited papers. In "Have Referees Rejected" he presents a quantitative study. Campanario focused on the 400 most-cited articles, selected those for which he had commentaries (205), and located 22 papers of the 205 (10.7 percent) that had problems being published. Some were accepted after revision or after authors challenged the referee's evaluation; others were rejected outright. Three of the 22 were not only highly cited, but were the most highly cited paper of the journal in which they were published. Some papers were rejected because referees felt that the findings were not sufficiently important; others because (in Campanario's words) they "clashed with existing ideas and methods."[33] One study was rejected by the prestigious journal *Science* because the referee maintained the work was "not of sufficient general interest" and "should not be published in any journal." After being published by another prestigious journal, *Nature*, the paper became the second most cited article in the following three years. It is true that the papers listed in *Citation Classics* obviously were published eventually. But as Campanario points out, we may speculate that there were other papers that would have been cited heavily but because of delays produced by poor refereeing and rejection never saw the light of print. Other papers covering the same topic may have gotten there first, preventing the rejected papers from being published anywhere else.[34] A result similar to Campanario's—the rejection of later classics—was obtained (by other researchers) for papers in economics, though the economics study seems interested in compiling a list of famous rejected *authors* as much as famous rejected *works*.[35]

A minimal inference we can draw from Campanario's (and the economics) study is that referees sometimes make poor judgments about the quality and importance of papers. "Something must be wrong with the peer review system when an expert considers that a manuscript is not of enough interest and it later becomes a classic in its discipline."[36] This inference, we should note—and Campanario is aware of this—presupposes that the papers in question were not revised before winning acceptance to another journal. Without knowing the truth of this assumption, no conclusions can be drawn about the quality of the initial refereeing, let alone the role of conservatism in the process. In any case, the implication of poor referee judgment does not in itself suggest that the papers were rejected because the ideas were unfamiliar. On the contrary, Campanario cites instances in which papers were rejected because "it is doubtful whether the methods given are sufficiently new or valuable to warrant publication in such detail."[37] In these cases, referees do look for a new element in publications. (It is unclear why they did not find such an element in a publication that was destined for a warm reception.) Still, Campanario's paper suggests that at least some of the papers examined were too innovative to be accepted initially. Campanario writes, "prejudice and resistance to new ideas may rob readers of the opportunity to learn of these advances. To avoid this, referees should receive directions from journal staff to allow a bit more originality and creativity and the peer review system should balance quality control with the encouragement of innovative ideas."[38]

To this it may be added that once a view is in the literature, criticisms of it and even retractions are not given enough attention. Fraudulent articles that were retracted continue to be cited, a study of medical literature showed. In reviews of literature in education, critiques and replies are mentioned only 8 percent of the time; and in medicine, letters to the editors are often ignored in literature citations and are not indexed in Medline.[39] The scant attention given to criticisms of published views is not evidence of conservatism per se, since innovative articles might receive the same sort of entrenching treatment. But the phenomenon could certainly contribute to a conservative outcome.

There are also arguments—armchair arguments, we may call them—according to which it stands to reason that an innovative thesis, when first introduced, will be resisted. First, it is human nature to hold on to earlier beliefs—we saw that in our examination of ideological bias and belief-resistance in chapter 2. M. L. Johnson-Abercrombie writes as follows of the "assumptions of the age": "Like the mores of a culture, they are anonymous and so all-pervasive as to be almost imperceptible. It requires an Einstein to offer an alternative." After quoting this, Malcolm Atkinson adds: "Even Einstein clung to conservative imagery when faced with the probabilistic implications of quantum mechanics."[40] Human nature, then, as revealed by empirical studies, gives us reason to expect resistance to innovation. Thomas Kuhn writes in a related vein: "Almost always the men who achieve these fundamental inventions of a new paradigm have been either very young or very new to the field whose paradigm they change."[41]

There are also psychologically based reasons to expect conservatism among reviewers and editors. To echo a theme from our discussion of ideological bias in chapter 2, "the process asks a referee to suppress humans' natural tendency to self-preservation. The referee must evaluate fairly a paper that may eviscerate the referee's life work."[42] Referees would lose their standing as authorities. Thus referees and editors are invested in the prevailing paradigm: referees, for the reason just noted; editors, because the reputation of their journal may plummet if they print manuscripts that many regard as speculative. (On the other hand, it may also plummet if it is perceived as boring and predictable.)[43] Group psychology plays a role too. Ian Douglas-Wilson writes: "The expert is as likely as not a member of an in group, recoiling from utterances that do not blend readily with a group's current thinking."[44] E. Rae Harcum and Ellen F. Rosen charge that "the evaluation process is often controlled by mechanisms that are similar to those of groupthink, thus limiting its effectiveness."[45] This concern of blind conformity may be exaggerated, as many referees think for themselves. But it may contain some degree of truth as well.

In addition, as explained earlier, the paradigm is likely to boast more support than the innovative thesis. This fact not only explains why conservatism is practiced; it justifies the practice.

David Horrobin, editor of a medical journal, raises another consideration that in his opinion makes rejection of true innovation expected.

> The towering achievements of science for the most part have their origins in brilliant individual minds. These minds are exceptionally rare. The concept of peer review is based on two myths. The first is that all scientists are peers, that is, people who are roughly equal in ability. The second myth is that in those rare instances in which someone who is exceptional does appear, the ordinary scientist always instantly recognizes genius and smooths its path. No one who knows anything at all about the history of science can believe for one second in either myth. Most scientists are not the peers of the very best, and most scientists follow the crowd when it comes to the recognition of brilliance. The *concept* of peer review [Horrobin is of course speaking about science—D. S.] is philosophically faulty at its core. Ordinary scientists consistently fight against or ignore the truly innovative.[46]

In short, innovation is likely to be resisted because less-than-brilliant minds will not recognize its merit. One would like to hear evidence for Horrobin's view, but if his thesis applies even in some cases, resistance to innovation is to be expected.

Finally, the very way journals operate, specifically their very attempt to be fair to authors, can stifle innovation.[47] Journals typically use more than one referee, and consider it ideal to have many. One would expect this system to produce a fairer outcome. After all, if two referees agree on a paper, that could be due to chance, but if fifteen agree, that is much more agreement than chance, and if two disagree, but thirteen of fifteen agree, the resultant judgment to accept the paper is valid. Now in the case of an innovative paper, it is likely that there will be more than one or more referees who display resistance; the referee reports are likely to exhibit a low degree of what is called "reliability," that is, agreement. The odds are therefore stacked against a controversial paper being accepted. The editor might wish to take this into account, but may not feel comfortable going against a significant number of referees, in a field in which he or she may not be expert.

In what follows I will present several responses to the arguments I've canvassed in defense of conservatism.

Responses to the Charge of Conservatism

Limiting the Phenomenon

Brilliant innovation is appreciated in certain fields. Consider philosophy. When the theory of reference was in the process of being radically reshaped by Saul Kripke, Hilary Putnam, and Keith Donellan in the 1960s, and the concept of knowledge was being transformed into a causal concept by Alvin Goldman, proponents of the new theories did not have trouble disseminating their new theories in print, even though the theories encountered resistance in the philosophical community and were open to formidable objection. Objectors raised problems in print, and proponents of the theories published replies, often refining the theories in the process. Thomas Kuhn's revolutionary ideas about the history and philosophy of science were resisted when they became public, but that is not the same as saying that they had trouble finding a publisher or a forum for discussion. On the contrary, Kuhn had invitations to present his ideas and was asked to publish them in the *Encyclopedia of Unified Science*, which he did.[48] In philosophy, conservatism may have power and force postpublication, but not necessarily in the prepublication peer review process. It is my impression that openness to new ideas continues to mark philosophy three and four decades later. It must be conceded that philosophy journals, publishers, and conference organizers have had their share of criticism for not being open to nonanalytic trends such as Continental philosophy, with the battles affecting the very style in which philosophy is done. But with regard to controversies within the analytic school, innovation is highly welcome.

One well-known philosopher wrote to me:

> I'm not sure that reviewing is so conservative. If it is thought that the stuff that gets published is fairly conservative, on the whole, then one reason for that might be that most of the stuff that gets submitted is quite conservative. (I realize there's a chicken and egg problem here, but we shouldn't assume that the source of the problem lies on the side of the reviewers.) As someone who does a lot of reviewing, I can add my impression that the stuff that gets published is, if anything, less conservative than the stuff that gets reviewed. I think reviewers are, in many cases, quite eager to see new ideas, and that new ideas get, on the whole, quite a good hearing. But this is only my subjective impression, and I have no idea how you would go about getting good data on this.[49]

Note that we should expect some of this attitude to be found in fields other than philosophy. After all, if eminent scientists complain about conservatism, and such scientists are often referees, wouldn't one expect that they would favor innovative papers, given their complaints? If so, why do innovative papers (as alleged) not get published? One possible answer: they are not being submitted.

Furthermore, despite the complaints we hear about conservatism, in several fields there may be institutional correctives to excess conservatism.[50] (1) Proliferation of journals: A paper rejected by top journals still has a good chance of finding a home. This fact by itself does not prevent conservatism from operating, since publication in a lower-echelon journal means that the paper may not be taken as seriously as it would be if published in a top journal. This is especially true in fields like physics where the top journals have a high acceptance rate (75–80 percent).[51] Publishing in a lower-tier journal could actually be a blight on an author's record. Perhaps what is needed, as Jonathan Adler suggested to me, is a division of labor—but not an overt one—between adventurous journals and conservative journals. Some top journals must be ready to accept "risky" papers. They must of course balance adventurousness with quality control. (In psychology, the journals *Behavioral and Brain Sciences*, *International Journal of Forecasting*, *IEEE*, and *Psychological Bulletin* are known to publish controversial papers.) In any event it is worth noting that the classic papers considered in Campanario's study and the parallel study in economics did (and the authors of those studies note this) eventually get published. (2) Openness: In some fields, conservatism is no problem, because the field is relatively open and has no paradigm. Of course the question arises why the field is relatively open—is it because there are no ideas in the field that have not met with resistance, is it because prior paradigms have been very problematic, and so on. (3) Quality control over quality control: In some fields there may be monitoring of refereeing and editorial decisions that prevents conservatism from dominating the field.

Quality Control vs. Innovation

Some not only argue that innovative papers should not be judged negatively more often than conventional ones, but, on the contrary, "propose that evaluations give priority to new ideas, even if they have reservations about some methodological details. The purists and doubters still have an opportunity to express their concerns later in signed publications."[52] How would this position be justified?

One obvious tactic is to argue that in any field avoidance of error has to be balanced against potential loss of truth. One therefore might take a chance on an innovative paper that, if true, yields an important truth, rather than foreclose the possibility of acquiring that truth. (In scientific parlance, type II errors are serious just as type I errors are.)[53] An exclusive concern with not publishing erroneous papers closes off promising avenues. Thus new ideas might be accepted despite their lack of empirical support, if there is a cost to not putting the ideas out for public consumption. This openness works best with safeguards. So, a journal might invite open peer commentary to accepted controversial papers, as per *Behavioral and Brain Sciences*; or it might provide space for replication studies, corrections of errors, and letters to the editor. Again, it might consider having certain papers published in the form of an abstract or a proposal, in order to solicit opinion. But the basic point is that fear of a theory's falsehood is not the decisive consideration in an editor's calculation.

Horrobin offers a related argument for publishing innovative papers.[54] Horrobin asks the question, "What is peer review for?" and notes that the usual answer is "quality control." But, Horrobin continues, this answer is not adequate, because we can further ask what quality control is for. In medicine, Horrobin argues, quality control is not an end in itself; it is a means to the end of curing, relieving, and comforting patients—in a word, improving the quality of patient care. Reviewers therefore should ask of a paper's thesis, "Is this a possible innovation that should be encouraged?" Accuracy must be balanced with creativity. "[I]f we are to deliver results, quality control can be only one side of the editorial equation . . . the other must be the nourishment and encouragement of high innovation. Innovations are often erratic, unsystematic, and difficult to deal with. . . . The quality controllers . . . rarely discover anything that matters."[55] Modern peer review practices would have blocked the introduction of lithium into psychiatric treatment because the researcher worked under primitive conditions and used crude experiments. In conclusion, Horrobin maintains that medical editors should ask themselves: "If the article is right, could it change medicine 5, 10, 20 years from now?" If it could, it deserves publication. As Alvin Goldman points out, an article that in the opinion of peer reviewers will properly raise the probability of a hypothesis in readers' minds from .15 to .45 is worthy of publication.[56]

A challenge to Horrobin's argument is that if standards are lowered a great deal to accommodate the innovative papers, the possibility of truth becomes too meager to justify accepting the paper. At a certain point we must say: this could be valuable to the medical community if true, but the probability of its truth is too low. Some medical editors make the point that publishing inadequately corroborated papers leads the public down the road of false hope and inefficient treatment—a point well borne out by the effects on the population of certain *published* "discoveries" that turned out wrong, in areas like breast cancer treatment. The hope of truth has to be balanced against the danger of false leads. Clearly any argument based on the disvalue of losing truth must strike a balance between likelihood of truth and the disadvantages of being wrong. But this is not so much an objection to the theory as a challenge to articulate how probability and utility should both be considered.

It seems that a standard calculation of expected utility will do the job here. Suppose the probability that proposed theory H' is false is .7 (the calculation includes data supporting the prevailing paradigm) and the probability that H' is true is .3. Let u1 be the utility (to society) if H' is true and is published, and let u2 be the utility to society if H' is false and is published. Let u3 be the utility to society if H' is true and is not published, and let u4 be the utility if H' is false and is not published. The expected utility of publishing H' is .3u1 + .7u2, and the expected utility of not publishing H' is .3u3 + .7u4. When (.3u1 + .7u2)' > (.3u3 + .7u4), H' should be published. However, we may need to adjust the utilities further to take account of the effects of inundation, if many more articles would be published using Horrobin's principles.

Because Horrobin frames his argument in terms of medicine, the argument needs to be modified if it is to apply in other fields. In philosophy and literature, for example, we could argue as follows: quality control is not an end in itself, and the peer review system may serve other ends besides truth, for example, the development of interesting controversies. Whereas in medicine, the efficacy of an approach (the goal of medical publishing) depends on its truth,[57] the goals of philosophy and literature may not require that an "efficacious" publication be a true one. On the contrary—it could be one that forces the paradigm to confront challenges and suggests a different perspective.

It is important to note that once values other than truth are introduced into the evaluation, true views might be suppressed in the name of other goals. Actually, this is not a difficulty in the eyes of philosophers like Philip Kitcher, who argue that certain types of research (for example, research into genetic differences between races) should not be published because of their potential to cause unjust social results.[58] For Kitcher, science's goals should not be truth alone. But others will disagree.

Medical editor Stephen Lock makes another suggestion: the balance between conservatism and openness to innovation should be determined by the stage of development enjoyed by a theory. At stage one, a new theory is at the stage of "speculation and hypothesis." In the case of the British Medical Journal, submissions in this category are published in a special section called "Unreviewed Reports," reserved for anecdotes or speculations based on slim data (but still reviewed). These do not appear in databases such as Index Medicus. Stage two is the stage of "discovery," and stage three that of "breakthrough" where "everybody has suddenly come to accept the thesis and wants to climb on the bandwagon."[59] Articles in the second category challenge the prevailing paradigm and editors have to consider the gains and losses of publishing. In the case of stage three articles, referees have to consider the negative aspect of proliferation of an already known view. (The final stage is "classic," which we need not look at now.)

Millian Arguments for Publication of Innovative Papers

Relevant to our discussion is a position taken by David Lewis with regard to another issue. Lewis considers whether it is proper to take into account, in a hiring, tenure, or promotion decision, whether the candidate has opinions with which the evaluator agrees. *De facto*, reports Lewis, this factor is not considered:

> I put it to you that an appointing department will typically behave as if the truth or falsehood of the candidate's doctrines are weightless, not a legitimate consideration at all. No speaker will ever argue that a candidate should rank high because he has the advantage of being right on many important questions, or low because he is sunk in all manner of error. . . . Most likely, there will be no mention of whether the candidate's doctrines are true or false. If there is mention, the speaker will make clear that what he says is a mere comment, not an argument for or against the candidate.[60]

Lewis sees a puzzle here. Do not universities seek to advance knowledge? If so, why not choose the candidate who will best further this goal by disseminating *true* opinions?

Lewis's question uses philosophy as a model. He recognizes that in fields like science and mathematics it is important that a candidate for appointment, promotion, or tenure have true views. But let us move into his discussion of answers to his question about philosophy, for aspects of the answers he considers apply to all fields.

The reply Lewis finds most effective is that members of a department enter into a treaty in which each side of a disputed philosophical issue agrees to ignore the advantage of believing the truth lest its view one day be perceived as false. This, though interesting, is of no relevance to us. En route to his own account, however, Lewis considers other advantages of allowing wrong opinions in one's department. For example:

DIVISION OF LABOR. The researcher who is not running with the crowd may do more to advance knowledge, if he does turn out to be right, just because he is not duplicating others' efforts. Even if we think it probable that he will fail because he lacks the advantage of being right, we can expect a more important success from him if he does succeed. It may be worth backing the long shot in the hopes of winning big.[61] Philip Kitcher takes a similar position with regard to the pursuit of scientific theories which the evidence suggests are inferior to a competitor theory. "We sometimes want to maintain cognitive diversity even in instances where it would be reasonable for all to agree that one of two theories was inferior to its rival, and we may be grateful to the stubborn minority who continue to advocate problematic ideas."[62] The community needs dissenters or at least people who pursue and work on one theory even if every individual scientist is rational in believing another theory. Interestingly, most of Kitcher's examples involve the utility of some scientists holding on to an old paradigm while the majority accepts the new, while we are interested in the opposite case (a minority believing the new).

CHANGE. He who is wrong today may be right tomorrow. If he is open to argument and not too proud to change his mind, his present errors may not persist. And he who is right today may afterward go wrong.

RISK OF ERROR. We might try for the candidate who has the advantage of being right, but we might be wrong ourselves and therefore choose the candidate who has the disadvantage of being wrong.

DIFFERENT QUESTIONS. Someone who has been wrong about the questions he has so far addressed may yet, if he has the virtues conducive to being right, have the advantage of being right about different questions that he will take up later.

DEAD DOGMA. The advocate of error will challenge those on the side of truth. He will keep them on their toes, compelling them to think of questions hitherto ignored, and causing them to improve their positions even more in order to answer his arguments.

Most of these arguments (all but "Different Questions") are variants of John Stuart Mill's arguments (in *On Liberty*; see chapter 1 of this book) for tolerating opinions other than one's own. They can be transformed, with some tweaking, into reasons for someone who holds the accepted opinion to recommend allotting journal space to views he or she regards as mistaken. Publishing an innovative article that referees think is wrong may lead to a large success; it may become accepted tomorrow (though here one could retort: let it be resubmitted tomorrow); it will challenge those on the side of truth to think of questions hitherto ignored, and improve their position. These, notice, are *epistemic* advantages.

Unfortunately, in the absence of standards that the wrong opinion must meet in order to be published, the door would be open too wide. We would be left with the "let a million flowers bloom" approach that we considered in chapter 1, along with its disadvantages, such as inundation, decline of quality due to low incentive, and a total lack of quality control—many falsehoods will be believed. So some balance is needed between the need for evidence and the need to achieve the Millian goals. Here too a calculation of expected utility is called for. That having been said, we can still conclude that if Mill is right, the cause of truth could be well served—in some instances—by publishing articles that a referee or editor regards as mistaken. The question is: at what cost?

Problems with Epistemic Conservatism

Another strategy is to challenge the principle of EC head-on. This challenge can take two forms: show that EC is false, or show that even if true, EC does not justify conservative decisions in journal submissions, for additional conditions must be built into EC, conditions that are not satisfied in the case of scholarly submissions.

a. We have already canvassed the proposals for justifying EC and found some of them wanting.
b. A first stab in assailing EC itself is to argue that EC merely grants *permission* to hold on to one's prior beliefs. It does not mandate choice of the entrenched theory over the new one. Favoring innovation is then epistemically permitted. But the example of skepticism suggests this is wrong. It is not epistemically permitted to believe that we are brains in vats or are being manipulated by evil scientists.
c. The precise formulation of EC is a vexing matter. For suppose that person S believes that p due purely to a bias or wishful thinking. Is S really justified or rational in believing that p just because S believes it already? Intuitively, no.

But this objection is easy to handle. In the cases that matter to the present discussion, the entrenched theory will have a substantial amount of evidence in its favor and will not be under consideration only due to bias or wishful thinking. If we apply conservatism only in cases where there is substantial evidence in favor of a view, as is the case with paradigm theories, then conservatism is plausible. Since paradigm theories have substantial evidence in their favor, it is reasonable for someone who believes a paradigm to reject a theory opposed to it. However, one could object that conservatism is not plausible when a submission presents evidence against the paradigm, even if it does not match that in favor of the paradigm. Hence the principle of conservatism would not allow a referee or editor to reject an innovative theory when that theory is presented in a way that constitutes evidence against the paradigm.

To cut to the chase, suppose we reformulate EC in the careful manner suggested by Jonathan L. Kvanvig:[63]

> Necessarily, if S believes that p, believes that there is something that shows that S's belief that p is true, and believes nothing else that he takes to show that it is not the case that there is something that shows that S's belief that p is true, then S's belief that p has some presumption in its favor for S.

Kvanvig's version of EC applies only when the believer (S) does not believe anything that he takes to show that what he believes (p) is not shown to be true. Also, for Kvanvig, all that the principle of conservatism confers is *some* presumption in favor of antecedently held beliefs. This is not the same as saying that those antecedently held beliefs are justified *simpliciter* or are true. In sum, a careful statement of EC would not license rejecting innovative ideas just because they clash with antecedently held ones.

d. Perhaps EC should be used only when the evidence for each of two competing theories is equal in strength. If a paper succeeds in showing that one theory is more cogent than the other, EC would not apply. Innovative ideas that are underargued—and we have seen that innovative ideas often will be underargued—have little chance of being accepted, but conservative ideas that are underargued will not prevail against an innovative idea that is better argued. EC is only a tiebreaker.

e. Often it is only the referee who has a prior belief in the paradigm and is familiar with evidence for it. The editor may not be an expert in the field. Hence the editor may be in a different epistemic position than the referee—in particular the editor may not be in a position to apply conservatism to reject an innovative idea.

These objections, note, only address EC itself, not the evidential asymmetry argument. To meet that argument we must appropriate one of the other strategies mentioned, with Horrobin's and Lewis's seeming the most promising.

Conclusion

Ideological bias is not as self-evidently wrong as other kinds of bias, thanks to the principle of EC and to the reality that new ideas are not likely to boast the support that established theories have. Yet, despite the strength of conservatism, there are multiple ways of justifying the publication of innovative ideas that bust paradigms. The tricky question is how much evidence to require of the new kid on the block and, on some approaches, what utilities to consider and how to assign values to the utilities.

We have canvassed several strategies for removing the obstacle to innovation that is posed by EC. One general line of response is to identify goals of publication other than the avoidance of error or goals other than the delivery of truth. Another strategy is to attack the use of conservatism, either generally or in the context of publication specifically. Determining which if any of these responses are adequate—this I leave up to the reader.

Appendix

A Reductio Ad Absurdum of Conservatism?

An essay by Hugh Wilder helps us see what happens when conservatism is applied outside the context of refereeing for a journal or publisher.[64] Wilder's topic is not review of scholarly articles but grading of student papers. Wilder writes that he used to tell students that what position they take is irrelevant to the grade they will receive. What matters is the quality of your arguments, he would advise them: "[P]apers will be graded more on cogency of argumentation than on the substantive claims made. And of course students don't have to agree with me on substantive issues in order to get a good grade."[65] But he eventually abandoned this "principle of liberal tolerance" and decided to give lower grades to students whose work he disagreed with. Thus to use Wilder's own example a student who argued for the existence of God would receive a lower grade.

> I am suggesting that we take truth-value into consideration in determining grades, and to give good grades to papers which give good arguments for true beliefs. Since false beliefs stand a worse chance of being given good supporting arguments, papers expressing false beliefs stand a worse chance of being given good grades. . . . Arguments include conclusions . . . it is unlikely that cogent arguments will include false conclusions.[66]

I suppose Zeno and Berkeley would have received bad grades! Now Wilder's procedures do seem unfair. If the student's argument has no holes that Wilder can discern, then lowering the grade simply because the conclusion is in Wilder's opinion wrong is patently unfair. (I recall hearing a philosopher jokingly remark that the ontological argument for God's existence is unsound because its conclusion is false.) Admittedly, given his own beliefs, Wilder may have reason to apply epistemic conservatism (he does not use the term) and to reason that there must be some problem (as yet unspotted) with the student's argument. But the student has no reason to apply EC, and should be graded according to the reasonableness of his or her belief. For the student it is well argued and does not contradict his antecedent beliefs (because he has no antecedent beliefs on the subject).

If the student's argument has some obvious hole, then a lower grade seems called for, but not a lower grade than if the student were arguing for some conclusion Wilder agrees with. Finally, if the student's argument has a *subtle* hole, it seems unreasonable to expect the student, lacking skills, to have spotted it.[67] Therefore, the grade should reflect standards of argument required of a student paper, as opposed to standards that are used to judge work of a trained professional. Wilder might be warranted in going over a paper a second time if he disagrees with the conclusion, but if that second reading does not reveal any errors in the argument, he ought not lower the grade.

Some will take Wilder's argument as a sign that EC is wrong or even absurd; his application of it leads to a counterintuitive if not absurd conclusion. Should we generalize from the imputed failure of Wilder's argument and conclude that EC cannot be accepted? No: after all, the goal of publication differs from that of grading student papers. In student papers the student's goal is to present a good argument. In refereeing a journal submission the value one wants to find—bracketing the argument by Horrobin and Lewis we considered earlier—is truth; being well argued, or well argued given one's assumptions, isn't enough. So the approach of EC remains an option in the case of journal articles—if as a referee I think antecedently that a paper's conclusion is wrong, that gives me reason to reject it and live with whatever negative evidence it supplied.

Notes

1. My reason for adding "undue or improper" is that some conservatism may be perfectly proper. See below.

2. See R. E. Speier, "Peer Review and Innovation," *Science and Engineering Ethics* 8 (2001): 99–108.

3. Stephen Lock, "Letter to P. B. S. Fowler," *British Medical Journal* 290 (December 4, 1984): 1560.

4. Harry Redner, "Pathologies of Science," *Social Epistemology* 1 (1987): 224. See also his book *The Ends of Science* (Boulder, Colo.: Westview, 1987), chap. 6.

5. Graciella Chichilnisky in *Rejected: Leading Economists Ponder the Publication Process*, ed. George B. Shepherd (Sun Lakes, Ariz.: Thomas Horton and Daughters, 1995), 57, 67.

6. Shepherd, ed., "Foreword," *Rejected*, vii.

7. David F. Horrobin, "Peer Review: A Philosophically Faulty Concept Which Is Proving Disastrous for Science," in *Peer Commentary on Peer Review*, ed. Stevan J. Harnad (Cambridge: Cambridge University Press, 1982), 34.

8. J. Scott Armstrong, "Barriers to Scientific Contributions: The Author's Formula," in *Peer Commentary*, ed. Harnad, 167.

9. Sue P. Ravenscroft and Timothy J. Fogarty, "Social and Ethical Dimensions of the Repeated Journal Reviewer," *Journal of Information Ethics* 7, no. 2 (fall 1998): 45.

10. Richard Whitley, *The Intellectual and Social Organization of the Sciences* (Oxford: Clarendon Press, 1984), 27, quoted by Redner, "Pathologies," 226.

11. Geoffrey Burbridge, quoted by Eliot Marshall, "Science Beyond the Pale," *Science* 249 (July 6, 1990): 16.

12. Gordon Moran, *Silencing Scientists and Scholars in Other Fields: Power, Paradigm Controls, Peer Review, and Scholarly Communication* (Greenwich, Conn.: Ablex Publishing Corporation, 1998); Brian Martin, *Suppression Stories* (Wollongong: Fund for Intellectual Dissent, 1997),

13. Gordon Moran, "Peer Review and Academic Paradigms," *Journal of Information Ethics* 7, no. 2 (fall 1998): 21.

14. See Karl Popper, *Conjectures and Refutations: The Growth of Scientific Knowledge* (New York: Harper and Row, 1963).

15. Moran, *Silencing*, 21.

16. Moran, *Silencing*, 88–100.

17. See R. G. Newcombe, "Towards a Reduction in Publication Bias," *British Medical Journal* 295 (1987): 656–59; J. Scott Armstrong, "Peer Review for Journals: Evidence of Quality Control, Fairness, and Innovation," *Science and Engineering Ethics* 3 (1997): 63–84. I mention a few more suggestions below.

18. See M. Wolman, letter to the editor, *Scientist* 1 (1987): 10.

19. See William Lycan, *Judgment and Justification* (Cambridge: Cambridge University Press, 1988), chap. 8.

20. Gilbert Harman, *Thought* (Princeton, N.J.: Princeton University Press, 1973), 159; see also *Change in View* (Cambridge, Mass.: Harvard University Press, 1986), 59–60. Harman follows the approach of W. V. O. Quine. Harman and Quine present descriptions of epistemic practice without endorsing the notion that epistemology is normative. But I take the principle as normative.

21. Jonathan L. Kvanvig, "Conservatism and Its Virtues," *Synthese* 79 (April 1989): 143–63.

22. Thomas Kuhn, *The Structure of Scientific Revolutions* (Chicago: University of Chicago Press, 1962).

23. Skinner might have wanted a different term!

24. Charles Willard, *Social Epistemology* 1 (1987): 279. (Response to Harry Redner, "Pathologies of Science.")

25. See Lawrence Sklar, "Methodological Conservatism," *Philosophical Review* 84, no. 3 (July 1975): 374–400; David Goldstick, "Methodological Conservatism," *American Philosophical Quarterly* 8 (1971): 186–91; Richard Foley, "Epistemic Conservatism," *Philosophical Studies* 43 (1983): 165–82; Jonathan E. Adler, "Conservatism and Tacit Confirmation," *Mind* 99 (1990): 559–70, and "An Overlooked Argument for Epistemic Conservatism," *Analysis* 56, no. 2 (April 1996): 80–84; David Christensen, "Conservatism in Epistemology," *Nous* 28 (1994): 69–89; Kvanvig, "Conservatism and Its Virtues."

26. See Sklar, "Methodological Conservatism"; Foley, "Epistemic Conservatism."

27. All these approaches are criticized in Christensen, "Conservatism in Epistemology."

28. See Christensen, "Conservatism in Epistemology," 70 and 85, note 5.

29. To be sure, someone who does not antecedently accept EC could resist EC on the grounds of conservatism itself, arguing that he antecedently rejects conservatism and is entitled to stick by that. But if he argues this way, he obviously is using EC after all.

30. See David W. Sharp, "What Can and Should Be Done to Reduce Publication Bias? The Perspective of an Editor," *JAMA* 263, no. 10 (1990): 1390–92.

31. See H. W. Holub, G. Tappeiner, and V. Eberhaster, "The Iron Law of Important Articles," *Southern Economics Journal* 58 (1991): 317–28.

32. Juan Miguel Campanario, "On Influential Books and Journal Articles Initially Rejected because of Negative Referees' Evaluations," *Science Communication* 65 (1995): 304–25; "Have Referees Rejected Some of the Most-Cited Articles of All Times?" *Journal of the American Society for Information Science* 47, no. 4 (1996): 302–10. I thank Prof. Bella Haas Weinberg for pointing me to these papers.

33. Campanario, "Have Referees Rejected," 306.

34. Campanario, "Have Referees Rejected," 308.

35. See Joshua Gans and George B. Shepherd, "How Are the Mighty Fallen: Rejected Classic Articles by Leading Economists," *Journal of Economic Perspectives* 8, no. 1 (winter 1994): 165–79; the articles are listed also in *Rejected*, ed. Shepherd, 3. In psychology, see the following articles in *Psychological Bulletin*, in which authors of highly cited articles comment on their experiences: J. Cohen, "Fuzzy Methodology," *Psychological Bulletin* 112 (1992): 409–10; L. J. Cronbach, "Four *Psychological Bulletin* Articles in Perspective," *Psychological Bulletin* 112 (1992): 389–92; R. J. Douglas, "How to Write a Highly Cited Article without Really Trying," *Psychological Bulletin* 112 (1992): 405–8. I thank Aaron Levine for the economics reference and Liora Schmelkin for the psychology references. For more examples from the medical realm, see David Horrobin, "The Philosophical Basis of Peer Review and the Suppression of Innovation," *JAMA* 263 (1990): 1438–41.

36. Campanario, "On Influential Books and Articles Initially Rejected," 321.

37. D. Burk, "Enzyme Kinetic Constants: The Double Reciprocal Plot," *Trends in Biochemical Sciences* 9 (1984): 202–4.

38. Campanario, "Have Referees Rejected," 308. He cites Horrobin, whose views are quoted below.

39. Liora Schmelkin makes this point in "Peer Review: Standard or Delusion." On fraudulent articles, see M. P. Pfeiffer and G. L. Snodgrass, "The Continued Use of Retracted, Invalid Scientific Literature," *JAMA* 263 (1990): 1420–23; the 8 percent figure is from F. B. Murray, J. Raths, and L. Blanteno, "The Decoupling of *RER* Articles, Critiques and Rejoinders in the Educational Literature," *Review of Educational Research* 66 (1996): 657–58. See also Cronbach, "Four *Psychological Bulletin* Articles in Perspective."

40. Malcolm Atkinson, "'Peer Review' Culture," *Science and Engineering Ethics* 7 (2001): 195. The quotation from M. L. Johnson-Abercrombie is from *The Anatomy of Judgment* (London: Hutchinson, 1960).

41. Kuhn, *Structure of Scientific Revolutions*, 90.

42. *Rejected*, ed. Shepherd, 127.

43. This was noted by Hilary Kornblith in personal correspondence with the author.

44. Ian Douglas-Wilson, "Editorial Review: Peerless Pronouncements," *New England Journal of Medicine* 296 (1977): 877. See also B. Barber, "Resistance by Scientists to Scientific Discovery," *Science* 134 (1961): 596–602.

45. E. Rae Harcum and Ellen F. Rosen, *The Gatekeepers of Psychology: Evaluation of Peer Review by Case History* (Westport, Conn.: Praeger, 1993), 4. They credit the term "groupthink" to I. L. Janis, "Groupthink," *Psychology Today* 5 (1971): 43–46, 74–76.

46. Horrobin, "Peer Review," 34.

47. The phenomenon I am about to describe is explored by Dominic V. Ciccheti, "Referees, Editors, and Publication Practices: Improving the Reliability and Usefulness of the Peer Review System," *Science and Engineering Ethics* 3 (1997): 51–62. See also Armstrong, "Peer Review for Journals."

48. Kuhn, *Structure of Scientific Revolutions*, preface, viii.

49. Hilary Kornblith (personal correspondence). One could argue (as David Johnson pointed out to me) that innovations by known philosophers are more likely to be accepted than innovations by unknown philosophers. But even if this is true, the charge of conservatism fails, at least in part.

50. I thank Jonathan Adler for this point, as well as for the specific examples of institutional correctives.

51. This answer does not work for grant applications; see Speier, "Peer Review and Innovation."

52. Harcum and Rosen, *Gatekeepers of Psychology*, 177.

53. This is the approach taken to religious belief in William James's classic "The Will to Believe."

54. David Horrobin, "The Philosophical Basis of Peer Review and the Suppression of Innovation," *JAMA* 263, 10 (1991): 1438–41.

55. Horrobin, "Philosophical Basis of Peer Review," 1439.

56. Alvin Goldman, *Knowledge in a Social World* (New York: Oxford University Press, 1999), 263–66.

57. I put aside here the instrumentalist view that efficacious results may come from false theories.

58. Philip Kitcher, *Science, Truth and Democracy* (New York: Oxford University Press, 1999), pt. II.

59. Stephen Lock, *A Difficult Balance: Editorial Peer Review in Medicine* (Philadelphia: ISI Press, 1986), 81.

60. David Lewis, "Academic Appointments: Why Ignore the Advantage of Being Right?" in Cahn, *Morality, Responsibility, and the University*, 233.

61. Lewis, 237, referencing Philip Kitcher, "The Division of Cognitive Labor," *Journal of Philosophy* 87 (1990): 5–22. The other reasons I cite for ignoring the advantage of being right appear on p. 238.

62. Kitcher, "The Division of Cognitive Labor," 7.

63. Kvanvig, "Conservatism and Its Virtues," 160.

64. Hugh Wilder, "The Philosopher as Teacher: Tolerance and Teaching Philosophy," reprinted in Peter Markie, *A Professor's Duties: Ethical Issues in College Teaching* (Lanham, Md.: Rowman & Littlefield, 1994), 129–41.

65. Wilder, "Philosopher as Teacher," 129.

66. Wilder, "Philosopher as Teacher," 136.

67. Wilder explains that he does not wish to turn his students into misologists, haters of reason. Wilder realizes that the obvious reply to him is that he is confusing truth with what-Wilder-takes-to-be-truth.

CHAPTER FOUR

⌒⌐

Peerless Review:
The Strange Case of Book Reviews[1]

The Problem with Book Reviews

In a 1994 letter to the *Proceedings and Addresses of the American Philosophical Association*,[2] Tibor Machan, an exponent of libertarian political philosophy, complained about a brief book note that was published by the journal *Ethics* and that evaluated a work by two other philosophers sympathetic to libertarianism. The reviewer had written that he is "unconvinced by the main argument of the book," and also that "It is unclear, in the end, how the authors propose to derive a natural right to liberty from the premise that freedom is a necessary constituent to human flourishing." In addition to these criticisms, the reviewer poses several questions about the book and then declares "I can find no answers to these questions in this book."

Machan's letter assails the reviewer's statement. The answers to the reviewer's questions *are* in the book, argues Machan. Hence, he infers, there is a high probability that the reviewer did not read the book carefully but merely skimmed it. While such conduct is bad, says Machan, the problem is broader. He continues:

> More important than this particular instance of malpractice, however, is the custom in *Ethics* of offering these slipshod royal pronouncements as reviews. They ought to be scrapped, period. They are gratuitous, whether positive or negative.
>
> In my view it would be a good start for *Ethics* to list as "books received" the volumes it deems unworthy of serious reviewing and skip those irritating "this won't do" and "that's a fine job" bits, demeaning thereby most works people

spend years to prepare. If they believe they should do more than just list such books as "received," they ought to just provide a brief description of the book—maybe reproduce the jacket cover—instead of acting in their current off-handish, high-handed fashion.

It's about time to stop the charade and produce either serious treatments of our colleagues' works or just skip it. Insults, explicit or tacit, are no substitute for arguments and they certainly tend to undercut that favorite process of many who are very well received at *Ethics*, namely, authentic, serious and decent normative discourse. And these Caesar-like "thumbs up," "thumbs down" pronouncements are certainly little more than insults.[3]

The review in question was an entry in the "Book Notes" section of *Ethics*, which publishes briefer assessments than a full-fledged review. Hence the reviewer may have been constrained by word limits to make any judgment a summary one. In fact the reply to Machan by Gerald Dworkin, editor of *Ethics*, implies that the issue Machan raises is whether "Book Notes" should be replaced by a list of "Books Received," not whether the publication of book *reviews* is being called into question by Machan's objection. Thus Dworkin implies that Machan's only quarrel is with a particular feature of his journal known as "Book Notes." Clearly, however, the issues Machan raises are germane to conventional-length reviews as well. I have in mind here shorter reviews of the 500- or 750-word variety—where it is difficult for reviewers to argue in detail and therefore all too easy to give a "thumbs-up" or "thumbs-down" judgment to a claim in the book, or even a central thesis or argument, without adequate explanation.

Machan's letter should make us realize that book reviews are indeed an anomaly in scholarly publishing, an exception to the conventions that apply to other published manuscripts. My rationale for including a chapter on book reviews in this work, in fact, is that book reviews call into question the commitments of professional publications to peer reviewed work. Book reviews are not peer reviewed, and they violate other canons of scholarly publishing. They themselves are peer reviews, but often particularly bad peer reviews.

First of all, book reviews are generally accepted as submitted, subject to minor copyediting changes. Because they are not reviewed carefully by peers and are not commented on before publication, book reviews differ not only from refereed submissions but even from invited articles. Invited articles usually elicit some comments from editors, necessitating revisions. Rarely are even such comments offered on reviews. Again, invited articles may have to be redone before acceptance; book reviews usually are taken more or less as is. In a nutshell, *book reviews essentially are exempted from the peer review process.*

It is not difficult to see what could justify the exemption. Reviewing the reviewers is simply impractical. For a book review to be peer reviewed, the peer reviewer would have to read the book and reflect upon it at least as carefully as the original book reviewer. But that means, in turn, that every book review will require *two* people to read the book.[4] Furthermore, one peer reviewer normally is insufficient in the case of articles—two or three is the norm. Book reviews will of necessity violate peer review conventions, unless two or three people besides the book's reviewer read the book. This, however, would obviously be cost-inefficient. If having multiple readers of a book is an unwise investment of resources, then journals would seem to have but two other options: eliminate book reviews, or violate the canons of peer reviewing. Critics of book reviewing could argue that the former course is preferable, while advocates opt for the latter.

Furthermore, book reviews that candidates for appointment, promotion, or tenure have written generally do not count significantly for or against the candidate. Some committees count them not at all; others may ask candidates to handle them only *en bloc*, listing them in a single line of the *vita* as "Reviews published in . . . ," with no detail required about what books were reviewed, and no offprints requested. Some schools count book reviewing as service to the profession.[5] Because a reviewer is likely to have her review accepted as is and the review is likely to be ignored by personnel committees, a scholar's incentive to produce a superior work is diminished that much more. Imagine now that the candidate knew that his or her review might be rejected entirely. Considering the time it takes to do a review, and the hassle it could bring about with the book's author, would the person agree to write the review at all? Book reviews need to be published more or less automatically if the enterprise is to stay alive.

In short, the reasons that book reviews are not subjected to the same level of peer review as articles are cogent. But the bottom line is, someone who truly values peer review might wish to abolish the entire practice of published book reviews. (Insisting that journals allow letters responding to reviews would help ameliorate the problem, but journals are unlikely to accommodate, especially when they publish many reviews.)

Book reviews differ from articles in a second respect as well. Readers of published book reviews are given various kinds of judgments that they do not find in scholarly articles that critique other people's work. How good is the writing style? Is the prose lucid? Is the work well organized? Are there typos? It is true that novels and collections of poems routinely are subject to published evaluations that comment on style, but surely scholarly articles never are; only scholarly books lie open to criticisms of this sort. In fact, if someone

were to write an *article* critiquing someone's book, the writer would not include this sort of information on style and organization, but would cut straight
to substantive points. But in a book review—there these matters are commented on. Criticisms of the "gotcha" variety (this or that tangential comment is wrong, this or that text is incorrectly referenced, this or that source is
not cited, etc.) abound in book reviews. Many reviewers feel the need to show
how smart they are—few scholars are comfortable writing reviews that are all
praise. Sometimes this incentive to show one's mettle leads to good criticism,
but sometimes it leads to unseemly nitpicking.

This leads to a third point. Not only are book reviewers licensed to criticize a work's style and packaging, they may do so without furnishing supporting evidence. Reviewers often write things like, "this book is not well
written," without anyone demanding grounds for the assertion. (Although
reviewers sometimes like to quote a bad sentence or two, this is not required.)
The reader might be expected to assume that evidence exists but cannot be
adduced due to space limitations. Judgments about style, however, are not
only subjective; they are difficult to back up by argument. In a word, the reviewer is not held accountable for certain sorts of evaluation. When it comes
to criticisms of style, the journals *Noûs*'s and *Mind*'s system of having an author see a review in advance and respond to the reviewer makes a negligible
difference. Author and reviewer could debate interminably over whether a
book is written well or poorly.

Fourth—and this is Machan's point, extended from book notes to book
reviews—judgments in book reviews about *substance* are often summary and
undefended. The late Hector Neri Castaneda, founding editor of the philosophy journal *Noûs*, is reputed to have said: "you don't need to justify praise;
you do need to justify criticism." Reviewers often flout this advice and prof-
fer criticism without furnishing a justification of the criticism. Is that entirely
their fault? No. In, say, a 500-word review, it will generally take 300–350
words to convey a clear idea of what the book is about. That leaves precious
little space to *argue* for anything. Obviously some arguments can be ex-
pounded within that frame, but many cannot. The reviewer must articulate
a bottom-line evaluation, and is not expected to defend it elaborately as
would be done in an article. Insults are therefore common. The reader assumes the existence of evidence, when in reality the evidence could be weak
or nonexistent.

Something is wrong here. A book review in essence is a signed and *published* peer review—but in some instances, it is a peer review of an unhelpful
or even bad sort. A referee ticks off things that strike him or her as wrong
without giving a detailed explanation of the criticisms, an explanation that

would enable the book's author to respond. We have seen in previous chapters that confidential peer reviews themselves are in need of improvement. A "thumbs-up/thumbs-down" judgment just won't cut it in a peer review. *Published* peer reviews (book reviews) should not be held to standards that are lower than those applied to unpublished reviews that are the bread and butter of peer reviewed scholarly journals.

What indeed could motivate a reviewer to provide careful arguments in a short review? As the editors of a journal titled *Review* related in 1979—that journal consists almost entirely of reviews—"to tell a scholar that he has only 400 to 750 words is to suggest that the assignment isn't all that important—in effect, that he is being asked to provide filler, and often he responds with just that."[6] When journals ban footnotes from reviews, as they often do, this message emerges even more loudly.[7] To be sure, by and large, reviewers take their responsibilities seriously. They want to be fair, and their name does after all appear on the review. Slipshod reviews do not help a reviewer's reputation.[8] All that having been said, the degree of conscientiousness is likely to be lessened by the knowledge that the review will be published without being peer reviewed; and as we have seen already, faculty up for promotion and tenure will know that the review will not count much, if at all.

There is a fifth problem with book reviews: they are liable to be affected by numerous personal factors. Different reviewers have different conceptions of a review's purposes and criteria, as well as different ways of weighing strong and weak points. Steven M. Cahn has rightly emphasized that sympathy for another author is a virtue in scholarship. Accordingly, Cahn takes to task those book reviewers who "focus almost exclusively on a work's perceived weaknesses while saying little, if anything, about its possible strengths."[9] But whether a reviewer highlights the good or the bad is affected by various factors: the reviewer's temperament—is he or she kind or instead begrudging and jealous; and the reviewer's status in the profession—a reviewer may feel obliged to come up with criticism because a bland review will be perceived as a sign of a weak critical acumen (the review is after all signed). Also, reviewers are often selected by editors precisely because they are known to *lack* sympathy for the book's position—they have an ideological bias that will make the review more interesting to readers. And then at the other end of the spectrum is the sweetheart review—one gets to review a friend's book. In general, since reviews are written with the reviewer knowing the author's identity and affiliation, the same concerns about bias that arose for peer review, and were solved by blinding, arise here—with no chance for blinding.

These five criticisms undermine the system of book reviewing as we know it. But while some scholarly journals do not publish reviews, others publish a spate of them; and notwithstanding the issues I've raised, many scholars confess to turning to the book review section of a journal first.

A Putative Rejoinder

You might be tempted to dismiss all objections to the practice of scholarly book reviews by saying that, if taken seriously, these objections would undermine much of ordinary practice across our entire culture. Reviews of creative works are a staple of our society. Who seriously objects to the practice of publishing reviews of movies, plays, television shows, wines, and restaurants? Most publications that provide such reviews have reviewers who issue *ex cathedra* judgments. Nobody except their target objects to that, so why make a fuss over scholarly book reviews?

But this attempt to put scholarly reviews in the same boat as other reviews does not produce an effective reply. To begin with, one person's *modus tollens* is another's *modus ponens*; if scholarly reviews are comparable to, say, film reviews, then indeed the practice of reviews is in trouble across the board. Second, it is specifically scholars who make fusses about canons for review and acceptance of scholarly works—far more than do artists, filmmakers, and restaurateurs. The scholar's problem with book reviews is a charge of hypocrisy or inconsistency. Third, most reviewers of restaurants, films, concerts, and so on, write regularly for their publications. They are likely to show certain temperaments and proclivities that readers will become aware of. If the movie reviewer for a certain publication tends to review romantic comedies more favorably than action films, a reader will usually know this when reading the review and will adjust her own attitude to the product under review. By consistently reading the reviews of a particular reviewer, the reader becomes used to the criteria that reviewer uses, and knows whether he or she accepts those criteria. But scholars do not often know a reviewer's proclivities, and as journals reach out to a greater variety of reviewers, it is difficult to know where a particular review "is coming from." Fourth, some magazines publish not only their own reviews but summaries of other reviewers' evaluations (in the form of stars or letter grades). These references to other reviews give readers a fuller basis for expectation and judgments. No comparable system exists for scholarship. Authors and publishers may collect reviews of their books, but who publishes such a collection about individual works? Nobody. Readers' impressions of a book's quality often are based on just one review.

The journals *Noûs* and *Mind*, among others, send book authors advance copies of reviews of the book in order to forestall ill-considered criticisms and put reviewers on perhaps scrupulous watch. When people have to confront a person they are criticizing they are more likely to guard their words. There is no question that this leads to a fairer, more rigorous review. At the same time, no one would claim that an author's review of the reviewer's draft amounts to peer review. The author has no power to recommend rejection of the review. A book's author is hardly an impartial referee for his or her own work. Imagine designating author X a reviewer to decide on whether an article critical of her work should be published.[10]

No matter how we slice it and no matter whether authors can review the review before publication, no matter whether book authors are granted space to reply, the initial assumption that a book review is accepted unless there are grounds to reject is perplexing. Of course to some extent book reviews are merely invited articles. But given the lack of safeguards and the potential for abuse, are book reviews a good idea?

The Purposes of Reviews

To assess the criticisms we have canvassed, we need to raise some foundational questions: What are the purposes of book reviewing? Do what Machan calls the "royal pronouncements" meet those aims?

I suggest we classify the reasons for book reviews into three categories: consumerist, credentialist, and conversational approaches.

Consumerism: A first version of consumerism maintains that book reviews exist to apprise readers of what books are available and what the books are about. In this latter conception, book reviews are a kind of information service. Since information about availability can be gleaned from advertising no less than from reviews, the function of describing what the books are about should be declared the more central of these two by someone who advocates the consumerist view. However, it is clear that the information service conception is inadequate anyway, because reviews typically do more than inform; they are not plot summaries, they furnish evaluations.

Hence a more adequate version of consumerism would maintain that reviews serve an evaluative and not merely descriptive function for consumers. They furnish readers with evaluations that will help them decide which books to purchase or to borrow from the library. And of course reviews serve to give libraries good criteria for purchasing a book.

This conception, too, fails to justify the practice of book reviewing as it presently exists. Why are reviews done of books and not of articles? In many fields, articles are where the action is, so would not a critical survey of articles be at least as useful for individuals and libraries as a survey of books? Also, why do reviewers describe only select parts of the book? If the purpose of reviews were to inform, why not review many more books than presently are reviewed? It is difficult to see how these questions could satisfactorily be answered in a conception that sees book reviews as akin to a *Consumer Reports* for academia.

Credentialism: In this conception, reviews furnish a record of evaluations to enter into a book author's dossier. Certainly reviews serve that purpose, but if reviews are justified as a form of credentialism, why review books of senior people at prestigious institutions who have nowhere further to go?[11] Why not review more books to take account of more authors? Why not publish reviews almost as soon as the book comes out, as major newspapers and popular magazines do, instead of waiting several years? Why allow such a hit-or-miss pattern to what gets reviewed? None of these questions can be answered satisfactorily by a credentialist approach.

Conversationalism: This brings us to the third conception of the purpose of book reviewing: they provide discussion of issues in the field. For many scholars, unfortunately, the gossip value of reviews is higher than their value as serious contributions to discussion of an issue. Scholars will often know that a book received a nice/hostile review in journal A, but will not be conversant with the issues the review raised. I take it that the "conversational" value of reviews should not lie in gossip, but in the reviews' impact on considerations of issues. This is why often reviewers are chosen who have ideological biases: the conversation is more interesting that way.

It is at this precise point that Machan's criticism finds an anchor. When reviews make flip judgments unaccompanied by argument, the result is that no serious discussion of the issues is advanced. Worse, authors do not get to reply.

Stargazing

The aims of scholarly conversation are frustrated still more if Machan is correct about another charge:

> Nearly all the books given *bona fide* reviews are published by Harvard, Princeton, Oxford or Cambridge University Presses—written, also, mostly by the folks at elite institutions—testifying to a habit of stargazing that isn't becoming to philosophers.[12]

In his reply to Machan, Gerald Dworkin, editor of *Ethics*, the journal that published the review that offended Machan, writes that

> Such presses do in fact predominate . . . but I can assure Professor Machan that this is because there tends to be a correlation (imperfect, to be sure, which is

why each decision is made quite independently of the book's publisher) between the most important and significant philosophical books, the most acute
and interesting philosophers, and the most prestigious presses.[13]

There are two possible versions of this argument. (a) In one version, we have
a variation of the inductive argument we encountered in the chapter on bias.
The selection of books to review itself is based on known correlations between
being published by a prestigious press and carrying significance, acuteness, and
interest. No one thinks the correlation is perfect, but it is thought good
enough to merit selecting books for reviews based upon who published them.
(b) The editor or book review editor makes an independent selection of what
to review based on interest, acuteness, and so on. Then the editor discovers
that the presses that dominate the selection are the prestigious ones. If (b) is
the correct interpretation, then someone at the journal must either read the
book or else must project based on the publicity, the book jacket, the introduction, or some other guide.[14] In any case, though, if Dworkin is claiming
that the correlation is discovered through the examination described in my
account of (b), it is but a short step to using (a), since a correlation has been
determined to exist. This does not mean that every book put out by a prestigious press is reviewed, or that no books by nonprestigious presses are reviewed. It does mean that, in assigning books for review, the editor or book review editor concentrates attention on prestigious-press books, resulting in
these being reviewed more than books from nonprestigious presses.

Is the correlation accurate? One editor who has worked for both Princeton University Press and Penn State University Press argues that belief in the
supposed correlation is a bias, "an irrational preference with no basis in fact."
After all,

> Is there any difference in the decisionmaking processes at the more and less
> prestigious presses? In fact there isn't. Editors at all university presses seek re-
> views from the best readers they can find, anywhere in the world, and present
> the reports and their own recommendations to editorial boards consisting of
> faculty members. Is there anything about those editorial boards that would
> make a difference? Not in my experience. . . . And what about the editors
> themselves—is there any reason to believe that editors at more prestigious
> presses make better decisions? Not at all.[15]

I think Dworkin would respond as follows. It is not the identity of the referees or the composition of the editorial boards or the decision-making ability of
the editors that creates a difference between prestigious and nonprestigious

presses. Those factors, he could concede, may very well be equivalent at the different presses. It is rather two factors that explain the difference: (i) the standards used in making a decision to publish or not publish based on reports, that is, how the editor of the press decides what to accept based on reports; and (ii) the quality of the submissions received. If presses are *perceived* to be of differing quality, rightly or wrongly, then even allowing for the fact a book author can submit to several publishers at once, we fully expect that the submissions to the respective presses will not be the same. Top-level authors will shun low-prestige presses, and younger authors will aim for the most prestigious presses. The cycle is self-perpetuating: because of differences in perception, there will be differences in reality. One cannot claim *both* that members of the profession are biased toward certain presses *and* that submissions to the various presses are comparable in quality. A corollary of this explanation, of course, is that if we could eradicate differences in perception, we could eradicate differences in reality.

That said, I do believe that not everything published in "top" journals or by "top" presses is as persuasive and as good as everything published under lower-prestige auspices. Time and again philosophers write effective and even devastating replies to "prestige" journal articles and effective if not devastating book reviews of "prestige press" books. They find holes in an author's central argument, indirectly exposing thereby the poor judgment of the original referees (chapter 1, p. 1). But this argument establishes only that some books produced by lower-prestige presses may be better than some books produced by high-prestige presses. It does not alter the fact that by inductive reasoning, journal editors (or their book review editors) may find books produced by high-prestige presses to have a greater likelihood of being high quality than books produced by low-prestige presses, and therefore more worthy of review.

Dworkin's approach presupposes that the book review section should be devoted to the *better* books. On the consumerist and credentialist models, there is no reason for this preference. On the conversational model, the books to be reviewed are those that will excite the best discussions. "Important, significant, acute and interesting" books would seem to be right for this purpose.

On Changing the System

If reviews are to improve, a change in the attitude to them is needed across the board, on the part of editors, on the part of universities, and on the part of reviewers. There are several suggestions that would improve book reviews as we know them.

- Have someone referee the review, despite the complications that introduces.

- Allow more space to the reviewer, encouraging review essays, and ask the reviewer to use the liberalized space to produce arguments in lieu of subjective impressions. With electronic journals space constrictions are no excuse.
- Minimize negative remarks about style unless they can be backed up by a few examples; allow complimentary remarks without examples.
- Send reviews to the author before publication to elicit his or her feedback. (The *Noûs* and *Mind* system.)
- Have reviews evaluated by tenure and promotion committees, increasing the incentive to produce quality. Again, this may cause complications (who can judge the book if not another reader?), but the problem is not insuperable.
- Have books reviewed in an "author meets critic" format, along the lines of a feature in *Philosophy and Phenomenological Research*, where several reviewers assess the book's thesis and argument, each focusing on a different feature, and the author then replies.
- Publish correspondence reacting to reviews, with the maximum length determined on a case-by-case basis. The correspondence should not be of the thumbs-up/thumbs-down variety, nor should it be modeled after, say, Amazon.com's reviews. Rather, we are talking about thoughtful, reasoned discourse.

These are all good suggestions, and strikingly simple. They require no elaboration except to say that Internet publication would allow for the space required to carry out some of these tasks. But let James Hoge and James L. W. West III make the final point:

> As long as universities fail to reward worthwhile reviewing and as long as editors pay little attention to reviews, we may continue to expect many reviewers to write hurriedly, to impose lax standards, and to turn out comments that are more often "cute," emotive, or biased than fairminded or painstaking. Such performances, often shot through with backscratching and cronyism, will not be taken seriously by universities, and so the circle will go on and on.[16]

Notes

1. Soon after thinking up this title, I discovered the same pun in the title of D. E. Chubin and E. J. Hackett's *Peerless Science: Peer Review and U.S. Science Policy* (Albany, N.Y.: SUNY Press, 1990).

2. Tibor Machan, *Proceedings and Addresses of the American Philosophical Association* 68, no. 2 (November 1994): 88–90. The review in question is of Den Uyl and Douglas Rasmussen, *Liberty and Nature: An Aristotelian Defense of Political Order* (Chicago: Open Court, 1991).

3. Machan, *Proceedings*, 89.

4. I thank Steven M. Cahn for this point.

5. James O. Hoge and James L. W. West III, "Academic Book Reviewing: Some Problems and Suggestions," *Scholarly Publishing* 11, no. 1 (1979): 36. Also see Lynette Felber, "The Book Review: Scholarly and Editorial Responsibility," *Journal of Scholarly Publishing* 33 (2002): 166–72.

6. Hoge and West, "Academic Book Reviewing," 37.

7. Hoge and West, "Academic Book Reviewing," 40.

8. The last three sentences are taken almost verbatim from an e-mail sent to me by Hilary Kornblith.

9. Steven M. Cahn, *Saints and Scamps: Ethics in Academia* (Totowa, N.J.: Rowman & Littlefield, 1986), 47.

10. *Noûs*'s and *Mind*'s system of placing authors in dialogue with their critics is a good precedent to follow in the case of articles. See chapter 6.

11. Clearly senior people seeking a different job, or a merit raise, will benefit from good reviews, but there are many at the top schools who have nothing to gain because they already have enviable positions.

12. Machan, *Proceedings*, 89.

13. Gerald Dworkin, *Proceedings and Addresses of the American Philosophical Association* 68, no. 2 (November 1994): 91

14. I thank David Berger for raising possibility (b).

15. Sanford G. Thatcher, letter to the editor, *Proceedings and Addresses of the American Philosophical Association* 68, no. 5 (May 1995): 107–8.

16. Hoge and West, "Academic Book Reviewing," 41.

CHAPTER FIVE

What Should Count?

Why couldn't God get tenure? Because He wrote only one book, and it wasn't refereed.

—Academic jokelore.

Jean, a freshly minted Harvard Ph.D. in philosophy, has just landed a position as an assistant professor at Dumont University. Dumont is not in the same league as Harvard or Princeton, but it is a respected school that expects scholarly productivity of its faculty. Jean's position is of that increasingly rare breed—a tenure track job. She is eager to begin compiling a record of publications that down the road will earn her tenure.

As a graduate student Jean was ranked highly by her mentors, and her name has been circulating in the publishing grapevine. No sooner did she earn her doctorate than she received an e-mail from a graduate professor. He had been contacted by a university press to edit an anthology in philosophy of language—her specialty. With his own plate already full of unfinished commitments, he decided to turn this one down. However, he recommended Jean to the publishers in strong terms as someone who is on top of the literature and reliable, and possesses good judgment. Jean is highly flattered and undertakes putting together the collection.

A few days later Jean receives a letter from the *Philosophical Review* inviting her to do a 500- to 750-word review of a posthumously published new book by Donald Davidson, with whose work her dissertation dealt. The thought of publishing in such a fine journal on such a famous author excites her: what a wonderful opportunity, she thinks. She gets to work immediately.

Not long afterwards comes a letter from a well-known philosopher who has heard wonderful things about Jean's work. He invites her to contribute to an anthology he is editing called *New Essays in the Philosophy of Language*. Jean jumps at the chance.

Her lucky string keeps going. She submits a paper to a conference and it is accepted.

Next comes a chance to actually author a book. There is no good up-to-date "single author" text introducing students to the philosophy of language, and a well-known publisher would like her to produce one. The thought of doing the book is sweetened yet more by the nice royalty offer that comes along with the project.

In total, in the first few weeks of her job, Jean has landed a book review in a well-known journal, an article in an anthology that is sure to be read and respected, editorship of a collection, an offer to do a textbook, and a spot on a conference program.

After this rousing start more invitations follow for articles and book reviews, offers to do a second text, and other attractive options. Jean is riding high. The run continues: after publishing part of her dissertation, Jean and a colleague collaborate on an article and publish it in a good place. Then she posts a lot of her work in progress on the Internet.

Jean is also highly knowledgeable on social issues and assumes the role of public intellectual, contributing to public debate. Widely read highbrow magazines carry her political writings; newspapers of distinction present numerous op-ed pieces by her. Space in these venues is at a premium, but Jean is good and gains the coveted spot.

Six years later Jean's tenure committee convenes. And then the other shoe falls. Every single one of the projects that had so excited her is now being questioned by her evaluators.

Textbooks don't count.
Reviews don't count.
Anthologies don't count.
Oral presentations don't count.
Invited contributions don't count.
Coauthored pieces don't count.
Internet postings don't count.
Her work as a "public intellectual" doesn't count.

Ultimately, Jean is turned down for tenure.

This may seem outrageous to you, but it doesn't strike everyone that way. Real-life variants of Jean's situation can be found. There are schools in which junior faculty find themselves in a precarious position if they accept offers like those that came Jean's way. Indeed they would be well advised to turn down such offers. In fact, there are often other constraints: some schools count a book for tenure or promotion only if it is published with a major university press. Favorable external reviews are not enough; the publisher has to be prestigious.

The consequences of junior faculty living under Dumont's policy would be quite negative for the professional field to which they belong. The impact would be felt by scholars and students. Granted, in some areas there are already too many textbooks, as people, including senior faculty, write them for money. But in other areas there wouldn't be enough textbooks, or enough high-quality textbooks, without the Jeans of the world writing them. Without the Jeans of the world there also wouldn't be enough articles to fill certain anthologies, conferences would be understaffed, and so forth. Alternatively, there would be such books and articles, but people as talented as Jean would not be writing them or participating in conferences. Applying Dumont University's standards would be harmful, in a word, to the dissemination of knowledge to other scholars and to students.

Certain jobs need to get done in a well-functioning profession; certain types of scholarly work need to be produced; certain types of settings need to exist (such as symposia). Surely there is something anomalous about saying that anyone who actually does the jobs or joins the settings is putting himself or herself into a precarious position. *Prima facie* there is something fundamentally wrong with a system that prevents much work that is (1) of quality and (2) beneficial to professors, students, and society from being helpful to professional advancement. You might retort that, by my logic, a candidate's regularly taking out the garbage or making coffee (tasks beneficial to the profession) should count toward tenure credentials. But obviously taking out the garbage and making coffee are not in themselves professional activities that call upon philosophical skills (or whatever skills the candidate's field requires). Someone has got to write the textbooks, someone has got to do oral presentations. And these, unlike garbage-dumping and coffeemaking, require philosophical ability.

I recognize full well that Jean's situation is a caricature. Also, some educators would feel that more disturbing than the fact scholars like Jean get turned down is that people of lesser ability and productivity are awarded tenure and promotion. Insofar as tenuring mediocre faculty prevents good faculty from rising through the ranks, I agree that tenuring the mediocre is a problem. But apart from this factor I think Jean's case is worse. I need not deny that in some schools the reverse phenomenon may exist and that it is a problem—it is simply not my topic now.[1]

Should Unrefereed Invited Work Count?

I want in particular to address one question posed by Jean's dossier. How should a member of an individual's committee for tenure or promotion weigh unrefereed as against refereed material? Universities face this issue when they weigh an invited article. Let us consider this example and then turn to *unsolicited* unrefereed electronic work.

Some years ago I invited an assistant professor at a major research university to contribute to an anthology of new essays that I was editing. I did not know this individual personally, but his published work had left me with the conviction that he would be the best person to write on a particular area that needed coverage. Before extending the invitation I confirmed my positive assessment of this scholar by consulting my colleagues and friends in the field. Thus this invitation in no way betokened a friendship with the invitee, but was based on my evaluation of his previous work.

Much to my surprise and chagrin, this young assistant professor turned my invitation down. The reason, he explained, is that senior colleagues had cautioned him against publishing in anthologies as opposed to refereed journals. When he would apply for tenure, the pieces in anthologies would be counted far less than pieces in refereed journals, if at all, and so the time he needed to write the anthologized article would be better spent on trying to write an article (on the same or a different subject) that would undergo competitive peer review. Accepting invitations, he was told in effect, should be the luxury of the secure and famous.

I was disappointed over losing what I expected to be a splendid contribution, and lamented the senior colleagues' attitude (or the attitude they were saying *others* would have). After all, when the candidate would come up for tenure or promotion, his work would be sent out for review by outside specialists anyway, regardless of where it was published (in addition to being reviewed by colleagues). Members of the tenure or promotion committee would consult these outside personnel evaluations; and when they did, they would have plenty of evidence concerning the quality of the anthologized article. They could have a dozen or so evaluations in hand—far more than the journal editor had—and some were likely to be from experts of greater renown and experience than the referees that the invitee would have had for a refereed submission. If the evaluators are superior in number and quality to the potential referees, why should it matter that the piece was not refereed?

Also, if the articles were submitted to a refereed journal and rejected, one wouldn't know who the referees were and probably wouldn't know their reasons for rejection: how, therefore, could one judge the quality of their particular reviews? By contrast, the personnel letters would be signed and could serve as a check on a referee's recommendations. By soliciting further evaluations of refereed published material and being prepared for the possibility of a bad report, universities seem to be admitting that there is a higher court than the original referees, a court that uses perhaps still higher standards. That court should be able to decide equally well the quality of an invited published work. Complicating the picture, there is empirical evidence to suggest that articles in peer reviewed journals often are really invited articles. If an article thought to be peer reviewed received a fine reaction and was influential, are we supposed to retract our favorable view of it when we learn that the editor invited it?[2]

Any assumption that an invited piece signals nothing more than a friendship is unfounded and unfair without hard evidence. Indeed, in the particular instance I cited, I had formed my opinion of this individual by conducting my own "peer review" process when I reviewed his articles and solicited opinions of others. Besides, academics often form "friendships" like this: X has heard of an article Y wrote and would like a reprint. X likes the article and asks Y to "send more stuff." X then sends Y some of his own material. Y likes X's material. Out of this mutual respect for the other's work a friendship grows. The two scholars may meet personally only rarely, perhaps at conventions, or they may never meet. But they become friends, via correspondence, because they value each other's scholarly abilities. The assumption that an invitation from a "friend" is unrelated to the invitee's competence is gratuitous, indeed false in many cases.[3]

This is not to say that a tenure committee member can be expected to differentiate the kind of case in which people become friends out of mutual respect for each other's work from cases in which an editor invites a schoolmate or cousin or lover. Furthermore, an invitation does not usually entail a positive evaluation of a *particular* piece already written but rather of the author's *previous* work. Acceptance to a journal, by contrast, testifies to a *particular* piece's quality. But once again, that work will be evaluated by scholars when the time comes for a decision about tenure or promotion and may even be assessed in print before then. Remember, too, that an editor will want to protect his or her own reputation and to that end will want papers that meet a high standard. For that reason the editor is unlikely to invite a paper *only* as a favor.

Consider this analogy. When a speaker is invited to a forum, it is without prior knowledge and review of this particular speech. Yet (1) one would not normally infer that the invitation is due to friendship alone; and (2) if someone finds the speech to be of high quality and hears others praise it as well, it would be absurd to moderate that assessment just because the speech was not subject to *prior* review. As with good invited speeches, so with good invited articles. And let us not forget that a policy of disparaging unrefereed pieces would diminish the works of Plato, Aristotle, Descartes, Hume, Kant . . . and of course God.

I am not denying that the fact a piece was peer reviewed creates a certain presumption of quality. We have here a reasonable inductive argument. But even if the fact it was peer reviewed were truly sufficient for its having high quality (which it is not—recall the comments to the contrary in the introduction, p. 2, chapter 1, p. 17, and chapter 3, pp. 91–92), being peer reviewed is not *necessary* for high quality. Non–peer reviewed works can also be good. It hardly seems necessary to point out that some peer reviewed articles are accepted with minimal revisions, suggesting that peer review is not always necessary to improve quality, and that a paper might be of high quality even before the review process. If a work is invited, there is some presumption—let it be small—that it will be in this category. I also do not deny that if there were no peer review system at all, committees would have a very tough time sorting out the wheat from the chaff. But it would be doable.

It might be replied that outside evaluators for a tenure/promotion case are not likely to be as demanding as referees and editors for a competitive journal. When a personnel evaluator decides whether to recommend X for tenure and promotion, the evaluator is not normally forced to choose between X and someone else, to compare X to other candidates. But journals are competitive, and so a positive recommendation from a referee means more than a positive recommendation in a personnel evaluation.

This argument is specious. The referees' original reports were not made in the context of a competition. As a rule, referees for a journal article are not comparing the article to other articles that were submitted to the journal.[4] They are offering a noncompetitive evaluation. Furthermore, as the Peters and Ceci 1982 study showed,[5] referees may be ignorant of the most recent work on a subject and thus cannot even do a good job of comparing an article to other *published* ones. An *editor* perhaps makes a competitive decision; but an editor will not generally have read submitted papers carefully and will instead adjudicate the competition by contemplating what topics most need coverage or by comparing the language of different referees' reports. Since an individual referee's report is usually not straightforwardly based on a competitive evaluation, the editor may not have a direct way of ranking two "competing" submissions.

Personnel committees, on the other hand, are often asked to offer comparisons—not only about where candidates rank relative to others in the field but also where particular works rank and what those works have contributed. Evaluators often say things like "this is the best piece I know of on the subject . . ." or "it's one of the two or three best." Why not count such praise of an invited article if one counts it for a refereed article?

There are further points in support of counting invited articles heavily.[6] First, many scholars are more familiar with key anthologies in their fields than with journals (in part because anthologies are used in courses). Presumably publishing is intended to benefit scholars, to "spread knowledge." If more scholars would read a paper in certain anthologies than would read it were it to appear in a journal, surely this ought to be significant in assessing the publication's value to the field. Second, it seems unfair to in effect force beginning professors to decline invitations. A young scholar may have a better chance of making a reputation by publishing in a well-placed anthology than by publishing in a journal. Any good publication leads to expanded contacts and further opportunities. Several volumes of mostly invited essays have had great impact on the philosophical profession (*Midwest Studies in Philosophy*, for one). I know of no one who disparages the quality of those books just because many of the essays are invited.

Howard Stein, an eminent philosopher of science, complains about a case in which a colleague who was up for promotion had produced work that was highly regarded but which the administration found insufficient because some of it was presented at symposia or in invited collections:

> If this policy is maintained, it will be necessary for the Department of Philosophy . . . to warn all its members who have not yet achieved tenure, or who have tenure but have not achieved the rank of full professor, to *refuse* to participate in invited conferences or to give invited addresses if their papers are to be published in connection with those events—and also to refuse to contribute invited papers to scholarly collections—unless they are willing to have such work ignored as far as the furtherance of their careers at this university is concerned.[7]

Stein's conclusion is fundamentally correct, but perhaps overstated. Even if Jean's work is discounted entirely vis-à-vis tenure, her work is not irrelevant to professional advancement. If people see her name on a program, or hear her speak, this benefits her professionally. You would not list a lunch conversation with a famous philosopher on your resume, but you also would not say that the meeting did nothing for you professionally. Presentations mean exposure. Hence it would not really make sense for someone to turn down invitation after invitation for the reasons Stein gives. But this actually strengthens my criticism. The young person must say yes for professional reasons and must also say no for professional reasons. Since this contradiction exists only because of the policy that I am criticizing, this counts as an additional argument against that policy.[8] In all likelihood, under the policy Stein bemoans, fewer junior faculty and even fewer associate professors would participate in the programs he describes, surrendering thereby important opportunities in order to pursue writing for refereed journals.

The "Prestige" Factor

The issues I have raised resurface when we turn to another question: should a hiring, tenure, or promotion committee count publications by "top" journals with high rejection rates (say, 90 percent) more than publications in journals with lower rejection rates (say, 80 percent)?[9] The putative grounds for doing so would be that the odds of getting the paper into A were 10 percent lower than the odds of getting it into B, and that the quality of submissions to A will be higher since scholars tend to submit work there first. Acceptance by journal A will thus signal that the paper has survived a stiffer competition, and to that extent it will provide stronger testimony to the paper's high quality.

This argument overlooks a few points. First, though authors count a journal's reputation perhaps more than any other factor in deciding where to submit an article,[10] the appearance of an article in a lower-prestige journal does not entail that a higher-prestige journal rejected it. What if the author sent it in to the better journal, was warned of a large backlog, and withdrew it? An author who is not a gambler might well have decided to send articles to journals with higher acceptance rates and quicker response times in order to secure birds in hand and move on to other projects. Authors lacking in self-confidence may think mistakenly that their work would not be accepted by the better journal. An author may fear that a top journal would reject his article because it published other articles on that topic recently, and indeed the journal A may reject the piece only for this reason. An author may just not be savvy about where to send a paper. Where an article winds up is often the product of extraneous factors—for example, the candidate's personality, how many pages a journal is willing to publish, even the referee's age (younger referees are reputed to be harsher than older ones, though some studies suggest otherwise). Or a journal may just make a bad decision.

But the greatest concern about asking "Where did this appear?" is that it produces bias, the same fault that blind refereeing was designed to remove. Jonathan Vogel suggested to me a wonderful formulation of the bias problem, modeled on Plato's "Euthyphro question": "Is it published in journal X because it's good, or is it good because it's published in journal X?" Scholars in various fields have reported to me that some articles made their reputation more on where they were published and less on the quality of the work. Clearly contributions ought to be evaluated by their inherent merits. Yet when a personnel committee takes into account where something appeared, that sends a message that evaluators *ought* to evaluate an article at least partly by who published it.[11] Indeed, what is most intriguing about the question "Where did it appear?" is that it utilizes an inductive argument of the type we discredited in chapter 2 in connection with *ad hominem* and affiliational bias. While in those cases the inductive arguments were based on the person or his affiliation, and in the case at hand it is based on the journal, in neither case does it seem right to bypass the step of getting the paper evaluated in order to be sure that a generalization that holds much of the time holds this time.

In the case of books, committees often ask, "Which press published this?" Books published by "prestigious" university presses are counted more heavily than books published by other presses. Here again we must ask why, putting aside the question of how "prestige" is defined. If two books receive the same postpublication evaluation from outside evaluators, why should a book published by Arcane University Press count less than a book by Renowned University Press? Is there a tacit assumption that only if Renowned rejected the book would the author go with Arcane? Such an assumption is unfounded. Perhaps Arcane actively recruited the book. Perhaps the author heard from Arcane while Renowned was dragging its feet and, wanting a bird in hand, chose to accept Arcane's offer. Perhaps Arcane made a better royalty offer. Perhaps Renowned really meant it when it said that the book didn't "fit into our plans."[12] Those who think that a book published by Renowned should count more might be assuming that Renowned selects from among a fitter set of candidates. In the previous chapter, I indeed suggested that Renowned's overall submissions would be of higher quality than Arcane's. But it hardly follows that a particular author had a work accepted by Arcane *only* because of inferior competition. The acid test of quality is postpublication review. What if Arcane's book got a better postpublication book review than Renowned's (from reviewers with similar abilities at judgment)? Why not just impute a mistake to Renowned's editors and concede that Arcane's is a better book?

An editor who has worked for both the Princeton University and Penn State University Presses attacks the notion that a book's imprint is an indicator of its quality:

> Is there any difference in the decisionmaking processes at the more and less prestigious presses? In fact there isn't. Editors at all university presses seek reviews from the best readers they can find, anywhere in the world, and present the reports and their own recommendations to editorial boards consisting of faculty members. Is there anything about those editorial boards that would make a difference? Not in my experience. . . . And what about the editors themselves—is there any reason to believe that editors at more prestigious presses make better decisions? Not at all.
>
> This bias, then, is just that—an irrational preference with no basis in fact.[13]

We encountered this passage in chapter 4. There the issue was whether *from the point of view of a book review editor*, a book published by a prestige press can be assumed to be more significant and of better quality than one published by an unprestigious press. I argued that if certain presses are perceived as unprestigious, this was bound to affect what gets submitted to that press, even given the allowability of multiple submissions, so the review editor may make his decisions about what to review on the basis of an induction. But in the present context we want to know whether a book for which one has postpublication evaluations in hand should be assumed inferior because it was published with a less prestigious press than the committee's preferred presses. Here I think the answer is absolutely not. Were great works of philosophy judged by "Which press was it published by?" Merit is merit, and postpublication reviews, published or unpublished, can detect it.

Let me repeat verbatim a point made in the previous chapter. Not everything published in "top" journals or by "top" presses is as persuasive and as good as everything published under lower-prestige auspices. Time and again philosophers write effective and even devastating replies to "prestige" journal articles and effective if not devastating book reviews of "prestige press" books. They find holes in an author's central argument, indirectly exposing thereby the poor judgment of the original referees. If anything, a personnel evaluator will have one advantage that the original referees did not: hindsight. By the time the evaluation is written the reviewer will be aware of something the referees could not know—namely, how well the article or book has been received and has withstood *public* scrutiny. Needless to say the personnel referee's evaluation should not slavishly follow others' reactions, but an awareness of those reactions will help the evaluator form a more meaningful assessment. Nobel laureate Rosalyn Yalow originally had her prize-winning work rejected, and J. R. Mayer's 1842 paper reporting the first law of thermodynamics was rejected by a leading journal and accepted by a relatively obscure one.[14] The value of their ideas is better judged after publication than before. (We saw many such examples in chapter 3.) Philip Gossett is correct to point out that "In some cases a short article in a conference report may transform a field and be *prima facie* evidence of international stature."[15]

At this point someone might object that I have been too generous to outside evaluators for hiring, tenure, and promotion. Letters of recommendation can be exaggerated and written irresponsibly. Assuming an honest evaluation is not always warranted, and we have to be wary of evaluation inflation.[16] Furthermore, an evaluator who is called upon to offer an opinion of a candidate's *oeuvre* perforce does not examine each thesis and point of the candidate with the same care that a referee does. The evaluator will form an overall opinion and cast it in the form of a few sentences. The outside evaluator, unlike a referee, is not likely to plumb the deepest strengths and weaknesses of an article to convey a truly reliable assessment of its merits. A truly conscientious evaluator will probe as deeply as a referee, but that is the exception, not the rule. By and large external review letters are like the conventional-length book reviews I spoke of in chapter 4: cursory and apodictic rather than fully reasoned out.

To begin with fears of irresponsible evaluation, would this not call into question the wisdom of relying on those letters altogether? If those evaluations are to be the core of personnel decisions, we have to assume a basically honest and dependable system. As for the claim that the evaluator will not probe the article as a referee would, it doesn't matter if this is the case. Awarding someone tenure or promotion is not tantamount to proclaiming his or her positions to be correct, his or her arguments impervious. If it were, then whenever a reply is published to a tenured professor's article, that should be grounds for saying tenure was a mistake, which needless to say it is not. Doing high-quality work and being correct are not equivalent except in certain fields, specifically in the sciences, and even there the correlation is imperfect. Great philosophers often have views that most people reject, but this does not diminish the quality and importance of their work.[17] Personnel evaluators can spot quality and importance.

A remaining argument for weighing certain organs of publication more than others is the argument from status. Every department in a research university wants its members to be people of status and stature in the field. Top journals and top presses create that status. Also, the impact of a work is greater when the work emanates from certain journals or presses.[18]

This argument cannot be dismissed lightly. But it plays off of a situation that needs to be remedied. In effect the argument gives an imprimatur to a form of bias, in fact, snobbery. The perception of what constitutes status should itself change once publication in those journals or by those presses is seen not to *necessarily* spell higher quality. Letters to potential evaluators could emphasize that they are to comment on quality and not be influenced by provenance. Furthermore, if there is a concern with status, then, as noted before, some anthologies reach larger audiences than most journals; and an invitation from certain editors might carry its own prestige.[19]

Two concessions must be made. First, when it comes to hiring decisions, looking for candidates with peer-reviewed works with prestige journals or presses is a good mode of operating. It is much more efficient and cost-effective to pare down a large initial pool of candidates by identifying candidates who have published in peer-reviewed journals, unless the invited articles listed are known to the search committee. Letters of recommendation that accompany dossiers are all invited by the candidate rather than the school, and tend not to focus on individual works. So they are not as helpful as postpublication letters for tenure or promotion. Second, the distinction between prestigious and nonprestigious journals is relevant when evaluators decide whether to be impressed by the *quantity* of a candidate's publication. Ten papers in relatively undemanding journals may be less impressive than five in very exacting ones. Hence I am ready to countenance an adjustment of *quantity* requirements based on the journals' rejection rates. But quality is quality no matter where it appears.

Should Unpublished Works Count?

Would my arguments on behalf of invited pieces apply to unsolicited papers in unrefereed electronic journals? Not all do. Publication in electronic journals, as opposed to publication of an invited piece in the company of prominent authors, carries no "status" and makes no statement about how others regard the author. Universities would like at the very least the prestige factor of an invited piece. But the argument that quality is quality, and can be judged so by personnel evaluators, applies to unsolicited and unrefereed, as well as invited, print publications.

A fair question to hurl my way at this point is: wouldn't all your arguments support counting unpublished, privately circulated manuscripts as much as journal articles and invited pieces? Why not just rely on outside evaluators here too? If the evaluators say the work is good, grant the tenure or promotion; if their judgment is unfavorable, reject the candidate. Why insist on the candidate publishing at all?

The form of this objection is *reductio ad absurdum*; but is the conclusion really absurd? Publication is said to be essential for disseminating knowledge. But what if someone frequently presents work in oral form? Better, what if

Smith e-mails or even snail-mails unpublished work—good work—to every member of a professional association and pays them to actually read it? Won't more people then read it than if it were in a print journal (and Smith would also gain some notoriety, so Smith's name would be better known)? Some important papers (for example, David Kaplan's "D-That" back in the 1960s) were originally circulated widely but not published immediately, achieving a degree of status and fame in the process.

The key advantage of publication is that it provides an access point for the scholarly community; by means of indexes, book catalogues, advertisements, library records, citations, and so on, scholars both in and out of one's field can locate the work for generations to come. Unpublished work, particularly outside one's field, cannot be accessed this way and is therefore not of lasting value. That, I believe, is the best argument for demanding publication.

Theodore Benditt amplifies this point. He points out that scholars have a responsibility

> not only to preserve knowledge left by others but to preserve the knowledge they themselves possess. . . . For future generations, tradition includes us, includes who we were and what we did and thought. Therefore these things must become part of the record. Future generations can decide what is worth preserving and what is not. For us, the task is to preserve the ideas that constitute part of the ongoing tradition, by presentation or publication or other forms of reproduction that will be available to others.[20]

In other words, publication is required because professors are duty-bound to share their work with the larger community—including future generations.

At the same time, as Benditt's closing words suggest, ideas can be perpetuated in forms other than traditional publication. And Benditt's argument for publication brings us full circle to chapter 1, raising anew the question of whether peer review is defensible. For his argument invites the question of why we would not want *all* that we think to be passed on to future generations. The concerns, methods, and standards of the next generation may be different from ours, and work ignored in one period may become vital and show new merit in another.[21] Referees and editors shape their disciplines according to fads and fashions of their own time. We need to think about how scholars will think in later times, as well as how rapidly tides may turn in our own. The longer view articulated by Benditt leaves us wondering whether, by being as selective as we are and by privileging some modes of dissemination over others, we are neglecting future generations. Or perhaps the opposite holds: we serve future generations best by preventing them from being inundated.

If electronic works can be indexed, accessed, and archived as are print volumes—and certainly accessing a given subject is easier in an electronic medium—then they should be eligible for postpublication review just as other nonprint works (e.g., videotapes) are. Content, not medium, is crucial. High quality in unpublished but accessible works deserves the same ranking as quality in print volumes (though one might evaluate impact separately). Electronic communication expands scholars' networks of contacts and leads to further opportunities.

Let me emphasize that a candidate for tenure or promotion (or hiring) would be *wise* to submit material to prepublication peer review. Doing so would prevent committees from judging him or her adversely, and would maximize quality since the author would profit from peer review and possibly from the extra incentive of knowing a work will be peer reviewed. One might argue that there is even an obligation to submit some works to peer review.[22] But after the fact, that is, given that the person has not submitted work for peer reviewers to judge but has accepted an invitation, the work should be judged by postpublication review.

These reflections bring us to the subject of Internet "publication," to which I turn in chapter 6.

Summation

To sum up, I have argued that the practice of discounting certain sorts of publications and presentations in tenure and promotion decisions sits un-easily with the fact that those sorts of work contribute significantly to the profession. By treating the refereed work as the gold standard of professional approbation, the scholarly community may have unfairly belittled quality work of capable scholars and discouraged some from placing their work in forums that are more likely to reach a large audience than refereed journals are. In certain ways—notably by its ability to speak from hindsight—postpublication peer review is a more reliable guide to quality and of course impact than the refereeing process. Committees no doubt want their de-partments to have "status," but if they would cease to view status as depen-dent on where something appeared and view it instead as dependent on postpublication reception, the objection to ignoring where the work ap-peared would fall away.

None of this alters the reality that scholars are consumers and will usually prefer to read works that come with prior approval. Experts are proxies for their readers, preventing inundation. Peer review creates a more competitive environment and therefore a higher-quality set of submissions. It also improves work, making it likely that the published version of a manuscript will be better than what came over the transom. All this I concede, in fact insist on. Even so, however, this does not settle the question of how to weigh items that were not subjected to competitive refereeing when we have other instruments by which to evaluate them.

To return to hapless Jean, let us hope that her next university will give Jean's invited publications their due and will accord greater weight to those of her publications and presentations that are the lifeblood of the profession.

Notes

1. Collaborative publications are another source of difficulty for authors. In the sciences multiple authorship has become so common in medical journals that it has been jokingly referred to as the disease "polyauthoritis." See V. K. Kampoor, "Polyauthoritis Giftosa," *Lancet* 34 (1994): 1039. I thank Edward Reichman, M.D., for the reference.

2. See M. S. MacNealy, B. W. Speck, and N. Clements, "Publishing in Technical Communications Journals from the Successful Author's Point of View," *Technical Communication* 41 (1994): 240–59, which found that editors had solicited 25 percent of the papers.

3. These points would suggest also that friends may serve as outside evaluators on a tenure or promotion case. But I have reservations about extending the argument this far.

4. An *editor* perhaps makes a competitive decision; but an editor will not generally have read submitted papers carefully and will instead adjudicate the competition by contemplating what topics most need coverage or by comparing the language of different referee's reports. Since an individual referee's report is usually not straightforwardly based on a competitive evaluation, the editor may not have a direct way of ranking two "competing" submissions.

5. See chapter 2, p. 7.

6. I will not argue the point here, but I think that well-done book reviews ought to be counted more heavily than they normally are even though they are not subject to peer review. See chapter 4 for what I mean by "well-done."

7. Howard Stein, letter to the editor, *Proceedings and Addresses of the American Philosophical Association* 70, no. 2 (November 1996): 161. Stein felt so strongly about this matter that he suggested a demotion in his own rank to the level of associate professor.

8. The last three sentences are taken almost verbatim from comments by David Berger.

9. This is not to say that greater prestige *invariably* is attached to a higher rejection rate.

10. See *Scholarly Communication: The Report of the National Enquiry* (Baltimore, Md.: Johns Hopkins University Press, 1979), 49. This, however, is not a recent survey.

11. See also Gordon Fellman, "On the Fetishism of Publications and the Secrets Thereof," *Academe* 81 (Jan.-Feb. 1995): 27.

12. As economics drives university presses to seek broad and fashionable subjects that will interest general readers, specialized works will fit less and less into their plans. If universities are to grant tenure, they will have to drop the demand for producing a book with university presses as a condition for tenure.

13. Sanford G. Thatcher, letter to the editor, *Proceedings and Addresses of the American Philosophical Association* 68, no. 5 (May 1995): 107-8. I quoted this letter in chapter 4 as well.

14. See Rosalyn Yalow, "Competency Testing for Reviewers and Editors," in *Peer Commentary on Peer Review*, ed. Stevan J. Harnad (Cambridge: Cambridge University Press, 1982), 60-61; Andrew W. Colman, "Manuscript Evaluation by Journal Referees and Editors: Randomness or Bias?" in *Peer Community on Peer Review*, ed. Harnad, 21-22.

15. Philip Gossett, *Proceedings and Addresses of the American Philosophical Association* 70, no. 5 (May 1997): 168-69.

16. On how truthful evaluations should be, see Paul Eisenberg, "The Truth, the Whole Truth, and Nothing but the Truth," in *Morality, Responsibility, and the University*, ed. Steven M. Cahn (Phliladelphia: Temple University Press, 1990), 109-18.

17. An interesting question is whether departments should consider the correctness of a philosopher's position in deciding whether to hire that person. See David Lewis, "Academic Appointments: Why Ignore the Advantage of Being Right?" in *Morality, Responsibility, and the University*, ed. Cahn, 231-42. Lewis recognizes that his view that the truth of a colleague's positions don't matter holds for philosophy but not necessarily for, say, science. See chapter 3 of this book, p. 21.

18. Cf. Gerald Dworkin's letter in *Proceedings and Addresses of the American Philosophical Association* 68, no. 2 (November 1994): 90-91, discussed in chapter 4. An author "would prefer a Press which has a larger advertising budget, which has a better distribution network, and whose lists tend to be scrutinized first by potential readers."

19. Some departments go so far as to count "Where were you invited?" as a criterion for evaluation. Perhaps this leaves too much to luck, as many invitations are generated by chance and networks. But if status is a consideration, then departments that consider the provenance of invitations are more right than wrong.

20. Theodore Benditt, "The Research Demands of Teaching in Higher Education," in *Morality, Responsibility, and the University*, ed. Cahn, 107.

21. David Berger reminded me of a text in the *Mishnah* (an ancient Jewish collection of texts, mostly legal in nature) that asks why minority opinions are preserved in the *Mishnah* along with the majority opinions, if the law follows the majority. One answer is so that a future court may rely upon the minority opinion to overturn the previous majority (*Eduyot* 1:4-5).

22. See Benditt, "Research Demands of Teaching"; Peter J. Markie, *A Professor's Duties: Ethical Issues in College Teaching* (Lanham, Md.: Rowman & Littlefield, 1994), 79; cf. Joe Cain, "Why Be My Colleague's Keeper: Moral Justifications for Peer Review," *Science and Engineering Ethics* 5 (1999): 531–40.

Benditt argues that the role of professor as teacher implies a commitment to test one's ideas by having them evaluated by others in the field. The reason for this requirement, he explains, is that we owe it *to our students* to undergo such professional review before we place our own ideas before them; we must be sure of the ideas' quality. Likewise, Peter Markie states:

> [I]f we develop theories of our own that we would teach as alternatives of equal standing to the other major views in the field, we must first present our theories for expert evaluation. . . . Our theories do not equal the other alternatives in standing until they too have undergone expert review, and we may not present them to our students as though they have. (79)

In Benditt's and Markie's conceptions, then, peer review of scholarship serves teaching.

This argument can be criticized in various ways. First, many will find it simply counterintuitive. Does a professor violate academic ethics if he or she presents a personal viewpoint to students before hearing from a journal editor, conference chair, or book publisher? Such a demand seems unduly stringent, and is violated regularly. Second, the argument is limited in that many ideas that professors develop have no bearing on what the professors teach. A separate argument would be required for submitting to peer review those ideas that will not be taught. Third, Markie concedes that teachers who do not present ideas as their own to students have no duty to publish those ideas. He also agrees that presenting a new idea is acceptable as long as its untested character is noted. Fourth, for purposes of teaching one could solicit feedback from colleagues and acquaintances in the field instead of going through a refereeing process. Cognizant of this possibility, both Benditt and Markie imply that feedback from colleagues is not as significant as feedback from referees. But it isn't really clear why. Whose judgment is better—referees' or acquaintances'—depends on which group is more capable and which group will read the work more carefully and responsibly. Many authors circulate drafts widely before submitting a paper for publication. If the response of their readers is favorable and the readers are of high caliber, that can serve as well as or better than formal refereeing. Referees can be careless in reading, while talking to one's reader personally can create a fairer hearing of problematic and controversial points. Fifth, the author/teacher may be the biggest expert on the particular field in question.

Some of these criticisms can be met, and indeed Benditt and Markie subtly engage some of them. In any case, the question that Benditt and Markie answer is not the same one as I ask in chapter 1, and their answer is not compelling as a response to my question. They are addressing this question: (1) Why should a professor seek peer review of his or her ideas? Their answer is that the ideas need such review before being presented to students. But I was asking a different question: (2) Why do journals insist on reviewing work before publishing it? It seems implausible that the answer to *this* question is "because they want to make sure that students learn correctly from this professor." In other words, Benditt and Markie at best explain why a professor who is committed to teaching his or her own ideas should take advantage of existing mechanisms for peer review; they do not explain, nor, I think, do they aspire to explain, why those mechanisms exist to begin with, or why they should determine what works get published.

⌒⌐

CHAPTER SIX

Where Do We Go from Here?
Peer Review in the Age
of the Internet

Scholars often associate the Internet with undisciplined, frequently unreliable discourse. Stevan Harnad, one of the most prolific and respected champions of using digital technology to disseminate scholarship, describes what he believes is scholars' typical attitude to the Internet, circa 1995:

> The Internet was created, and is continuing to evolve, as the result of a collective, anarchic process among computer programmers ("hackers") and professional, student, and amateur users. . . . Hence it was perfectly natural to imagine that this creative and enterprising anarchic spirit, which has proven so effective in forging these remarkable new tools, should also be the means of deploying them. Indeed, the rapid proliferation of bulletin boards, discussion groups, alerting services, and preprint archives, complemented now by simple and powerful search and retrieval tools, all pointed in the direction of a new "ultrademocratic" approach to information production and distribution in this new medium.
>
> Problems immediately manifested themselves, however, in this informational utopia: discussions would wax verbose and sometimes abusive; misinformation was difficult to distinguish from information; an ethos of egalitarian dilettantism prevailed; and, worst of all, serious scholars and scientists distanced themselves or kept their distance from the Net, concluding, understandably, that it was much too chaotic and undiscriminating a medium to be entrusted with the communication and preservation of their substantive ideas and findings. . . . [T]he [electronic] medium is still [in the mid-1990s] widely perceived as unfit for serious scholarship, more like a global graffiti board for trivial pursuit.[1]

No topic related to scholarly publishing has attracted as much recent commentary as the impact of the Internet on scholarly communication. Of the countless articles that have appeared on the subject, the overwhelming majority—this, contrary to what one might expect from Harnad's depiction of the situation less than a decade ago—advocate, if not salivate over, the electronic posting of scholarly work. Yet despite this general agreement, there is widespread disagreement about the *best* way to utilize digital technology in scholarly communication, and in particular about the best way to develop a filtering system such as peer review. Some argue that with digital technology we no longer need peer review; others, that peer review can now be conducted among a wider group of peers; still others, that peer review should remain in place exactly as it is utilized in print journals. Appointment, hiring, and promotion committees still exhibit skepticism about the value of electronic publishing, reflecting perhaps Harnad's 1995 analysis. Let us first review the advantages and disadvantages claimed for electronic scholarly publishing, and then examine competing proposals for how peer review should (or should not) be utilized in the new environment. Unlike other chapters in this book, this one is more a survey of existing positions than an argument for one. Nonetheless it fleshes out discussions we had in chapter 1 (on peer review and the marketplace) and chapter 5 (on how to assess works that were not peer reviewed), and ties in to examinations of bias and conservatism. It is, in short, a fitting capstone to the book.

An Assessment of Electronic Publishing

Advantages of Electronic Publishing

Some authors speak of the impending demise of scholarly journals. One writer, predicting (in 1996) that the demise will take place in ten to twenty years, calls print journals "an awkward artifact, though a highly developed one, of the only technology available over the last few centuries for large-scale communication."[2] Why is digital technology claimed to yield a better product?

Cost

Prices of journals and books are steadily soaring, making it increasingly expensive for libraries to acquire print volumes. In addition, storage space is shrinking. As fields become increasingly specialized—partly as a consequence of growth in knowledge—new journals appear, exacerbating the libraries' problems of money and space. As for books, university presses face financial challenges of such magnitude that some in academia are suggesting that producing a book, or producing a book with a university press, can no longer reasonably be made a requirement for tenure. An oft-remarked problem is that libraries in effect end up paying for the fruits of the research that their own universities support.

Electronic postings of work can be produced at costs that nowhere approach those of print journals and books, even allowing for such expenses as editors' salaries, copyediting, marketing, Internet access, and computer hardware and software. On the buyer's end, libraries may have to pay a subscription fee to an e-journal, but even leaving room for a healthy profit margin for the seller, it should be possible for the subscription fee to be lower than the fees of printed journals and the costs of books. Authors, it should be noted, much prefer that readers have low-cost, indeed free, access to their work.[3]

That electronic journals can be produced cheaply does not mean that libraries can buy them cheaply. Publishers may charge the same price for e-journals as for print volumes; and some publishers offer e-versions of print volumes only when the print volume is purchased too.

SPARC (Scholarly Publishing and Academic Resources Coalition) and BioOne are examples of proactive attempts by researchers in the sciences to provide electronic journals as alternatives to products of commercial publishers, correcting what BioOne calls "market dysfunctions." Their journals still lag behind print journals in prestige, but over time that could change. Institutional repositories, which would store works by the school's researchers and professors, are another way of offering scholarly information without commercial publishers.

While considering costs, let us not ignore the cost standpoint of the reader, the consumer of the knowledge. Such expenditures as travel to libraries, photocopying, mailing, and postage do not exist in the electronic medium.

Speed

In a print medium there are often substantial delays between submission of a manuscript and acceptance, as well as between acceptance and final publication. "In a culture where getting things out first is so important, delays of months or a year (or even longer) seem almost absurd when a message sent to an electronic mailing list can travel the globe in a matter of seconds."[4] Time will be taken up, of course, by the author's writing of the paper or book, referees' evaluation of it (assuming a system of peer review is applied to the electronic medium), and the author's response. But once the work is ready to go, it can be communicated without delay, if not immediately as a journal article, then as a preprint of a forthcoming article. There are no production queues. This point applies equally to scholarly responses to others' works: the responses can be distributed immediately.

Another advantage of electronic posting is that an author in a distant country can communicate his or her work immediately and need not be dependent on the vagaries of a snail-mail system that further delays the publication process, possibly depriving him, in some cases, of due credit for being the first to discover a particular point or argument.

The speed of electronic conversation has another advantage, noted by Stevan Harnad. At paper production tempos (lags of weeks, months, or years between messages), ideas that sprout one day could become forever lost. With electronic publishing they can be placed on record quickly and permanently.[5]

Distribution

Because journals and books are expensive, and academics' salaries are generally modest, many scholars cannot afford to purchase all the printed materials they need. Obtaining the works from libraries is not practical if the library itself does not acquire the journal or book. Books and journals can also be checked out or lost. Interlibrary loans take time. With electronic publishing not only can a researcher access materials from home, saving trips to a library, but anyone anywhere in the world can obtain a work. Third world countries can become equal participants in the international scholarly community; indeed, Paul Ginsparg calls his pioneering e-print system "a major boon to developing countries" by virtue of the low cost of the enterprise and the capacity for instant communication. Because of lower costs, Ginsparg says, graduate students can easily become part of the conversation too.[6]

Problems of Proliferation

There was a time when subscription to a few print journals gave a scholar adequate access to key papers in the field. With the proliferation of journals, journals are no longer a particularly useful guide, and readers will need to consult either a survey essay or an electronic source.[7]

Evolving Improvement of Content

"Learned inquiry is a continuum . . . reports of its findings . . . are milestones, not gravestones."[8] With electronic publishing, an author can continually revise a paper, and both the current and previous versions can be archived. In the world of print, it is true, an author might produce a second or third edition revising the previous edition; and sometimes an author might revise a published journal article and publish the new version in a book. But these are the exceptions to the rule that once an article appears in a print journal, it is cast in stone and not a jot or tittle may be changed. As Harnad explains, the effect of having authors and critics engage in continuing conversation, revision, and further discourse—a process he calls "scholarly skywriting"—is that research and writing cease to be separate activities.[9]

Varying Lengths of Works
Print media publish works of a particular length. But sometimes a scholarly work can be too long for a print journal article and too short for a printed book. Electronic publishing handles documents of any length. An author's full data can be appended to a study.[10]

Searchability
This is self-explanatory. You need not skim pages to find the key terms in which you are interested.

Research Tools
Thanks to hypertext, citations in text and footnotes can be linked to the article being cited, so that the reader may call up the cited article as desired. Multimedia links further enhance the value of citations.

Number of Articles Available
This is the one "advantage" that may be a disadvantage. Electronic communication makes more material ("information") available; but will the inundation prove too great? Of course much depends on the standards used by e-journals and on whether they use peer review. More on that later.

Disadvantages of Electronic Publishing
With all the advantages of e-journals, libraries face the challenge of archiving those journals as the electronic media and software needed for archiving undergo technological development and change.[11] Furthermore, if authors revise their publications in response to feedback, will a scholar be able to keep track of the various versions?

If the archiving problem is solved, the disadvantages of electronic scholarly publishing will be few. Some scholars are not technologically literate, and they will be at a disadvantage. This hardly seems a reason to hold up everyone else. There are dangers of power shutdowns, malfunctioning software, system failures, network breakdowns, and viruses.[12] But here, too, a cost-benefit analysis favors electronic media, assuming only that all information is adequately backed up. Both problems I mentioned—that not all scholars are technologically literate, and that digital technology might suffer glitches—will fade as time goes on. Computer literacy will become almost universal; and technological problems, it is hoped, will become fewer and easier to eliminate, even if new technology occasionally brings new problems. An issue that may not go away is copyright law: strict copyright laws and tight controls on fair use would hamper the distribution of materials. But so do controls over printed matter.

Remaining reasons for opposing the digital technology are really reasons for favoring printed journals and books over "e-" counterparts across the board, not only in scholarship. Being able to carry a book or a journal and read it anywhere is something people value. So is lining home shelves with attractive volumes. Browsing in bookstores is easier for some than browsing the Web. Printing out articles all the time is a nuisance. (Ironically, enormous amounts of paper are needed to work effectively with the paperless medium.) For some it's harder to read a computer screen than a printed page.[13] Without question, then, scholars would have to part with some features they value if all scholarship goes electronic. But it seems well worth it.

I am reminded of a comedian who poked fun at society's infatuation with computers by reflecting on the excitement people feel over reading the news on the Web. Imagine, he said, that things were the other way around—that for centuries people got their news from a computer, and then someone had the bright idea of printing a newspaper. You could read it at the breakfast table, in the subway, in the bathroom. What a great idea, we'd say! At last, you don't have to turn on that machine each time! The comedian has a point, I think, but not one forceful enough to override the advantanges of Internet publishing.

Quality Control and Peer Review in Internet Publishing

What would happen to peer review if publications were e-based? The answer is: as much or as little as we want to happen, for there is much flexibility in how peer review could work on the Net.

The word publishing has taken on new meaning today. Whereas once publishing required an editorial staff and a press—a "publisher"—today "anyone equipped with a computer, a modem, and a connection to the Internet can be a publisher."[14] Some but not all e-journals are peer reviewed. As things stand, publishing in an electronic journal is not valued as highly by hiring, tenure, and promotion committees as is publishing in a paper medium. (Obviously, I am speaking of publishing in journals that are purely electronic, as opposed to publishing in journals that appear in both a print and an electronic version.) In 2000, Indiana University conducted a case study of a fictional assistant professor of English who had published one article in a peer reviewed print journal, had another one accepted but not yet published, and had also published two articles online. One of the online articles was posted on a website and was not peer reviewed; the other was peer reviewed and published in an online journal. The non–peer reviewed article had 725 hits, the peer reviewed one had 127 hits. The result? The "candidate" was turned down because the committee members felt they had no clear guidelines for evaluating the online articles (as well as the online courses the candidate had developed).[15] Because of the low prestige of e-articles, there is a movement to have authors of e-articles keep the copyright so as to be able to submit them smoothly to prestigious print journals. But perceiving competition, editors and commercial publishers will not necessarily consider such publications for print volumes.

In the chapter titled "What Should Count?" I argued that in cases of unrefereed electronic publications, just as in cases of invited articles, postpublication review by outside referees should be the determining factor, and that online publications that elicit high praise from postpublication reviewers should count, perhaps heavily. If my arguments there were sound, a committee should utilize outside readers and be prepared to render a favorable judgment based upon their evaluations. Be that as it may, the discussion that follows would be short-circuited if certain proposals were opposed simply on the grounds that tenure and promotion committees would insist on some level of refereeing more stringent than that put forward in the proposal. In an idealistic spirit one could say that we must ban such arguments and assume instead that whatever proposal is put forward would be acceptable to a committee, since the committee would realize the proposal's wisdom. Realistically, though, I think that peer review would have to be implemented in a form similar to that used by print journals and publishing houses in order for committees to take the publications seriously. And that practical argument could be the best argument for retaining the peer review system, even if ideally committees ought to rely on postpublication reviews, and further, even if digital technology makes possible *many more* postpublication reviews (online, independent of the tenure and promotion process) than the print medium does. Furthermore, the present hierarchical system of journals and presses provides incentives for people to do their best work. If there were no peer review system, or standards were relaxed, the quality of work would fall off considerably.[16]

As we go through the various suggestions for using the Internet to either jettison or improve the refereeing process, it is interesting to bear in mind that these suggestions had been made in the age of print as well. Among these suggestions are: (A) make referees more "accountable" by signing their reviews (a theme we touched on in chapter 2); (B) increase the number of referees; (C) use open peer commentary, whereby a paper is published with many replies in the same issue;[17] (D) have reviewers see each other's comments after they have written their reports, thus in effect subjecting each set of referee's comments to peer review; (E) publish the referee's report together with the paper; (F) give the author a chance to reply before the decision is made. These strategies do not absolutely require digital technology, but they can be implemented most easily with it. The computer, then, allows the implementation of strategies that were proposed before the online revolution.

Proposal 1: Eliminate Prepublication Peer Review

This once-radical suggestion is associated with Paul Ginsparg, founder of the Los Alamos e-print archives. (Ginsparg is now with Cornell University.) Unrefereed, or mildly refereed, e-prints are posted on a website. Authors can go on to do with the e-prints as they please, including submitting the articles to a peer-reviewed journal. But except for the demands of tenure and promotion committees, there is little point in that, since the e-prints receive feedback from the wider community, which is more feedback than peer review affords. Authors may revise regularly.

The obvious problem with this proposal is inundation—how does a reader know which e-prints to look at, if e-prints lack the certification of peer review? Now, as Ginsparg notes, pre-Internet physics had a tradition of preprinting articles. Authors would photocopy and mail copies to the wider community before sending the work to a refereed journal. (In other fields this was done on a much more limited basis.) It is this tradition, he says, that makes physicists more accepting of the e-print system. Further, critics argue, there are other features of their discipline that make physicists receptive to e-prints, making it questionable whether dispensing with peer review is a step that could be taken in other fields. I will rehearse now objections that have appeared in the literature. But I do so with some reservation, because Ginsparg's idea has been implemented not only in fields of physics besides high-energy physics, but in disciplines outside physics altogether, such as economics and, in Japan, philosophy.

1. To do physics at all, you need grants, and to get grants, you need the endorsement of referees. So papers in physics already must have merit since the research was likely to have been done under a grant. In fields not controlled by grants, the model may not work.[18]

2. In physics, acceptance rates to print journals are about 75 percent. Hence the decision to publish online without peer review does not alter the "acceptance" rate as much as it would in, say, English or philosophy, or in the top medical journals, where rejection rates are in the area of 90 percent. Most of the physics papers are destined for publication in a peer reviewed journal anyway.[19] Harnad suggests that peer review is here exercising an "invisible hand": "remove that invisible constraint—let the authors be answerable to no one but users of the Archive (or even its self-appointed "commentators")—and watch human nature take its natural course, standards eroding as the Archive devolves toward the canonical state of unconstrained postings: the free-for-all chat-groups . . . —until someone reinvents peer review and quality control."[20]

3. In a 1995 editorial, Jerome P. Kassirer and Marcia Angell, editors of the *New England Journal of Medicine*, articulated the policy (tracing back to 1974 and previous editor Fritz Ingelfinger) that the *Journal* would not consider for publication any work whose substance has been reported elsewhere. E-mailing copies of one's work to one or two dozen people would be allowable, but not posting a manuscript on the Internet to which anyone can gain access. "Medicine," they wrote, "is not physics: the wide circulation of unedited preprints in physics is unlikely to have an immediate effect on the public's well-being even if the material is biased or false."[21] In an interview, Kassirer is quoted as saying that physics researchers constitute a small community, "and what they put out on their website is not going to affect the health of thousands or millions of people"[22] This is presented only as an argument against using Ginsparg's system in medicine, but it could be used against Ginsparg's idea in other areas like mental health. The objection has little if any hold in the humanities, and there opposition to e-prints would have to rest on other grounds. In medicine itself, however, Ronald Laporte et al. published a piece in the *British Medical Journal* called "The Death of Biomedical Journals"[23] that favored e-prints (albeit with a form of peer review), and to which Kassirer and Angell were reacting.

4. Ginsparg himself identifies features of the physics community that make it especially receptive to his system.

A well-defined and highly interactive community of voracious readers with a pre-existing hard-copy preprint habit, with a standardized word processor and a generally high degree of computer literacy, with a rational means of assigning intellectual priority (i.e., at the point of dissemination rather than only after peer-review), and with little concern about patentable content—all of which may be regarded as momentary historical accident—is there some more abstract characterization of the required autonomy that allows a circumscribed community to flourish rather than suffocate in its own unreviewed output stream? Again it will be easier to argue these issues in retrospect someday, but at least one noteworthy feature can be identified: in my own research discipline, the author and reader communities (and consequently as well the referee community) essentially coincide. Such a closed peer community may signal a greater intrinsic likelihood for acceptance and utility of free electronic dissemination of unreviewed material.[24]

But suppose we were to extend Ginsparg's models outside physics (as has been done anyway). Even if quality control is not as serious a problem in physics as in other fields, one cannot avoid facing the challenge Alvin Goldman sets before Ginsparg: finding a means of "product identification"—of knowing which products to read.[25] It will be harder to identify the best papers because of a glut of others. When papers are peer reviewed, as one moves down the hierarchy of journals, one anticipates diminishing quality. How does a reader anticipate quality in an unrefereed system?

Ginsparg's answer is that since thousands of peers will be reading the material, authors are circumspect and likely to do their best lest they go through embarrassment.[26] But doing one's best does not guarantee a good piece of work. Here the differences between physics and other fields kick in yet again— physics papers have already probably been refereed in connection with grant applications, so there is some prior presumption of quality; physics has high acceptance rates anyway; and so on. In other disciplines, the problem of product identification remains. Perhaps reviews posted and linked to the article will help, but how do the earliest readers know where to find quality?

Certainly survey articles are helpful in identifying the best papers. But they represent only one person's opinion. Another method, Goldman notes, is to use filtering systems such as GroupLens. GroupLens matches Professor X to a certain number of other professors who have given similar ratings on articles that all or most of them have read. Then when Professor X queries a title she has not read, the system makes a recommendation, based on the article's ratings, by the matching numbers. Goldman objects, however, that if Professor X has wide-ranging interests, GroupLens will not help. The system does not compare articles on different topics in a single science, let alone in different branches of science. Professor X's matching group will probably not have read the articles X is querying. And with tens of thousands of science articles published electronically each month, how can we have a guarantee that X "will query just those superior papers that will elicit enthusiastic rankings?"[27]

Another difficulty is that tenure, promotion, and salary increases depend upon a hierarchy of journals, providing incentive to authors to do their best work.

Ginsparg concedes that peer review has value, but he does not think it worth the cost:

> This is not, however, to argue that peer review cannot in principle provide sub-stantial added-value to the reader. One of the foremost problems at present is the large amount of information lost in the conventional review process, with the end result only single one-time or all-or-nothing binary decision. Although this may somehow be adequate for the purpose of validating research for job and grant allocation, it clearly provides little benefit to the average reader.[28]

In a similar vein, Jean-Claude Guedon writes: "For promotional purposes, for prizes, for grant awards, for teaching purposes, the printed record remains cru-cial, but for the day-to-day workings of the laboratory, once the retrospective bibliographic search has been covered, it is of relatively little importance. Sim-ilar circumstances prevail in the social sciences and the humanities."[29] When one realizes the number of hits on an unrefereed website, one realizes that read-ers are willing to read plenty of material lacking the certification of peer review. All that having been said, readers can't read everything, and they will want some way of knowing which are the best items, even if they want more access than access to the best. Reader feedback to e-prints will help in this regard, but does everyone who reacts have the credentials and expertise to react?

Proposal 2: Conventional Peer Review ("Business as Usual")

At the opposite end of the spectrum from Ginsparg's proposal is the sugges-tion that peer review go on as usual. A few referees will receive submissions electronically and submit their reports; if the paper is accepted, the article is posted online, and that is the end of the matter. Readers can submit replies to the journals as is now the case with print journals, and the author can re-ply, but no special effort is made to recruit responses.

This system does not avail itself of increased capabilities for more, and more interactive, feedback presented by online publication. The increased possibilities lie in two areas: predecision correspondence and postpublication exchanges. Let us turn to proposals that exploit these possibilities.

Proposal 3: Open Peer Review

In this system submitted papers are posted on the Web and all readers are invited to submit commentary.[30] The commentaries are used by the editor in lieu of invited, selective referees' reports. You might wonder: isn't the article in effect "published" when it is on the journal website? The answer to that is no: publication involves a certain permanence. Papers that undergo open review are withdrawn from the website if they are rejected. In this regard the plan differs from Ginsparg's system. But it could equally be argued that the paper should stay on the site in case it will be of use sometime, somewhere.

One could justify open peer review by reference to an argument we encountered in chapter 1. There is, we said, a problem of authority when peer review is limited to a few. If one or two of the peer referees do not like an author's ideas, arguments, orientation, methodology, organization, or even writing style, their opposition will often ensure (pending whether revisions are invited) that the ideas will not appear in print where the author wants them and will not reach the hoped-for audience. Should we not be concerned that the one or two referees—along with the editor who trusts them—might be mistaken? Chance would have yielded the same agreement or disagreement. Often the wider reception of an article does not match two referees' recommendation. Replies often point out gaping holes and serious errors in published works. By the same token, what if a rejected article contains crown jewels, as happened in the case of Nobel Prize–winning work that was originally rejected?[31]

With open review, authors lose the privacy and confidentiality they enjoy under the conventional system. That, however, may be all to the good—knowing their work will be circulated widely, they would strive to make the original submission as good as possible rather than merely submit mediocre work to test the waters in a relatively private fashion. Harnad has criticized the open review system, nonetheless, on the grounds that the self-appointed commentators will not necessarily be qualified specialists. "Are those who have nothing more pressing to do with their time than this really the ones we want to trust to perform such a critical QC/C [quality control/certification] function for us all?"[32] Furthermore, what happens to problems of referee bias in such an arrangement, where an author's brother-in-law, housekeeper, ex-spouse, and—if you will say that respondents must have some appropriate affiliation—chief competitor can respond? Peer review degenerates into a polling system, where thumbs-up or thumbs-down judgments are what matter and the process by which decisions are reached becomes irrelevant. True, an editor could study the quality of the reports, but editors would have a tough time rendering correct judgments accurately, especially when the volume of reports is large. In general, an article may precipitate so much diverging comment that an editor will not be able to sort it all out.[33] A far more sensible idea is for the editor to select reviewers; nevertheless, if one insists on keeping within the spirit of open review, the editor should choose more than the usual two or three referees, and people can request to be reviewers. Admittedly this system, like traditional peer review, is only as good as the editor's assessment of who is a good judge in the field.

Besides the potential for biased or incompetent feedback, another drawback of open peer review is that authors may be reluctant to submit even good work because of the very public way in which the work will be evaluated and in which a paper's rejection is known to all. I grant that once a work is accepted, there will also be public exposure and evaluation, but the author in that situation has the psychological benefit of knowing the work has passed the test of peer review.

Craig Bingham has raised a further point about open review.[34] In open review the fate of a rejected paper will often become known. Once a paper has been rejected by peer groups, it will be difficult for the author to get it published in another journal. First of all, to raise again a problem I raised earlier, the second journal might regard the wide distribution of the paper by the first journal to constitute publication. Second, available referees may have been "used up" the first time. The more "peers" comment on an article, the more difficult it would be for an author to get a fresh hearing if the paper is rejected and then submitted to another journal. He or she may wind up with the same referees.

Finally, in chapter 3 we noted that adding referees hurts the chances of a controversial, innovative paper.

Proposal 4: Closed Peer Review, Open Commentary

This system keeps peer review closed, in two senses: (i) limited to specifically appointed referees and (ii) confidential and private. However, once the article has been accepted, it is posted online and public responses are invited from a wide range of experts. The responses are then posted online with the article. (The original referees' reports could be published as well and linked to the published article as commentaries.) Authors can write rebuttals to those responses, or revise the articles in response (in which case a particular commentary will only be linked to an earlier version of the article which remains archived). This system is closed in the sense that the editor publishes only invited responses, but it is open in the sense of being public.

An open commentary system is used in the print journal *Behavioral and Brain Sciences* (edited by Harnad for over two decades) and in Harnad's e-journal *Psycoloquy* (the first peer reviewed fully electronic journal). Each print issue of BBS contains a large number of invited responses to an accepted paper. Harnad insists that open peer commentary is "an extremely powerful and important *supplement* to peer review, but no *substitute* for it."[35] Referees' reports, Harnad explains, are written for authors, editors, and possibly other referees; open peer commentaries are written for the entire learned community. But both are forms of quality control. It is the "skywriting" that takes place, the ongoing revision of a paper in response to critics, that marks the main difference Harnad sees between print and electronic media.[36]

Harnad's proposal that the open peer commentary take place in a single journal issue is superior, I think, to suggestions that view continuing discussion as open-ended. Surely something can be said for allowing an author to move on to other projects once a work has been published, give or take an occasional reply article. Continuing commentary and a continuing expectation that one will respond to critics will make authors revisit "old stuff," to the detriment of new research. A time limit on discussion would be helpful in this regard.

One other problem that the open commentary format solves is the lack of peer review for book reviews (highlighted in chapter 4). Book reviewers would have greater accountability, since others who have read the book can send in reactions to a review. Knowing a response could be published should induce the reviewer to be careful. The aim of allowing responses by others is not to turn journal book reviews into Amazon.com. With some quality control exercised, replies to reviews can be a valuable and interesting feature of an e-journal.

Proposal 5: Public Peer Review
(with or without Later Open Commentary)

Suppose that peer review (i.e., the decision-making process) is conducted as a dialogue between the author, reviewers, editor, and perhaps a small panel of consultants, and that the dialogue is available online. This process allows all parties to interact and learn from each other.[37] Since the dialogue is public, the editor and reviewers are open to scrutiny, increasing the chances of detecting unfair practices and subjecting editorial decisions to a form of peer review. Furthermore, authors and reviewers can respond promptly to criticisms and misunderstandings.

But there are also disadvantages. The process may take longer than a standard peer review process, and debates can be interminable unless a judicious editor knows when to close the book.[38] Finally, to repeat an earlier point, authors may be reluctant to submit even good work because of the very public way in which the work will be evaluated.

Other disadvantages have been noted by Craig Bingham, of which I shall mention two.[39] (i) If the first reviews are by senior researchers of powerful positions and high reputation, others may be reluctant to issue comments in disagreement with those reviewers. Bingham suggests that the senior people will want to see their opinions challenged by newcomers, but this strikes me as overly sanguine. (ii) Editors will feel increased pressure since readers will have the referees' reports available and can question editors' decisions. Bingham believes that on the whole an editor who explains his reasons is better off than one who can hide the reasons, but this remains to be seen.

Summary

There are numerous ways in which peer review could be implemented—or not—in an electronic medium. It seems to me that for most fields, forgoing peer review and relying on e-prints is not feasible; the "success" of the e-print archives in physics may not be suitable as a model for all fields, even though it is used. At the same time it seems stodgy and unimaginative to take the business-as-usual approach and refuse to make changes in the traditional peer review system. But what changes should be made? Open peer review, I have argued in concurrence with Harnad, is too subject to abuse, and creates problems for rejected articles when they are submitted to other journals. I favor Harnad's approach of prepublication peer review without publicity, plus postpublication open commentary with author response. Although the system per se does not need electronic capabilities to introduce interactions between authors and reviewers, the procedures can be implemented far more efficiently online. Such interactions can be part of the peer review process, but in blinded form, and continue after acceptance of the manuscript. The effects of these methods must be studied carefully, since they will induce delays in editorial decisions and may lead to interminable debates; but not to experiment at all seems to me a bad decision.[40]

Conclusion: Revisiting Some Earlier Questions

Digital technology has the potential to revolutionize scholarly communication. In the introduction to this book I listed a set of questions forced upon us when we contemplate the possibility of online publishing. Let me repeat those questions and sketch my answers. First to reiterate the questions:

Should this increased capacity for communication be accompanied by an effort to exploit the possibility of instant communication, relax standards of peer review, and present more material quickly for consumption and review by the entire scholarly community? Or is there inherent value in the current high rejection rates? Furthermore, since many electronic journals are unrefereed, how should unrefereed electronic material, such as papers on a website, be evaluated by hiring, tenure, and promotion committees? Should the peer reviewed publication continue to be the gold standard of scholarship in evaluating applicants for job vacancies, tenure, and promotion? Is there value in utilizing selected experts as confidential reviewers, or should we invite input from all those who are interested in a subject?

Now my answers:

Q. Should this increased capacity for communication be accompanied by an effort to exploit the possibility of instant communication, relax standards of peer review, and present more material quickly for consumption and review by the entire scholarly community? Or is there inherent value in the current high rejection rates?

A. Good work is good work. But peer review tries to ensure that work that is produced is good, and it motivates scholars to produce their best work. Quality would suffer if authors were held to a low standard or no standard at all. Furthermore, scholars as readers need a way of knowing what is good and what is not, and to meet inundation problems they'd be willing to trust peer review, knowing it's not infallible. Similarly, an admissions committee to a school may trust certain standardized tests as barometers of quality while knowing full well they are not infallible. Still, it is unlikely that rejection rates must be as high as they are, since good material ends up in lower-tier journals. So some relaxation of standards is appropriate once the space constraints of print journals are not operative. In addition, as I noted in chapter 5, we may wish to archive material that does not pass peer review in case it becomes relevant in the future. Publishing and certification are thus "decoupled."

Q. Since many electronic journals are unrefereed, how should unrefereed electronic material, such as papers on a website, be evaluated by hiring, tenure, and promotion committees? Should the peer reviewed publication continue to be the gold standard of scholarship in evaluating applicants for job vacancies, tenure, and promotion?

A. My reply is my argument in chapter 5: There is no good reason why unrefereed materials that are subjected to responsible postpublication external review should not count as much as similarly reviewed materials in peer reviewed journals. Schools are conscious of the prestige factor, of course. But once the idea sinks in that postpublication review is more important than prepublication review, the very concept of what constitutes prestige will change. To think that merit is possessed only by peer reviewed articles, or only by publications in certain journals or with certain presses, is to show a bias. I still think an author is *wise* to publish in peer reviewed journals, so that what is produced will be better than what was submitted, and so that appointment, tenure, and promotion committees will not minimize the work. If authors stop producing in peer reviewed journals we can expect a general decline in quality, which is surely undesirable. But once an author has chosen to post material electronically or to accept an invitation to write (an invitation which should be taken to confer a certain status, by the way), the quality should be what counts. This is the whole point of a committee having postpublication review by experts.

Q. Is there value in utilizing selected experts as confidential reviewers, or should we invite input from all those who are interested in a subject?

A. Steve Fuller helpfully distinguishes "relative peers" and "absolute peers." The latter are experts in the particular specialty of the manuscript; the former are other scholars with related expertise but not in that precise area.[41] Relative peers can contribute an interspecialty or perhaps interdisciplinary perspective. A psychologist can critique a paper on rationality or epistemology, a philosopher of science or ethicist can critique a psychologist or medical researcher's work on peer review, a sociologist can critique views on the philosophy of science—all from a vantage point different from the author's. Nonexperts are thus a bulwark against conservatism, as they are not wedded to assumptions of the specialty.[42]

These, it seems to me, are appropriate responses to some of the challenges which confront scholars and scholarship in the age of the Internet.

Appendix

On Increasing the Number of Referees

It is often said that having a multiplicity of journals mitigates the problem of referee bias, assuming that the same referees are not used across different journals.[43] Authors find democracy "between, not within, journals."[44] Furthermore, the more a particular journal approaches the ideal of multiple reviews the more meaningful the sample of referee opinion is and the lower the probability of a biased review dominating an editor's decision. With peer review taking place on the Net, there is likely to be an increase in the number of referees and hence, it seems, opportunities for a better review process.

Using more reviewers makes an editor's job easier in those cases where a clear consensus ("high reliability") can be found among the many referees. At first glance the convergence of, say, fifteen reviewers on the question of whether a paper should be accepted or rejected settles the issue decisively. But in truth agreement on the bottom line does not spell consensus. Having multiple referees can therefore complicate an editor's task.

Consider the case of two referees. Suppose that two referees recommend rejection/acceptance of an article. Have the referees reached a consensus? Not necessarily, for, quite apart from the problem that the sample size is too small to build on, consensus on the bottom line does not entail consensus on the strengths and weaknesses of the paper. Referees may recommend acceptance or rejection for different reasons. That which is a weakness according to referee #1 may not have been noticed by referee #2 at all; in fact, a feature that referee #1 disliked may be one that referee #2 liked. Is there consensus nonetheless because they agree on the bottom line?

The situation described is not uncommon, as has been documented by D. W. Fiske and L. Fogg in their pointedly titled article, "But the Reviewers Are Making Different Criticisms of My Paper! Diversity and Uniqueness in Reviewer Comments."[45] Fiske and Fogg are not disturbed by the diversity of reviewer comments, however.

> We very rarely saw any criticism that we were inclined to question, on the basis of internal or other evidence, such as the reviewer's stating that a statistical test had a particular assumption. Also, in instances in which we consulted the original manuscript, we found no reviewer criticisms with which we disagreed. . . . Finally, it was very uncommon for an editor to indicate disagreement with a point made by a reviewer.[46]

This response seeks to moot the issue of whether reports that raise different criticisms represent a consensus. The response does not engage that issue at all; it only says (a) that the existence of different sets of criticisms of the same article does not entail that the criticisms are not sound; (b) that the criticisms are in fact sound.

Psychologists E. Rae Harcum and Ellen F. Rosen object to the argument of Fiske and Fogg. First of all, they think that cases in which referees advance differing criticisms are cases in which referees disagree:

> In the context of an evaluation, one would reasonably infer that a failure to comment on a point constitutes an approval or endorsement of that point, or at least a subthreshhold level of disapproval.[47]

Harcum and Rosen go further:

> If *all* of the criticisms are valid, and not trivial, [as Fiske and Fogg claim], when the evaluations are not consistent, then *each* evaluator has obviously missed several real deficiencies in the submission.[48]

Referees who recommend rejection may recommend it on differing grounds. Thus referee A may raise criticism X, while referee B raises criticism Y. Does B's silence on the criticism A raises mean that B does not endorse that criticism? This analysis strikes me as incorrect. Harcum and Rosen assume that a referee's report raises every objection that crosses the referee's mind. What if the referee is simply selective in the choice of criticisms?[49] In addition, the key question should not be, Did the referee think of this criticism? Rather, it is: Would the other referee agree with the criticism if it were posed to him or her?

Suppose, however, that we conclude Harcum and Rosen are mistaken, and the absence of a particular criticism from a referee's report does not *entail* that the referee disagrees with the criticism. It is still *possible* that the referee does not agree with the criticism, or would not if it were brought to her consciousness. Editors will typically not know whether referees agree on particular criticisms, and in some cases the question is crucial. Suppose there are four reports, each recommending rejection, each presenting a different criticism. If only one of the four referees endorses each particular criticism, the paper would have to be accepted, because each recommendation is nullified by the silence of the other three. The point here is that with multiple reviewers the editor is thrown into a sometimes hopeless task. Multiply the number of reviewers, and the problem of determining consensus expands proportionally.

Apart from this, imagine if every journal used fifteen referees. The demands on scholars' time would be tremendous. Finally, suppose an author's paper is rejected and the author submits the paper to another journal. Given that the pool of referees for a given subfield is small, won't it be likely that the next journal will draw on many of the same referees, thereby dooming the paper? There are, to be sure, disputes over whether a journal should use a referee who has rejected the paper for another journal.[50] But here we are speaking of using several referees who have already refereed the piece.

For this reason, the solution of having many referees is more difficult than it seems. Add to this a point we noted in chapter 3—that the more referees there are the more we need to be concerned that a controversial paper is likely to receive negative reports—and it becomes clear that an editor has his or her work cut out.[51] The increase in referees associated with Web publishing needs to be handled wisely.

Notes

1. See Stevan J. Harnad, "Implementing Peer Review on the Net: Scientific Quality Control in Scholarly Electronic Journals," in *Scholarly Publishing: The Electronic Frontier*, ed. Robin P. Peek and Gregory B. Newby (Cambridge, Mass.: MIT Press, 1996), 108–9. On the "democratic" character of the Net, see also Gordon Graham, *The Internet: A Philosophical Inquiry* (London: Routledge, 1999), chap. 4.

2. Andrew Odlyzko, "Tragic Loss or Good Riddance? The Impending Demise of Scholarly Journals," in *Scholarly Publishing*, ed. Peek and Newby, 91–101. The quotation is from page 91.

3. Stevan J. Harnad, "The Invisible Hand of Peer Review," *Exploit Interactive*, issue 5, 3, www.exploit-lib.org/issue5/peer-review/ (accessed October 3, 2003) [this volume, pp. 235–42].

4. Robin P. Peek, "Scholarly Publishing, Facing the New Frontiers," in *Scholarly Publishing*, ed. Peek and Newby, 10.

5. Harnad, "Implementing Peer Review on the Net," 114.

6. Paul Ginsparg, "First Steps toward Electronic Research Communication," in *Gateways to Knowledge*, ed. Lawrence Dowler (Cambridge, Mass.: MIT Press, 1997), 49–50 (also at lanl.arxiv.org/ftp/hep-th/papers/macros/blurb.tex).

7. A similar argument is found in Paul Ginsparg, "Winners and Losers in the Global Research Village," 6, xxx.lanl.gov/blurb/pg96unesco.html.

8. Harnad, "The Invisible Hand of Peer Review," 4

9. Harnad, "Implementing Peer Review on the Net."

10. Jean-Claude Guedon, "The Seminar, The Encyclopedia and the Eco-Museum as Possible Future Forms of Electronic Publishing," in Peek and Newby, eds., 80.

11. On these issues, see, for example, Jeff Belle, "Revenge of the Librarians," *Econtent* 25, no. 5 (May 2002): 28–33; Lee Van Orsdel and Kathleen Born, "Big Chill on the Big Deal," *Library Journal* 128, no. 7 (April 15, 2003): 51–56; Richard Quandt, *Library Trends* 51, no. 3 (winter 2003): 349–76. I thank Pearl Berger, Dean of Libraries at Yeshiva University, for these references and for discussion of issues facing libraries in the age of electronic communication.

12. Duly noted by such e-enthusiasts as Peter Roberts, "Scholarly Publishing, Peer Review, and the Internet," *First Monday*, issue 4, www/firstmonday.dk/issues/issue4_4/proberts/ (accessed October 3, 2003).

13. See Richard C. Hsu and William E. Mitchell, "Books Have Endured for a Reason. . . . ," *New York Times*, May 25, 1997, F12.

14. Jerome P. Kassirer and Marcia Angell, "The Internet and the *Journal*," *New England Journal of Medicine* 332, no. 25 (June 22, 1995): 1709–10.

15. Vincent Kiernan, "Rewards Remain Dim for Professors Who Pursue Digital Scholarship," *Chronicle of Higher Education*, April 28, 2000, A45–46.

16. Alvin I. Goldman, *Knowledge in a Social World* (New York: Oxford University Press, 1999), 178.

17. Harnad, former editor of *Behavioral and Brain Sciences*, endorses open peer commentary but only as a *supplement* to blind review. See his "The Invisible Hand of Peer Review," *Exploit Interactive* 5, www.exploit-lib.org.

18. See Hal Varian, "The Economics of the Internet and Academia," in *The Economics of Information in the Networked Environment*, ed. Meredith Butler and Bruce Kinga (Washington, D.C.: Association of Research Libraries, 1996), 46; Goldman, *Knowledge in a Social World*, 177.

19. See Harnad, "Invisible Hand," 2.

20. Harnad, "Invisible Hand," 3.

21. Kassirer and Angell, "The Internet and the *Journal*," 1709–10.

22. Katie Hafner, "Physics on the Web Is Putting Science Journals on the Line," *New York Times*, April 21, 1998, F3.

23. Ronald Laporte et al., "The Death of Biomedical Journals," *British Medical Journal* 310 (1995): 1384. Such a method was tried, however, by the "World Journal Club," which has since disappeared from the Web. See Craig Bingham, "Peer Review on the Internet: Are There Faster, Fair, More Effective Methods of Peer Review," in *Peer Review in Health Science*, ed. Fiona Godlee and Tom Jefferson (London: BMJ Books, 1999), 221, note 3.

24. Ginsparg, "Winners and Losers," 7.

25. Goldman, *Knowledge in a Social World*, 175–80.

26. Ginsparg, "First Steps."

27. Goldman, *Knowledge in a Social World*, 178. It can be argued that with the advent of desktop publishing, publishing costs are lower than they have been previously, so the need to limit what is published is no longer great. Hence a postpublication filtering is preferable. Also see Varian, "Economics of the Internet and Academia," 50.

28. Ginsparg, "Winners and Losers," 6. In recent work, Ginsparg has suggested ways of introducing peer review into his system. See "Can Peer Review Be Better Focused?" arxiv.org/blurb/pg02/pr.html.

29. Jean-Claude Guedon, "The Seminar," 79.

30. See LaPorte et al., "Death of Biomedical Journals."

31. See chapter 3, pp. 10–11; chapter 5, p. 13.

32. Harnad, "The Invisible Hand of Peer Review," 2.

33. See Craig Bingham, "Peer Review and the Ethics of Internet Publishing," in *Ethical Issues in Biomedical Publication*, ed. Anne Hudson Jones and Faith McLellan (Baltimore, Md.: Johns Hopkins University Press, 2000), 108.

34. Bingham, "Peer Review and the Ethics of Internet Publishing," 108.

35. Bingham, "Peer Review and the Ethics of Internet Publishing," 108.

36. Interestingly, Harnad does not reject the notion of unrefereed discussion entirely. He allows for discussion by "a closed group of specialists with read/write privileges" as a useful complement to traditional peer review. See Harnad, "Implementing Peer Review on the Net," 115.

37. See Bingham, "Peer Review on the Internet," 214–22; "Peer Review and the Ethics of Internet Publishing," in *Ethical Issues in Biomedical Publication*, ed. Anne Hudson Jones and Faith McLellan (Baltimore, Md.: Johns Hopkins University Press, 2000), 91–109.

38. Bingham, "Peer Review on the Internet," 216.

39. Bingham, "Peer Review and the Ethics of Internet Publishing," 107–9.

40. For an analysis of how academic communities could be reshaped by electronic communication, see Robert J. Silverman, "The Impact of Electronic Publishing on the Academic Community," in *Scholarly Publishing*, ed. Peek and Newby, 55–69.

41. Not only have there been proposals for open review by scholars, whether they are experts or not, but there is dispute over including nonacademics, such as contract researchers, in the process of peer review. See the debate between Steve Fuller, "Response to the Japanese Social Epistemologists: Some Ways Forward for the 21st Century," *Social Epistemology* 13 (1999): 291–92 and Hidetoshi Kihara, "The Extension of Peer Review, How Should It or Should Not Be Done?" *Social Epistemology* 17 (2003): 65–77. Fuller uses the terms "absolute peer and relative peer" on page 293. The suggestion to include nonacademics stems from a breakdown of the simple picture of knowledge in which scholars are its producers and nonscholars are its consumers. Nowadays there is talk about knowledge being coproduced or co-constructed. I think that to some extent it is good for academics to be reminded that their work often seems . . . "academic" (often a synonym for "irrelevant"). See also the expanded circle of reviewers proposed by the Canadian biomedical editor Peter Singer, "When Shall We Be Free," biomedcentral.com/meetings/2000/foil/editorials/singer (accessed October 1, 2003).

42. See M. Wolman, letter to the editor, *Scientist* 1 (1987): 10.

43. Cf. Sue P. Ravenscroft and Timothy J. Fogarty, "Social and Ethical Dimensions of the Repeated Journal Reviewer," *Journal of Information Ethics* 7, no. 2 (fall 1998): 45.

44. Sandra Scarr, "Anosmic Peer Review: A Rose by Any Other Name Is Evidently Not a Rose," *Behavioral and Brain Sciences* 5, no. 4 (1982): 237–38.

45. D. W. Fiske and L. Fogg, "But the Reviewers Are Making Different Criticisms of My Paper! Diversity and Uniqueness in Reviewer Comments," *American Psychologist* 45 (1990): 591–98.

46. Fiske and Fogg, "But the Reviewers," 597.

47. E. Rae Harcum and Ellen F. Rosen, *The Gatekeepers of Psychology: Evaluation of Peer Review by Case History* (Westport, Conn.: Praeger, 1993), 13.

48. Harcum and Rosen, *The Gatekeepers of Psychology*, 13.

49. Atara Graubard Segal made this argument to me.

50. See R. L. Meile, "The Case against Double Jeopardy," letter, *American Sociologist* 12 (1977): 52; Ravenscroft and Fogarty, "Social and Ethical Dimensions."

51. Outstanding and poor papers are likely to elicit agreement by referees, whereas papers in the middle are likely not to. See Ronald N. Kostoff, "The Principles and Practices of Peer Review," *Science and Engineering Ethics* 3 (1997): 19–34.

SUPPLEMENTARY ESSAYS

~~

Ethics and Manuscript Reviewing

Richard T. De George and Fred Woodward

Publishing is a partnership between author and publisher, but it is most successful when both parties follow ethical practices and communicate to the other their expectations of the publishing process.

Of the natural antagonism between authors and publishers, Jacques Barzun observes: "Authors, as everybody knows, are difficult; they are unreliable, arrogant, and grasping. But publishers are impossible—grasping, arrogant, and unreliable." Manuscript reviewing, which lies at the heart of scholarly publishing, generates much of the friction. Such reviewing ultimately determines what gets published and what does not. Although editors differ among themselves, as do reviewers, an important function of the review process is to identify manuscripts that make a contribution to knowledge and from that point of view deserve publication.

Within the scholarly world, publishing is a means by which scholars or professors achieve recognition and sometimes advancement and tenure. Their interest in getting published may overlap with a publisher's desire to print what advances knowledge. Yet even if the aims of publisher and author do not overlap significantly, since each is dependent on the other, issues of fairness arise.[1] Are the ground rules for manuscript reviewing fair to all concerned? Are they uniform and uniformly understood? Can they be faulted from an ethical point of view or improved?

One might argue that reviewing manuscripts is the job of editors, that they are professionals at it, and that they both know how to do it and do it well. For them ethical issues raised from the outside would be extraneous and beside the point, and might well seem to be attempts to get them to change their procedures, not for justifiable reasons, but for reasons of political correctness or vested interest.

Nonetheless, it should not be controversial to claim that the basic moral rules that govern human transactions in other realms should apply in the review process as well: both sides should be truthful, arrangements should be fair to all parties, the rights of all affected should be respected, and conflict of interest that leads to unfairness should be avoided. Not only should following these precepts be uncontroversial, but they would also in no way conflict with the freedom of presses and journals to publish what they wish or to publish material that advances knowledge or enriches the store of human interpretation and the appreciation of human values.[2] In our ethical considerations we shall put our emphasis especially on moral rights and correlative duties or obligations.

Our concern is to look at the manuscript review process, to evaluate actual practices, and to argue for the need for more explicit guidelines that can help make many of the current practices both ethically justifiable and acceptable to all. There will always be grey areas. Guidelines can never substitute for judgment, for one must judge when and how to apply the guidelines. Yet guidelines can help assure all those engaged in the process that it is a fair one.

Authors' Rights

No author has any right to have his or her manuscript accepted or published by any press or journal, no matter how good it is or how good the author thinks it is. No press or journal has any obligation to publish any particular manuscript, again no matter how good it is. Comparable in some ways to the doctrine of employment-at-will,[3] this might be dubbed the doctrine of publishing-at-will. Implicitly, both authors and editors subscribe to this doctrine. Yet, just as the doctrine of employment-at-will should not ignore workers' rights, the doctrine of publishing-at-will cannot justly deny authors all rights in the publishing process. For instance, authors have a right to expect they will be treated in certain ways. If a book manuscript comes over the transom, then the author has no right to expect any particular kind of treatment until the editorial process has begun, if it is started at all. Such authors take their chances, for no one can force any editor to consider their work; simple submission of a manuscript carries with it no automatic right to review.[4] This is compatible with the claim that from the perspective of good business practice, even the over-the-transom submission deserves the consideration of a reply. If the authors have queried and received some encouragement to submit their manuscripts, however, they have a right to fair consideration. What constitutes fair consideration is the issue.

What rights do authors have, and what obligations on the part of editors correspond to authors' rights?

We suggest that what is fair is what both parties with appropriate knowledge agree to as fair. Central to ethics in the review procedure are truth and candor. With respect to an author, an editor usually operates from a position of power.[5] The abuse of that power is the prime cause for what either is or is considered unethical in the review process. From the point of view of authors, a manuscript that is sent to a publisher can seem to fall into a black hole. Control over the review process, with the author kept in ignorance of what is going on, is one of the keys to maintaining a publisher's power. Yet publisher and author are mutually dependent on one another, and although the publisher is in the position of power, the author has the right to respect and fair treatment.

The failure of many presses and editors is not that they act unethically, but that they act on an implicit agreement or contract. They know the conditions, but they do not share them with the author. The crux of what is ethical is most often not whether a manuscript is sent, for instance, to two or more reviewers, or whether it is sent for blind review, but that the author does not know how it is treated. There is no one ethically correct way to handle manuscripts. Many ways of dealing with manuscripts are ethically justifiable, but any of them is justifiable only if the author knows what the procedure is and agrees to the process that is followed. Part of what is necessary is making explicit the rules of the game. The problem is not one of getting all presses and editors to agree to follow the same rules and then to inform authors of them. This would be one possible ethical approach, but it is not necessary, probably not desirable, and presently not practicable.

Authors expect that editors will initially read or review their manuscript in whatever way the editor thinks sufficient to make some initial judgment. That is an editor's job and responsibility. What is due the author is that editors should do so within a reasonable amount of time, decide what further to do with the manuscript, and inform the author. How long a time is reasonable depends on a variety of factors. Surely a year is too long for such an initial reading, as is six months. Is three months too long? There is no ethically demanded period of time.

Journal editors typically do not communicate with the author at this stage, but simply send out the manuscript for review by readers. The "American Philosophical Association Guidelines for the Submission and Publication of

Philosophy Manuscripts" states that "unless authors are notified to the contrary, such evaluation procedures will normally not extend beyond four months from the date of receipt."[6] The total consideration process for a journal article, unless there are exceptional circumstances, usually takes less than six months. If more time is required, the author should be notified.

Since review of book-length manuscripts is often more complicated, consideration of the author requires that a publisher or editor notify the author of receipt of the solicited manuscript and give some indication of what will happen to it. At this stage perhaps this will be only an acknowledgment and an indication that the press will get back to the author with a report as soon as possible (if that is the truth), but within a period the editor anticipates and states. If the manuscript is 1,000 pages long and arrives at the beginning of the summer when many reviewers are unavailable, the time needed may be longer than if the manuscript is shorter and arrives at a more favorable time. What is important is that the author be given accurate information.

If the editor's judgment after an initial reading is negative, that should be communicated to the author soon after that decision is made. The editor has nothing to lose by delaying, but the author does. If an editor's initial reading results in the editor's decision to send the manuscript to one or more readers, the editor should so inform the author. The author has the right to know the status of the manuscript—that it has, for example, been sent to reviewers and that the reviews are expected within a specified period of time. If the reviews are delayed, additional reviews are necessary, or other reasons slow down the process, the author also deserves to know that the expected date for a decision has been moved back. Supplying such information may cause some extra work for the editor, and it certainly takes away some of the power that ignorance yields. If an editor keeps an author completely in the dark, the editor can do or not do whatever the editor wants. But so acting is hardly fair to the author. Keeping authors informed may raise the risk that some authors may deem the process too lengthy and withdraw the manuscript. That is a cost of supplying information and of keeping the process fair for all parties. Approval by an external review board can add to the time needed for a press to come to a final decision about a manuscript. The issue is not the time required but accurately informing the author about the time the process—whatever it is—will take and of delays, if they occur. This does not require that the author be informed at each stage what the interim reports are, although providing such information is by no means precluded.

The author has no right to choose reviewers or to know which reviewers the editor has chosen, although nothing precludes an author from suggesting or being asked by the editor for the names of possible reviewers. Yet peer review is the expectation of authors, and the usual practice of scholarly publishers.[7] If the peer review process is used, authors have the right to have their manuscripts reviewed by peers—that is, by scholars or teachers or others who are knowledgeable about the topic with which the manuscript deals.

Is it unethical for an editor to choose reviewers who are likely to agree with an editor's initial reaction? No, why should it be? If reviewers are objective—as they should be—choosing any such scholar should be acceptable. Choosing a reviewer whose inclinations the editor does not know does not guarantee objectivity. Indication that the editor is favorably or unfavorably disposed toward a manuscript may or may not prejudice a reviewer. But to argue that editors may not choose reviewers whose positions they know is much too strong a claim.

Would it be fair to an author for an editor knowingly to submit a manuscript to the author's enemy, or to someone who the editor knew would not give a more or less objective reading? The point of such an action would clearly not be to get an objective reading, but to provide the editor with a crutch to turn down the manuscript. Since editors may legitimately turn down manuscripts on their own, they may of course do so with the crutch of negative reviews they knew would be negative. To claim otherwise is to claim that authors have the right to be published by a particular press or journal—a claim we discounted at the start. The reason for an editor's seeking favorable reviews, and signaling this to reviewers, might be to convince the editorial board that an objective peer review has been conducted. What is unethical is not the choosing of the reviewers, but not being honest—if one is not—with one's own editorial board.

How many outside reviews are ethically mandatory? Surely the answer is there is no ethically demanded number. Two may be the norm in many presses and for many journals.[8] It is not ethically mandatory. Nor, if there is a dispute between or among reviewers, need an editor accept, reject, or seek more reviews. That is appropriately an editorial decision. An editor may trust one reader more than the other, may decide that a manuscript that requires three readers will not be approved by the press's board, or may have been only lukewarm about the manuscript to begin with. Authors may wish—even expect—a third reader. But expectations or wishes do not constitute rights.

Must the manuscript be sent for blind review, as some authors claim?[9] In our view no one has yet demonstrated that blind reviewing is ethically mandatory. On the face of it, withholding an author's identity from the reviewer would seem to increase the likelihood of an objective review, which is what most scholarly publishers and authors claim they want. Evaluations of the manuscript would be less colored by the reviewer's bias favoring or disfavoring the author's academic appointment, reputation, gender, race, and other characteristics extraneous to the work itself. Might not the publishing world diminish such discrimination—and certainly some of it exists—by blind reviewing? While the answer for most cases seems to be yes, a publisher need not have a uniform policy for all authors concerning blind reviewing.

Stanley Fish, for one, argues against blind reviewing by denying that "intrinsic merit" can be identified "independently of professional or institutional conditions."[10] It may make a great deal of difference who writes, as well as what is written. Although revealing the author's name to reviewers favors the better-known scholars, Fish claims that they have earned "the benefit of the doubt."[11]

Fairness for an author is not necessarily being treated in the same way as all other authors. Justice according to Aristotle means treating similar cases similarly; but not all cases are similar. If the philosopher John Rawls, whose book, A Theory of Justice, has received widespread attention from scholars in many fields, writes an article interpreting his earlier work or revising his views, an editor would appropriately wish the reviewers to know that Rawls is the author of the article they are reviewing. Only then can they put it properly in the context of his earlier work. Moreover, book publishers, whose investment in a given manuscript is considerably more than journal publishers', could argue strongly for taking extrinsic merits into account in making publishing decisions. For example, an editor may choose to publish an article or book by a certain author because it will attract attention or sell well simply because it is by that author. In such cases the editor may legitimately wish a reviewer to know who the author is.

Because blind reviewing is commonly employed by journals and because some see this as an ethical issue, authors have the right to know how their manuscripts will be treated so they can deal only with those publishers who conform to their preferences. Since authors frequently do not know what is possible and may hesitate to raise questions that could offend a potential publisher, editors should accept the responsibility for indicating to an author—perhaps in a policy statement sent to authors whose works are to be peer reviewed—what their standard practice is and, if blind reviewing is not their policy, whether it might be employed if the author so requests. As long as a publisher either makes available this latter option or clearly states to the author that policy prohibits it, there seems little if any ground for claims of unfairness. In any case, the editor who conducts the review knows the author's identity, and the final decision rests not with the peer reviewers but with the editor and/or the editor's board.

Authors' Obligations

What obligations do authors owe to presses or journals? The major one is truthfulness and disclosure. This means, among other things, that they should not misrepresent their credentials, make statements that are untrue or misleading, present as their own work that which is not their own, or agree to conditions or schedules they know they cannot fulfill or meet.

Authors are often in the dark about the acceptability of multiple submissions. This is one more area in which information is not readily available and not widely disseminated. What is appropriate for both authors and publishers on this issue? Many authors make multiple submissions of book manuscripts, in part because of the long time it take to get replies from publishers. This is less frequent with respect to journals. Are multiple submissions ethically justifiable? Again, there is no one ethically mandatory policy. But to keep the transaction between authors and publishers fair, each should keep the other informed. Many journals will not consider articles to which they do not have the exclusive option to publish if accepted. All concerned parties would benefit if this were stated when it is the policy. Presses seem to vary more in their policies in this regard, and presses may vary their policies according to the author or the work.

An author should inform the press if he or she is submitting the manuscript elsewhere. The editor may then decide to proceed with the manuscript or not. Since reviews cost money and the time of both presses and readers, it is unfair to presses to expect them to incur these costs without letting them know they do so at some risk.

Although this argument places the obligation on the author to inform publishers of multiple submissions, authors may not realize what they should do. Solving the problem is in the self-interest of publishers, who are the professionals and have the power and resources to effect a remedy. When acknowledging receipt of an invited manuscript, editors could inform the author of their policy with respect to multiple submissions and specifically ask whether the author is making or has made multiple submissions and, if so, whether the querying publisher has the right of first acceptance.

Of course, authors may lie. But unethical behavior on the part of some does not justify keeping authors in the dark about a publisher's policies. Nor is it necessary that a publisher have a uniform policy. It might be willing to work with multiple submissions from some authors and not be willing to spend the money to review a manuscript that only marginally interests them if the author is submitting the manuscript elsewhere. What is ethically mandatory is not that their policy be one way or another, but that they let authors know what their policy is so that authors in their turn can live up to the obligation of both sides to provide appropriate information.

Reviewers' Rights and Obligations

Reviewers have the right to anonymity if they request it, and it should be respected by all those who have access to their reviews.[12] Not to do so is to jeopardize the whole process. Only if reviewers are promised anonymity might they be willing to write a negative review if they feel one is deserved. We know from experience with letters of recommendation for students that very few letters that are open to the student's inspection will say anything negative about the student. Publishers should let reviewers know if the press will reveal their names to an author after a manuscript has been accepted. A press should respect a reviewer's preference not to have his or her name revealed to an author and should ascertain whether the author is willing to be identified before doing so. Although the press or journal may not release that information, the reviewer may identify him- or herself if he or she so chooses. No harm is done to the publisher by such a self-revelation.

If asked to review a manuscript they have already reviewed, should reviewers reveal that to the inquiring editor? The manuscript may have been revised in the interim. Nonetheless, a prior judgment on a manuscript is a pertinent disclosure. One has already formed an opinion and cannot pretend that he or she will give a second unbiased opinion, uninfluenced by one's first judgment. If the manuscript has been revised, a reviewer may well give it an objective appraisal. But the editor should know of the previous reading. Reviewing the same manuscript for two different presses, moreover, puts the author in double jeopardy if the review is negative. The danger is that a well-known author, seen as the obvious reviewer by several presses, might in effect be able to blackball a manuscript. Editors, aware of the fact that the reviewer has already reviewed the manuscript, should take that possibility into account, and they can do so only if informed by the reviewer in question.

Reviewers owe it to their peers to be as objective as possible. Anonymity is not license, and editors should hold (and should be known by authors to hold) reviewers accountable for what they say in their reviews. Reviewers have the obligation to read the manuscripts they agree to review and to do so with some care. Writing a negative report without reading a manuscript, or without reading all of it, is not unheard of. Reviewers should know in advance how long the manuscript is, what kind of a manuscript it is, and, if it is not blind reviewed, who the author is. To preclude people from reviewing the manuscripts of those whom they know is too strict. Some fields are small enough that all or almost all of those in the field know one another. Even where this is not the case, those best situated to render an objective judgment may well be those who know the author. But reviewers should disqualify themselves from serving as readers for those on whom they cannot render an objective judgment—possibly their former mentors or students, certainly their spouses or relatives, and just as surely their avowed enemies. Reviewing is a professional activity of trust and should not be used to get revenge. Editors cannot know in advance when this is a danger and cannot control the unethical acts of those they ask to review. But if the reviews reveal such unethical bias or motives, editors should not use such reviews to arrive at their final decisions.[13]

Reviewers owe those whose manuscripts they review confidentiality, and they also are ethically precluded from using for their own benefit the contents of the manuscripts they read. Legally they are not allowed to copy the text of the manuscript any more than they are allowed to copy the printed text. Furthermore, it is unethical to steal, borrow, or take any of the authors' ideas without attribution. One has no right to make attribution, without the prior consent of the author, to a manuscript that one has access to only in the process of a review. In this case the reviewer must distinguish between what he or she has access to by virtue of the position of reviewer and what is open to use as if it were the reviewer's own or as if it had been published.[14] The author did not choose to reveal the manuscript to the particular reviewer, who was chosen by the press's editor. Nor does the author agree to the review process with the understanding that anyone to whom the editor gives access to the manuscript and who wants to use the ideas contained and expressed in the manuscript may freely use or cite them. For this reason, it is also unethical to let others read a manuscript entrusted to one as a reviewer. Editors give manuscripts to reviewers as confidential documents for the specific purpose of review. Publishers can help educate reviewers of their obligations, routinely enclosing together with the manuscript a sheet of instructions with such reminders of confidentiality.

Just as publishers are expected to get to manuscripts as soon as they can and to let authors know the time frame in which they expect to operate, so reviewers should get to manuscripts as soon as they can and should let publishers know if they cannot meet an agreed-upon schedule. It is unethical to agree to read a manuscript within a certain period of time if the reviewer knows he or she cannot meet the deadline. Delays may occur, and in some cases they may be unavoidable. In such instances the obligation is to contact the publisher with that information and let the publisher decide whether the delay is acceptable. This is necessary if the publisher is to fulfill the obligation to the author, as we discussed earlier.

The decision to publish or not is one that is appropriately made by the publisher. The obligation of the reviewer is to provide the publisher with a fair review. The reviewer should not judge a manuscript from a less prestigious press any differently from one from a prestigious press. It is not up to the reviewer to decide that one press ought to publish poorer quality manuscripts than another, or to decide that a given manuscript is good enough for A but would not be for B. The manuscript should be judged on its merits, and its strengths and weaknesses indicated. A recommendation to publish should indicate a justifiable opinion that the manuscript is in fact publishable and that it advances knowledge or meets whatever other criteria the reviewer is using, which he or she should specify.

Obligations of Editors

In discussing the rights of authors and reviewers we have already frequently mentioned the obligations of editors. But we have barely mentioned the obligation of editors to their boards and presses or journals. We have emphasized truth, communication, and disclosure in the review process. The same values apply as well in dealings with editorial boards. A function of the board is to help make or approve policy, to accept or reject recommendations to publish particular works, and to decide which ones to publish, what risks to take, and so on.

Boards are usually at the mercy of the editorial staff. Each member of the board does not usually read all the manuscripts on which the board is asked to pass judgment. The members rely largely on outside reviews and on the recommendation of the editor(s). The obligation of editors is to present accurately and fairly whatever case they have prepared concerning the manuscripts they recommend to the board. The obligation not to lie or mislead means they cannot praise a manuscript they have not read as if they had read it. Must they present all reviews, good and bad, and may they appropriately discount some they think are prejudiced or poorly done? Since the ethical obligation is not to deceive and not to mislead, the answer is yes. It then becomes the editor's responsibility to persuade the board to discount the poorly done or prejudiced reviews. Editors should have the trust of their boards, and usually they get and keep this trust by being fair and objective in their presentations and recommendations.

Is there a conflict between obligations to authors and obligations to editorial boards? If there is, which takes precedence? While the answer might be "It depends," as a general rule editors are the paid agents of their presses and have the obligation to act as such. If loyalty to authors means that an editor fights for fair treatment and consideration for them, that is also part of what is expected of editors by most presses. If loyalty to authors means showing favoritism for one's friends, then that is usually inimical to the professional role editors play. The rights violated are not those of authors but of the press they are paid to serve.

Obligations of Publishers

Do publishers have an obligation to publish the best (and only the best) material they can? It would be strange for scholarly publishers to aim at less, within the parameters they set for themselves. However, a press may well choose to publish regional material, even though it might be of lesser quality than other works it could publish, in order to fulfill a part of its mission or to generate revenue, and because the publisher may feel the better material will find a home elsewhere. Those who manage a press have the obligation to manage it efficiently and to use the resources available to it as best they can. But publishing scholarly books with limited audiences may lead to the need for subsidies.[15] Scholarly presses have no ethical obligation to make a profit (how could they if they are not-for-profit organizations?), even though the director of the press has the obligation to be financially responsible in running the press. But like a private business, unless the press is financially solvent, it may not be able to stay in business.

The implication for reviewing is that editors have no ethical obligation to publish the best manuscripts, however these are defined, any more than any author has the right to have his or her manuscript published by a particular press. This does not justify discrimination based on gender, race, national origin, or other criteria inappropriate to the press and to the work being considered; but it relieves publishers of an obligation they cannot fulfill (and so one that they cannot have), and it admits that publishers have many considerations to balance in deciding to publish a manuscript—quality being only one of them.

The conclusion to which we come is very close to the place from which we started. Editors usually do know best most of the time what is required of them and how to handle manuscripts. Their major failing is the failure to acknowledge the power they wield vis-à-vis authors, and the tendency to adopt an almost paternalistic attitude that authors should trust them, and so need not be kept informed.

We have argued that publishing is a partnership, that authors are an essential part of the process, and that as such they have the right to know the rules governing the process in which they are key players. One way to provide them would be for all presses and journals to agree to a list of ethically defensible rules and to state them clearly and openly. This approach is neither necessary nor clearly the preferable approach. Different presses often appropriately follow diverse rules, and the diversity of presses is a publishing plus rather than a minus.[16] Such a state of affairs is ethically justified if most presses take upon themselves the obligation to inform authors and potential authors of their procedures, and if each press keeps those authors whose manuscripts it agrees to review informed throughout the process, and informs those who do the reviewing what its policies are. Ethical quandaries and possibly friction between authors and publishers would be lessened if both authors and editors clearly knew the rules and assumptions under which they were mutually operating.

Notes

We thank the following for their assistance and suggestions: Melissa Biederman, Michael Briggs, Colin Day, Charles Grench, Elizabeth Hadas, Beverly Jarrett, Cynthia Miller, and Donald McCoy.

1. There is surprisingly little written on the specifically ethical aspects of manuscript review. Alan Brilliant, "The Decision to Publish," *Scholarly Publishing* 11, no. 1 (October 1971): 55–57, briefly discusses the ethics of the decision to publish. Some others raise the issue of the "fairness" of the review process, without mentioning ethics. Literature exists on blind reviewing, including Stanley Fish, "No Bias, No Merit: The Case against Blind Submission," *Doing What Comes Naturally* (Durham, N.C.: Duke University Press, 1989), 163–79 [this volume, pp. 215–30], and Michael McGiffert, "Is Justice Blind? An Inquiry into Peer Review," *Scholarly Publishing* 20, no. 1 (October 1988): 43–48. There is considerable literature on ethics in publishing in the sciences, but this centers more on fraud in reporting research rather than on the ethics of the review process. *ACS Style Guide: A Manual for Authors and Editors*, ed. Janet S. Dodd (Washington, D.C.: American Chemical Society, 1986), prints "Ethical Guidelines to Publication of Chemical Research" as appendix 2, which lists ethical obligations of editors of scientific journals, of authors, of reviewers of manuscripts, and of scientists publishing outside the scientific literature. The July 1993 issue of *Scholarly Publishing*, dedicated to "The Ethics of Scholarly Publishing," focused primarily on problems raised by the publication of a controversial article written by Gordon R. Freeman, which he included in the special issue (December 1990) he guest-edited of the *Canadian Journal of Physics*.

2. "Ethical Guidelines to Publication of Chemical Research" is one of a number of documents that claim to give ethical guidelines, but how the norms they prescribe are obtained or defended is never made clear. Many of the guidelines are not ethically required, but are common sense, matters of etiquette, or ethical ideals. One receives praise for achieving ethical ideals, but failure to achieve them entails no ethical blame; one deserves blame for failure to fulfill one's ethical duties, but no special praise for doing so.

3. Employment-at-will is the doctrine that employers have the right to hire whomever they wish, and to fire for any reason or no reason; and that employees may work for whomever they choose who offers them work, and to quit whenever they want for any reason or no reason.

4. Journal manuscripts are frequently submitted over the transom, and this is the accepted practice of many journals. In such instances, the authors deserve fair consideration from the start.

5. An editor may well dance to the tune of a scholar who has a manuscript hotly desired by several competitors, but this is more the exception than the rule for most authors.

6. The "American Philosophical Association Guidelines for the Submission and Publication of Philosophy Manuscripts" were adopted (with the exception of an item on printing the date of receipt of the manuscript) by the Society of Philosophy Journal Editors. The guidelines are reprinted in Janice M. Moulton, *Guidebook for Publishing Philosophy* (Newark, Del.: American Philosophical Association, 1975), 11–12.

7. We do not here question whether peer review is ethically justifiable. We take it as a given. Stephen Lock and Jane Smith, "Peer Review at Work," *Scholarly Publishing* 17, no. 4 (July 1986): 303–16, argue that "peer review works," as does Margaret F. Stieg, "Refereeing and the Editorial Process: The Ahr and Webb," *Scholarly Publishing* 14, no. 2 (February 1983): 99–122.

8. The sixth responsibility for editors of the new 1993 "Research Communications Publication Policy of the National Research Council of Canada" specifies: "When a manuscript is deemed appropriate for consideration for publication, arrangements are made for it to be reviewed by at least two referees." The entire text of the policy is contained in *Scholarly Publishing* 24, no. 4 (July 1993): 274–80. The policy lists responsibilities of authors, editors, the editor-in-chief, reviewers, and the publisher. The policy does not say whether these are ethical responsibilities or other kinds of responsibilities but many are clearly not ethically required, even though ethically acceptable. The policy includes no justification or defense of the responsibilities it lists.

9. James M. Banner Jr., "Preserving the Integrity of Peer Review," *Scholarly Publishing* 19, no. 2 (January 1988): 112, argues for blind reviewing; Michael McGiffert, "Is Justice Blind? An Inquiry into Peer Review," *Scholarly Publishing* 20, no. 1 (October 1988): 441–48, argues for double-blind reviewing.

10. Fish, "No Bias, No Merits," 166. The fact that we quote Fish rather than some little-known person in literary studies shows that it makes a difference whom one quotes. This is simply another facet of the position Fish defends.

11. Fish, "No Bias, No Merits," 175.

12. Of course, any guarantee of anonymity is conditioned by the law. Just as U.S. federal courts have ruled that "confidential" tenure and promotion files must be made available to litigants appealing university decisions denying tenure, so it is possible that a future ruling could force a publisher to reveal the identity of a reviewer to whom it had promised anonymity. As with any right, the right to anonymity may conflict with and be overridden by other stronger rights.

13. This is consistent with our earlier claim that an editor can send a manuscript for review to an author's known enemy if the editor has already decided not to publish the manuscript.

14. "Ethical Guidelines to Publication of Chemical Research," adopted by the editors and Journals Division of the American Chemical Society in January 1985, in section c. 10, which discusses ethical obligations of reviewers of manuscripts, says: "Reviewers should not use or disclose unpublished information, arguments, or interpretations contained in a manuscript under consideration, except with the consent of the author. If this information indicates that some of the reviewer's work is unlikely to be profitable, the reviewer, however, could ethically discontinue the work." This is consistent with what we claim, since the latter involves the cessation of work. To hold otherwise would be to demand that even if one learned through reviewing a manuscript that one's work was useless, one could not stop pursuing it. That would require a greater division of what one knows as a reviewer from what one knows in other ways than can be reasonably expected. What of positively using an idea? The proper distinction here is claiming credit for an original idea one takes from another and developing one's own ideas sparked by reading a manuscript. The latter is ethically permissible; the former is not.

15. Richard Mohr in the Chronicle of Higher Education, "When university presses give in to bias, academic principle will be disregarded" (July 15, 1992, A44), argues that university presses have an obligation to be creative, to uphold academic principle, and to make public bold academic ideas. These are arguably part of the mission of a university press. Making money is not part of its mission, even if it is necessary for its existence. This is part of what it means to be not-for-profit.

16. It is because presses differ that scholars with new, unusual, and unorthodox ideas or points of view can sometimes get a hearing. A monolithic system, such as that which existed in the Soviet Union, tended to uniformity of view in the material that was published and was open, if not to explicit censorship, then frequently to self-censorship with knowledge of what would or would not be acceptable.

Why Be My Colleague's Keeper?
Moral Justifications for Peer Review

Joe Cain

Justifying ethical practices is no easy task. This paper considers moral justifications for peer review so as to persuade even the skeptical individualist. Two avenues provide a foundation for that justification: self-interest (the right behavior is that which maximally serves one's own interests) and social contract theory (the right behavior is that which best meets obligations set in binding social contracts). A wider notion of "interest" permits the self-interest approach to justify not only submitting one's own work to peer review but also removing oneself momentarily from the production of primary knowledge to serve as a rigorous, independent, and honest referee. The contract approach offers a nonselfish alternative and relies on four types of binding social contracts: those implicit in accepting funds, those implicit in asserted professional status, those to contribute what is of most value to society, and those to defend the ideals of the Academy. Efforts to restore respect for rigorous, independent, honest peer review should begin in earnest.

Introduction

Justifying ethical practices is no simple task. Constructing reliable moral justifications—i.e., reasoning grounded in sound moral philosophy—taxes even the best scholars. Complicating this situation, moral reasoning is pushed to the background in our age, as pragmatic, legal, partisan and *post facto* tactics rise to the front. It is not an easy task to convince skeptical audiences that, no matter what other tactic they deploy, justifications for conduct *ultimately* rely on some particular moral philosophy. Teasing that set of moral tenets from the rhetoric may take considerable effort. Nevertheless,

179

once explicit statements of a moral theory are in hand, a nonpartisan evaluation of that justification can begin: its validity, its soundness, its implications, and the value of its moral foundation. Only then do observers of a situation have solid grounds for fully assessing conduct. But to start, we must seek clear, consistent, and explicit reasoning.[1]

This is not rarefied conceptualization. Increasingly, training institutions are asked to add "ethics thinking" into their curriculum and to develop in the next generation of researchers skills for structuring and articulating justifications for their actions. Also, research communities are being asked for increasingly explicit discussions of their once largely invisible moral economies.[2]

In addition, though peer review is central to academic machinery, some recent studies—combined with numerous widely reported anecdotes and the general gossip within professional circles—raise serious questions about its day-to-day value as independent quality control (e.g., Stewart and Feder).[3] Favoritism, nepotism, and partisan vendettas are common claims in such reports. Pressed with demands for their own productivity, reviewers regularly provide only cursory inspection of documents. Editors and funding panels must filter out commentaries that promote competing agendas or that seem merely crass partisanship. Authors fear competitors serving as reviewers, as they might poach unpublished data or scoop conclusions.

If these reports are (even somewhat) true, the scholarly enterprise has a serious problem: in practice, peer review may be bringing us neither much quality nor much control. With so much invested in this process, its integrity is of paramount importance. If researchers and scholars systematically withdraw from peer review, professional research loses whatever status review otherwise delivered. Scholarship loses the certificates it previously offered. Readers lose the ability to assume the literature meets a rigorous professional standard.

This paper considers moral justifications for participation in peer review. Asking how to better manage peer review or how best to safeguard it against various unfairnesses is not the point.[4] Instead, I ask: Why should we participate in peer review at all? What justifications might researchers offer to defend its use? What moral theories satisfy us when we defend the practice? I consider peer review from the perspective of two moral positions: narrow self-interest and obligation resulting from social contracts.

Peer Review

Scholars and researchers—more importantly, their administrators and consumers of their productivity—use peer review as a key criterion for judging first-class from second-rate, whether that be for articles, journals, books, or research proposals—and now even films and websites. Manuscripts that fail peer review are relegated to low-status outlets. Grant proposals that fail peer review risk no community support. Such is the prestige of peer review that jobs literally depend on it. When academic employers assess job performance in this publish-or-perish world, peer reviewed output counts most. What's in peer review that invests it with so much authority?

Part of the answer is clear: peer review means approval. Approval by independent experts. It means one's ideas have been considered closely by a sample of peers, fellow specialists who understand (at least claim to understand) the subject and have the expertise to assess rigorously a manuscript's representation against the facts, methods, and experiences of the field. Passing peer review means passing muster. It means the author's thinking has been certified. Of course, that thinking is not certified to be *correct*; rather, it is certified to *merit* consideration, to be *worth* discussion. Any fool can print their ideas, but to get those ideas into a lead research article in *Science* or *Nature*, first an author must satisfy the reviewers.

Part of the cause in today's lapses in the peer review system stem from a collapse in the nature of the relationships between researchers and various communities in which they are members. Researchers increasingly feel no bond to participate in peer review processes (other than to extract for themselves its certifications). They feel their investments in those processes translate less and less into tangible, meaningful products or into results advancing their own enterprises. Added to this, institutions and collaborating partners—especially when working in highly competitive, highly lucrative research topics—often offer little encouragement for taking time away from pushing the research front ahead. An afternoon spent writing reviews means an afternoon lost on the next paper, the next grant, the next patent filing, or the next fortune-making innovation.[5]

This degradation of any sense of obligation to community—this rise of *individualism*—means some moral philosophies justifying peer review will meet unsympathetic audiences. For example, utilitarianism—crudely put, the right behavior is that which results in the greatest good coming to the greatest number of people—loses its force. Individualists reject a core assumption of utilitarianism; the target beneficiary is not any great number of people but the single researcher (or some small cohort of researchers within the community). Any defense of peer review designed to convince the next generation of researchers must, sadly, operate with the individualist as skeptic.

Two lines of argument can justify the practice of peer review while also satisfying the individualist. The first develops the position of the narrow pragmatist—crudely, the right behavior is that which maximally serves one's own interests. The second develops from social contracts, that in the process of committing to undertake certain kinds of activity, researchers bind themselves into various contracts with their professional communities. With the benefits of those contracts also come responsibilities; the right behavior, in this context, is that which best serves the letter (and perhaps the spirit) of those contracts. To be sure, these are not the only lines of argument that might defend peer review. The immediate goal here, however, is to engage individualists on their own ground.

Appeal to Self-Interest

Participation in peer review operates on two levels. First, an author agrees to submit his work—a finished manuscript, a research proposal, or the like—to evaluation by a sample of peer experts. Second, as experts themselves, researchers agree to serve, if asked, as evaluators of other work. Such evaluation is assumed to be rigorous and independent. It also is assumed to be confidential—between writer and reviewer—with an editor or administrator mediating the process.[6]

Submitting to Peer Review

Consider self-interest when an author agrees to submit work to evaluation (or insists on having work rigorously peer reviewed). The author gains expert advice and has the work examined for mistakes (be they simple or major; superficial or profound). Submission for review also open this possibility of a reviewer offering constructive criticism, identifying existing research along similar lines that has been overlooked, or disclosing otherwise unavailable information about related research. As such, the rewards for submission to review may become immediate and robust.

If the manuscript benefits, so does the author. Errors identified before going public means an author can avoid looking foolish, careless, or of dubious expertise. Conversely, knowing scrutiny will come means authors are likely to be more thorough and self-critical in their written products. Both avenues translate into better finished products and offer compelling selfish reasons for individuals to seek peer review.

Careers gain too. Well-produced research is appreciated. Reviewers remember superb manuscripts and projects. Such impressions inevitably creep into the daily chatter of colleagues and the informal circuit of information within disciplines. Reputations can be made and supplemented, intellectual territory may be claimed, priority can be informally bolstered, and collaborations or career promotions may result. Peer review for publication usually involves two or four colleagues of various career stages. Review panels for funding typically involve eight to sixteen usually senior or highly productive colleagues. Displaying one's expertise in these circles may be a very good idea indeed.

An author's status changes with peer review in a particular way. Such evaluation carries with it a process of validation, of legitimization. That stamp of approval means expert peers respect one's work at least enough to believe it merits or requires consideration. As such, a researcher becomes certified, eligible for the high table of community discourse. That's good for a researcher's own reputation, of course. Also selfishly, it's a kind of status employers love to note, and should the negotiation about one's position become an issue, it's precisely the kind of weight that might tip a balance.

Participating as a Peer Reviewer
Good reasons can be found for defending submission to peer review from a perspective of self-interest. All that is necessary is a simple widening of the boundaries of "self-interest."[7] But, this is only half the problem. Can self-interest also be used to defend the participation in the evaluating aspects of the enterprise, in the reviewing of one's peers? Leaving aside unwholesome motives,[8] five justifications rise to the fore.

Advocate for One's Own Standards
In acting as an evaluator of peer research, one serves not only as a deputy for the field but also as an advocate for one's own standards. Here is the opportunity to reject low and substandard work, i.e., work the reviewers themselves find poor or inappropriate. High personal standards can thus enter a research field. As a corollary, reviewers have the opportunity to interject new facts, techniques, and conclusions into a field's research domain by recommending—or insisting—an author make certain allowances or answer certain queries on those matters. This deputy function provides an opportunity for reviewers to lead, rather than follow.

Maintain Integrity of the Field's Knowledge Base
The absence of peer review risks the absence of a quality control mechanism for a field's literature, and therefore, for a field's knowledge base. The corresponding loss of accumulation—as any standard of reliability cannot be assumed—means one's own projects are put at risk. No researcher works without some recourse to that knowledge base. And, no researcher today has the capacity or patience to verify that foundation firsthand. Service as a peer reviewer contributes to maintaining the integrity of knowledge within a field.

It thus allows for the general and provisional accumulation of knowledge and facilitates the extension of one's own research program. In short, it means a researcher can assume certain things to be true and can move ahead from there. Nobel prizes are not awarded for reinventing wheels.

Maintain Integrity of Validation

Loss of peer review risks loss of validation even to researchers of the highest caliber. Passing low-grade and poor products degrades the outlets in which they appear and the institutions that serve as sponsors. Researchers have little patience for errant and unreliable information. Reputations sag quickly under such strain, and reputations for low standards are infectious. Once an outlet gains notice for occasional lapses of quality, the slide can be rapid and wholesale. Reviewers using the same outlets for their own work may suffer as a corollary: when the standards of an outlet are unpredictable, the validity of *all* contributions can become suspect.[9] Guilt by association cuts both ways.

High Reputation Leads to Increased Access

Researchers within a community often are well aware of who provides rigorous, reliable, confidential, and constructive examinations of scholarly materials. Those deputies are regularly sought out for advice and comment. For these deputies, such a preference offers substantial access to the cutting edges of research and thinking within a field. It provides the potential of steering research, for linking projects of possible synergy, for moving oneself into the social and intellectual center of a field. Helpful advice or constructive criticism as a reviewer in effect may be a substantial investment in one's own access to information contributing in the long run to an expanding research program, reputation, and career prospects.

Preserve Professional Autonomy

Funders increasingly insist on high, immediately tangible value for their support. As a mechanism for quality control, peer review offers a means for validating claims about results—not only to colleagues but also to funders both current and prospective. The failure of peer review mechanisms to maintain rigor risks eroding a profession's capacity to self-certify, to serve as the arbiters of reliability. In the absence of this capacity, funders might very well *impose* an external mechanism for certification so as to guarantee value for their expenditures.

Witness the massive administrative infrastructure surrounding use of animals in scientific research. This comes because those researchers are unable to produce an internal mechanism for rigorous adherence capable of persuading political constituencies they have matters well in hand. Autonomy was lost because self-regulation to a prescribed outside standard could not be guaranteed. Compare this to the near complete lack of external control for human research in the world's space programs. Here, patrons operate with the impression that professionals in the field are acting sensibly and responsibly, rigorously self-policing. Autonomy is thereby preserved.

For the individualist, active participation in peer review may seem wasteful at the outset. Such is not the case, however, as compelling justification for the opposite is easily grounded in self-interest theory.[10] Indeed, large contributions to mechanisms for peer evaluation may sharply enhance the programs and careers of individualists themselves.

Obligations Inherent in Contracts

No doubt, some will find a sole or heavy reliance on self-interest as a justification overcommitting, insufficient, or downright abhorrent. Certainly other categories of appeal exist. One—a far more controversial approach—is to ground that appeal in the theory of social contracts. (Rousseau[11] remains the classic starting point.) Such an appeal emphasizes contractual obligation and follows four distinct lines.

Contract Implicit in Research Funds

Most narrowly, when a researcher accepts funds for a project, that researcher agrees to undertake the work responsibly and reliably; in short, to serve the contract well and in good faith. But grants for research are more than simply pay-for-work contracts. There's an implicit social dimension, too. Consider scientific research. Normally, funders earmark support for *scientific* research into certain problems because they previously were convinced by that community's claims about its expertise in acquiring and producing relevant knowledge. The scientific community claims a special, superior epistemological status on the matter, and the funder displays its confidence in those claims with its offers of financial support. The Medical Research Council (U.K.) and the National Institutes of Health (U.S.), for example, generously fund *scientific* research into HIV—rather than, say, funding witch-doctor research into HIV, druid research into HIV, or psychic research into HIV—because they are convinced of science's superior potential for producing meaningful information. Part of science's special epistemological status derives from its quality control mechanisms, such as peer review. These help to ensure publications are reliable, cumulative, and good value for money.

Part of the reason a funder awards support to a *scientist's* proposal for work rests in the connections the researcher makes to science's special epistemology.

In the process of using that connection for support, researchers directly bind themselves into a contract. That contract obliges them to deliver the product as epistemologically promised, i.e., complete with certification through quality control mechanisms such as peer review. The special access to funds come with a price of prescribed standards of scrutiny. Simple reciprocity demands not just submission to review but also participation as a reviewer.

Contract Implicit in Asserted Professional Status

This contract-obligation-status argument provides a second defense. Scientists regularly use recourse to community standards when asserting the superior status of their knowledge about a phenomenon. When doing so, they imply they hold membership in that community and imply they are linked to its epistemology. Speaking "as a scientist" or offering a "scientific opinion" invokes a contract between oneself and the community such that one is bound by its obligations as much as one benefits from its rights and privileges. Membership may be open, but it is not free. Along similar grounds, embedded in professional status are implicit assertions of self-regulation and quality control (e.g., in engineering).[12] A decision to speak "as a scientist" morally obliges a researcher to *act* as a scientist, too. This means subscribing to its ideals, including participation as a peer reviewer.

Contract to Contribute What Is of Most Value to Society

The third use of social contract theory is much wider and certainly more controversial. Members of a society—the people who interact in its social space, make use of its infrastructure and opportunities, and claim membership— have an obligation to contribute to its advancement. This is not simply a matter of paying one's way: such as through prompt payments of taxes, donations to charity, and conformity to laws. There's more. One benefit specialized researchers draw from their societies is that of luxury of specialization. The best repayment for that luxury is one that makes good use of the skills derived from its activity. In other words, because society makes research specialization possible, the best way to satisfy one's return obligation to society is to make the best use of those special skills. In serving as an honest, rigorous, independent referee, the contract is not only served but served so as to maximize the return to society and to contribute most to its *additional* advancement.[13]

Contract to Defend Ideals of the Academy

Finally, also controversially, claims to membership in the Academy also bind researchers via a contract. To claim to be a scholar is to claim adherence to certain core principles of the Academy. These involve intellectual freedom. First is the principle of *universal participation*: access to knowledge must be open to all; all are free to contribute to its growth. Second is the *right to dispute*; dissent is allowed, even encouraged.

Crucially, the unfettered right to contribute that these principles assert does not imply the unfettered right to contribute *everything*. With the privilege of access comes obligation. Contributions and discourse are bound by principles of reason, decorum, and fair play. Thus, for example, contributors have no rights to contribute arguments with errors in logic, conclusions reaching far past their empirical warrant, or claims manifestly contrary to fact. Each violates the rules of discourse.

To ensure participants meet their obligations—and so are eligible for its privileges—the Academy imposes peer review as the best means for quality control. This process is intended to check the validity of logic, that conclusions are within reach of the data, that evidence is methodologically sound, and that manifest errors are avoided.

Claiming membership in the Academy is to claim not only an adherence to the principles of reason, decorum, and fair play. It also is to claim a willingness to contribute to the means of quality control, to the monitoring of others who claim the imprimatur of the Academy. This is a packaged deal, not a la carte. Claiming membership in the Academy implies a willingness not only to abide by but also to defend the core principles of universal participation and right to dispute. Neglecting to participate in peer review risks the consequence of these principles dissolving.

Consider this example. Articles for *Nature* meet a high standard because the journal imposes significant quality control.[14] In an environment where contribution is open to all, quality control is ensured via the mechanism of peer review. Removal or decline of expert review means a loss of quality control. To keep its high standard, *Nature* will seek alternative means to verify the quality of incoming work. For example, it might restrict the right of submission to a small group of certified, known-to-be-reliable experts. Thus, expert reviewers who use standards poorly or who withdraw from the review process entirely risk forcing a journal such as *Nature* to adopt alternative mechanisms of quality control. Those alternatives may have the consequence of violating the Academy's core principles of universal participation and right to dispute. So, *Nature*'s effort to maintain high standards—certainly laudable in isolation—may have a violently detrimental effect on intellectual freedom. All this is risked when peer review is widely treated as a trivial element of the research enterprise.

Conclusion

This paper develops two kinds of justifications for a simple claim: peer research is desirable and morally defensible. As researchers, contributors to the production of knowledge, and members of the Academy, we need to restore respect for rigorous, independent, honest peer review. Otherwise, we risk a serious erosion in the value of our common enterprise. Responding with the carrots of pragmatism and sticks of obligation may not be the most wholesome routes for developing that respect. Instead, they may only lay the foundation for additional treatment. At the least, we have *these* to rely on when attempting to draw individualists into the process. The remainder of the community may need less of an argument to elicit cooperation.

Long-term efforts to restore this respect will come only from within professional training. Just out of university, junior researchers may know a vast amount of content—facts, theories, techniques, equipment—in their professional fields. But there's more to the business of research and the Academy than content. Budgets and grantsmanship. Publications and conferences. Long-term planning and project management. Politics and collaboration. Community service and social contract. A lucky student is one who glimpses these while pursuing a degree. However, most process-oriented professional development currently is left either to accidental experience or to apprentice-style training in a postdoctoral environment. We learn, supposedly, by watching the masters. This no longer will suffice. We need to think about how to make professional training better.

To date, the *business* of research largely has been kept invisible to students and nonprofessionals. In the process, we are missing an opportunity to instill values crucial for the maintenance (or reinstallation) of high-integrity working environments. Those high-integrity working environments serve us all. They also go a long way toward repaying our obligations to the societies that surround us with the luxury to do the things many of us love most dearly: thinking, learning, and struggling to understand the world around us.

Notes

For critical comments, thanks to Rita Dockery and two anonymous reviewers.

1. For the novice, introductions to moral and critical reasoning include J. Rachels, *The Elements of Moral Philosophy*, 2nd ed. (New York: McGraw-Hill, 1993), and A. Thomson, *Critical Reasoning: A Practical Guide* (New York: Routledge, 1996).

2. For historical examples, see R. Kohler, *Lords of the Fly: Drosophila Genetics and the Experimental Control of Life* (Chicago: University of Chicago Press, 1994); E. Har-

cum and E. Rosen, *The Gatekeepers of Psychology: Evaluation of Peer Review by Case History* (Westport, Conn.: Praeger, 1993); S. Traweek, *Beamtimes and Lifetimes: The World of High Energy Physicists* (Cambridge, Mass.: Harvard University Press, 1988); D. Hull, *Science as a Process: An Evolutionary Account of the Social and Conceptual Development of Science* (Chicago: University of Chicago Press, 1988); and M. J. S. Rudwick, *The Great Devonian Controversy: The Shaping of Knowledge among Gentlemanly Specialists* (Chicago: University of Chicago Press, 1985).

3. W. Stewart and N. Feder, "The Integrity of the Scientific Literature," *Nature* 325 (January 15, 1987): 207–14.

4. For this, see D. Resnik, *The Ethics of Science* (New York: Routledge, 1998); A. E. Stamps III, ed., "Advances in Peer Review Research," special issue of *Science and Engineering Ethics* 3, no. 1 (1997): 3–98; B. Speck, ed., *Publication Peer Review: An Annotated Bibliography* (Westport, Conn.: Greenwood Press, 1993); and D. Chubin, *Peerless Science: Peer Review and U.S. Science Policy* (Albany, N.Y.: SUNY Press, 1990).

5. Poor institutional and professional mechanisms for credit certainly amplify the problem: time spent reviewing someone else's manuscript is time away from the next publication of one's own. If promotion is heavily dependent upon publication in peer reviewed outlets, institutions offer little incentive to meet the wider range of community responsibilities. Clearly, the credit mechanisms need to change.

6. The collapse of rigor, independence, and confidentiality are normative concerns assumed not at work in this discussion. How removing these assumptions affects the *practical* decisions is discussed by Harcum and Rosen, *The Gatekeepers of Psychology*; Resnik, *The Ethics of Science*; and Stamps, "Advances in Peer Review Research."

7. This approach is similar to, but not identical with, the discussion of "selfish altruism" in evolutionary biology: how can it make sense for natural selection to favor an organism's behavior that benefits other organisms at a cost to the giver? Most solutions to this problem widen the notion of "benefit," reminding us that what might be in our narrow self-interest may be more than meets our immediate attention. See E. Sober, *Philosophy of Biology* (Boulder, Colo.: Westview, 1993).

8. Examples of unwholesome motives for participation would be so that a reviewer may access unpublished data for the purposes of appropriation, or so that a project or publication can be stalled while competing work gains priority. See Hull, *Science as a Process*; Resnik, *The Ethics of Science*; and Stamps, "Advances in Peer Review Research."

9. This currently is the case with Web publishing. With pages of such radically uneven reliability, the working assumption of most scholars is to be extremely wary if not personally acquainted with the source's author. This also is useful for explaining why institutions within Academe are loathe to credit Web productions as legitimate publications. No mechanism currently exists for quality control or independent assessment; therefore, institutions have no means for validation.

10. Grounding this analysis in self-interest theory also opens the door for similar analyses about interests of colleagues, communities, institutions, and outlets.

11. J.-J. Rousseau, *The Social Contract* (1762), trans. M. Cranston (New York: Penguin, 1968).

12. See W. Krohn and E. Layton, eds., *The Dynamics of Science and Technology: Social Values, Technical Norms, and Scientific Criteria in the Development of Knowledge* (Dordrecht: D. Reidel, 1978), and E. Layton, *The Revolt of the Engineers: Social Responsibility and the American Engineering Profession* (Cleveland, Ohio: Press of the Case Western Reserve University, 1971).

13. One's own work—made possible through the privilege of a society—presumably advances society some; one's service to the obligation—the helping of others—advances it additionally. Picking up rubbish in the street also advances society in some sense, though only in a minimal way for someone specially trained in some other skill. Rubbish collection, laudable in itself, makes no use of the specialized expertise invested in the researcher. The claim here is that the nature of the contract makes those returning a maximum contribution for their draw in a morally better position than those returning a minimum contribution for their draw.

14. Instructions to authors appear in every volume, as do explanations of the journal's peer review process. Also, these now appear on the web: www.nature.com.

Peer Review Practices of Psychological Journals: The Fate of Published Articles, Submitted Again

Douglas P. Peters and Stephen J. Ceci

A growing interest in and concern about the adequacy and fairness of modern peer review practices in publication and funding are apparent across a wide range of scientific disciplines. Although questions about reliability, accountability, reviewer bias, and competence have been raised, there has been very little direct research on these variables.

The present investigation was an attempt to study the peer review process directly, in the natural setting of actual journal referee evaluations of submitted manuscripts. As test materials we selected twelve already published research articles by investigators from prestigious and highly productive American psychology departments, one article from each of twelve highly regarded and widely read American psychology journals with high rejection rates (80 percent) and nonblind refereeing practices.

With fictitious names and institutions substituted for the original ones (e.g., Tri-Valley Center for Human Potential), the altered manuscripts were formally resubmitted to the journals that had originally refereed and published them eighteen to thirty-two months earlier. Of the sample of thirty-eight editors and reviewers, only three (8 percent) detected the resubmissions. This result allowed nine of the twelve articles to continue through the review process to receive an actual evaluation: eight of the nine were rejected. Sixteen of the eighteen referees (89 percent) recommended against publication and the editors concurred. The grounds for rejection were in many cases described as "serious methodological flaws." A number of possible interpretations of these data are reviewed and evaluated.

Journal articles serve an important function in providing scientists with information about new ideas and discoveries in their areas of interest. Published papers also serve as vehicles for personal advancement, job security, and continued research opportunities. In academic settings the "publication count" is often a factor in determining salary or merit-pay increments, grant funding, promotion, and tenure (Gottfredson 1978; Scott 1974). Getting research published can also have consequences for entire academic departments. Summaries periodically appear in the literature that rank both the overall and the per capita productivity of departments of psychology (e.g., Cox and Catt 1977; Endler, Rushton, and Roediger 1978; Roose and Anderson 1970). Such rankings can establish a psychology department's reputation, which can potentially affect the number and quality of graduate students applying for advanced degrees, the awarding of competitive funds, and the pride and self-esteem of individual faculty members.

Although many are undoubtedly content with the peer review practices employed by modern research journals, a growing number of psychologists have raised important questions about the adequacy of the review system. Moreover, judging from the variety of disciplines represented by those calling for improvements in the review practices of journals, it would appear that criticism of the review process is not limited to one or two areas, but rather extends across many fields of science. (In the social sciences, see Brackbill and Korton 1970; Crane 1967; Gove 1979; McCartney 1973; Revusky 1977; Tobach 1980; Walster and Cleary 1970; in the physical and medical sciences, Cicchetti and Conn 1976; M. D. Gordon 1980; Harnad 1979; Ingelfinger 1974; Jones 1974; McCutchen 1976; Ruderfer 1980; Stumpf 1980; Zuckerman and Merton 1973.)

A major portion of the criticism of the journal review system has concerned the reliability of peer review. Empirical evidence concerning reviewer reliability has, until recently, been rather meager, considering the importance of this topic. Most of the reviewer-reliability literature has been contributed by social scientists, more specifically, by psychologists and sociologists. With a few exceptions (Crandall 1978a; Scarr and Weber 1978), the results of these investigations have not been encouraging. Interrater agreement between the reviewers of a manuscript, measured by a variety of rating scales and statistical analyses, is typically reported as low to moderate, with intraclass correlation coefficients of 0.55 at best (Bowen, Perloff, and Jacoby 1972; Cicchetti 1980; Cicchetti and Eron 1979; Gottfredson 1978; Hendrick 1977; Mahoney 1977; McCartney 1973; McReynolds 1971; Scott 1974). For instance, Scott (1974) reported that the degree of agreement between reviewers of manuscripts submitted to the *Journal of Personality and Social Psychology* was only 0.26, and Watkins (1979), using Kappa (K), the statistic that shows the degree of reviewer agreement remaining after correction for chance, found a near total lack of interrater agreement for reviews of manuscripts submitted to the *Personality and Social Psychology Bulletin*. McCartney (1973) examined 1,000 reviews of 500 manuscripts submitted to the *Sociological Quarterly* and found that one-third of the reviewer pairs for a manuscript were in complete agreement (i.e., both evaluated the manuscripts identically on a 5-point rating scale). Another one-third of the reviewers were in proximal agreement (i.e., they designated adjacent points on the rating scale). In the remaining one-third of the cases, the reviewers disagreed. While McCartney found some comfort in these data, it should be noted that the overall level of rater agreement is low after correcting for chance. Ingelfinger (1974) reported figures that showed that the degree of interreferee agreement for 496 manuscripts reviewed for the *New England Journal of Medicine* was below 0.30. Data of this type can certainly erode satisfaction with and confidence in the peer review system. It is not unusual to hear researchers express the belief that *chance* (e.g., reviewer idiosyncrasies, or the editor's choice of reviewers) had played a major role in determining the fate of a submitted manuscript.

The possibility of response bias[1] in the peer review process (e.g., institutional affiliation, paradigm confirmation or theory support, editor-author friendship, old-boy networks) has been another area of concern to scientists trying to publish the results of their research efforts. Although claims of reviewer bias have been made, and case histories revealing review prejudice can be found (e.g., the rejection of Garcia's original taste-aversion data by several leading journals—see Revusky 1977), little in the way of direct experimental testing of bias has actually been undertaken. Several of the published reports do, however, provide some support for the assertion of reviewer bias (Bowen et al. 1972; Cicchetti and Eron 1979; Crane 1967; M. D. Gordon 1980; Merton 1968b; Oromaner 1977; Yotopoulos 1961; Zuckerman 1970; Zuckerman and Merton 1973). In a recent investigation, Gordon (1980) analyzed 2,572 referee reports received over a six-year period from several prestigious physical science journals. Each set of reviews and manuscripts was coded in terms of the institutional identity of its authors and referees. The results revealed that major university referees evaluate papers from major universities significantly more favorably than papers from minor, less prestigious universities. This bias was not found for minor university referees; there was little difference in their evaluation of manuscripts from high- or low-status universities. Minor university authors were more frequently evaluated positively by minor university reviewers than by major university reviewers, while major university authors were more often rated favorably by major university reviewers. In considering these studies one must bear in mind Mahoney's (1977) point that most of the existing reports of reviewer bias involve post hoc correlational analyses, which limits the conclusions one can draw. However, in the rare instances in which the suspected sources of bias have been manipulated experimentally, evidence of reviewer bias has likewise been observed (e.g., Goodstein and Brazis 1970; Mahoney 1977).

In the present study we attempted to examine the issue of reliability and response bias in journal reviews, but instead of using indirect, correlational approaches, we decided there would be value in studying the review process directly, as it occurred in its natural setting. Recently published articles from mainstream psychology (research) journals were resubmitted to the journals that had originally published them. By adopting this procedure we hoped to be able (1) to assess the reviewers' familiarity with the author's field (which is often presupposed, but has not been tested), (2) to provide an ecologically valid study of the journal review system, (3) to examine reviewer reliability, and (4) to study response bias among journal reviewers.

Method

Characteristics of Journals Selected

Thirteen psychology journals publishing research articles were originally selected as the sources for the previously published reports. However, we learned during the study that one of the journal's publication criteria had changed with its new editor, and therefore we did not include the article taken from this journal in the analyses (Journal M; see table 3). Of the twelve journals studied, only two pairs overlapped in their respective specialty areas. Thus, our sample of psychological journals was fairly broad, with coverage including ten distinct areas each of which has separate divisional representation in the American Psychological Association (APA). The overall rejection rates for manuscripts submitted to these twelve journals was near 80 percent at the time the articles we selected were originally accepted for publication (Markle and Rinn 1977). These journals were also considered solid, mainstream purveyors of research by those working in the area, and are among the most prestigious journals in psychology in terms of where psychologists want to publish and where they expect important results to appear (Endler et al. 1978; Koulack and Keselman 1975; White and White 1977). An analysis of the overall "impact" these journals had on the field of psychology (i.e., the mean citation rate of a journal's article with respect to citations by psychology journals; see Garfield 1979a) revealed that ten of our journals were ranked in the top twenty for impact out of a list of seventy-seven source journals of psychology. Furthermore, the average annual citation frequency per article per journal in the *Journal Citation Report* (Garfield 1979b) for our twelve journals (one and two years after publication) was 1.15, which places these journals in the seventy-fifth percentile of all psychology journals listed in Garfield (1979a). All the journals we selected employ standard practice of nonblind reviewing; approximately half are published by the national organization, APA, and half are not. In addition, our sample (n = 12) represented approximately 70 percent of all prestigious ("prestige" criteria are presented below), nonblind psychology journals.

Procedure

One article was randomly selected from each of the twelve journals. The only constraint on the selection was that the article had to conform to our "prestige" criteria; that is, at least one of the original authors of each article had to have been affiliated with an institution with a high-ranking department of psychology in terms of prestige ratings, productivity, and faculty citations.[2] The articles chosen in our sample had the following characteristics: (a) With one exception (Journal H, see table 3), the original author(s) included someone from one of the ten most prestigious departments of psychology in the United States (Roose and Anderson 1979). (b) Authors were selected from the psychology departments with the thirty highest productivity rankings; 75 percent of the authors were from the top ten departments for their particular research area (Cox and Catt 1977). (c) Each article had at least one author from the top twenty-five institutions in terms of citations of faculty research (White and White 1977), with 50 percent in the first six (Endler, Rushton, and Roediger 1978). (d) The articles were selected from papers published between eighteen and thirty-two months prior to resubmission for this study. (e) The mean annual citation count in the *Social Science Citation Index* for our twelve articles was 1.5 for one as well as for two years following publication. Since, as mentioned, the average number of citations per year for articles in these journals during this period was 1.15, it seems that the reports we selected were above average in quality, using a citation count measure, for their respective journals. (The mean number of citations for all social science articles one decade following publication is 1.4; Garfield 1979b.)

Before we resubmitted the article as if for the first time, several alterations were made. First, the names (but not the sex) and the institutional affiliations of the original authors were changed to fictitious ones without meaning or status in psychology; for example, Dr. Wade M. Johnston (a fictitious name) at the Tri-Valley Center for Human Potential (a fictitious institution).[3] The titles of the original articles, the abstracts, and the beginning paragraphs of the introduction were slightly altered. It was hoped that these few changes would sufficiently disguise the resubmissions in the event an editor or reviewer made use of some mechanical filing system that would result in automatic detection (e.g., title, key words, or abstract files). The alterations to the original articles were always minimal and purely cosmetic (e.g., changing word or sentence order, substituting synonyms for nontechnical words, and the like). The meaning of the original articles' titles, abstracts, and initial paragraphs was never altered. The remainder of the introduction and the entire method, results, and discussion sections were typed exactly as they had appeared in print. To further guard against superficial detection, the format for presenting data was occasionally altered by converting graphs to tables and vice versa.

Each manuscript was prepared in accordance with the corresponding journal's instructions to contributors, and then sent to the journal that had originally published it with a cover letter requesting that it be considered for publication. Editors and reviewers had no advance knowledge of our efforts. They were informed about the nature of the project either when they detected that the manuscript was a resubmission during the review process, or when the study was completed. Since these events occurred at different times for the various journals, we asked all participants to keep the existence of our study confidential until the entire project was finished (i.e., when there were no more resubmitted manuscripts being reviewed).

Results

Reviewer Reliability

Nine of the twelve manuscripts were not detected (by editors or reviewers) as having been previously published. Since these articles had recently (within two to three years) received a positive evaluation that had resulted in their original publication, one might perhaps have expected a second review from the same journal to yield similar results, that is, acknowledgment of scholarship and recommendation for publication. However, as can be seen in table 1, this was the exception rather than the rule. Eight of the nine articles were rejected. Only 13 percent (4/30) [12 percent (3/26): figures corrected in proof—see table 1] of the editors and reviewers combined recommended publication in their journal. We should add that every editor or associate editor included in this sample indicated that he had examined the manuscript and that he concurred with the reviewers' recommendations.[4]

Table 1.   Evaluations of Undetected Resubmissions

Journal	Reviewers Only		Editors and Reviewers	
	Reject	Accept	Reject	Accept
A	2	0	3	0
B	3	0	5[b]	0
C	1[a]	0	1	0
D	2	0	2	0
E	2	0	4	0
F	2	0	3	0
G	2	0	4[c]	0
H	2	0	4[d]	0
I	0	2	0	4[g]
	16 (89%)	2 (11%)	26[e] (87%)[f]	4[h] (13%)[i]

a. The only reviewer of this article was the editor, who has therefore been included in this section.
Editorial Note: The figures with superscripts *b–i* are the ones the commentators saw. They were subsequently corrected by the authors as follows: $b = 4$, $c = 3$, $d = 3$, $e = 23$, $f = (88\%)$, $g = 3$, $h = 3$, $i = (12\%)$.

When we examined only the evaluations of the reviewers (n = 18)—which might be more meaningful, since the editors' decisions are not independent of the referees' evaluation—we discovered that an even smaller portion, 11 percent (2/18), found the papers acceptable for publication. Reviewers for seven of the journals (A–G) made clear, unequivocal recommendations against publishing the manuscripts (e.g., Journal A: "There are too many problems associated with this manuscript to recommend its acceptance for _____").

Two referees for the eighth journal (H) did not make any explicit statements regarding acceptability for publication, but their reviews were exclusively negative, perhaps best characterized as lists of errors, weaknesses, and shortcomings. We Xeroxed copies of these two indecisive reviews excluding journal identification, and asked six psychologists (all of whom serve as editorial consultants or editors) how they would rate the manuscript in question, on the basis of these referees' comments alone. A 5-point scale (McCartney 1973) was used, consisting of (1) major contribution: profound, theoretically important, very well conceived and executed, accept without question; (2) warrants publication: solid, sound contribution, accept with minor revisions; (3) sufficiently sound and important to justify publication if space permits; (4) poorly written—limited value, may be publishable if certain features are improved or extended, requires major revision; (5) insufficiently sound or important to warrant publication. The mean ratings for the two reviews were 4.8 and 5.0. Since these figures support our own interpretation (as well as the editor's) that clear rejection message was implied, we feel justified in classifying these reviews as "rejections."

Critical Comments Made by Reviewers

Perhaps the most serious objections that reviewers had about the manuscripts were directed toward the studies' designs and statistical analyses. Several referees detected methodological flaws in the papers we resubmitted. For example, Journal B: "A serious problem is the range of difficulty of _____ material within groups. No account of this range is given and no control of its possible effects is offered. Similarly, the comparability of material across groups is unknown"; Journal D: "Separate analyses of each test, on the assumption that groups are equivalent and then inferring gains, can be misleading . . . especially when analyses can be made directly"; Journal E: "I do not think that this paper is suitable for publication; further experimental work would be required"; Journal H: "It is not clear what the results of this study demonstrate, partly because the method and procedures are not described in adequate detail, but mainly because of several methodological defects in the design of the study"; Journal G: "Some other problems were . . . use of ANOVA for post-tests . . . loss of 3 children from Exp. 1 to Exp. 2."

Aside from the few cosmetic changes mentioned earlier, the manuscripts we submitted were identical to the original versions that had appeared in print. Several reviewers of the resubmitted papers criticized the authors' writing and communicative ability. For example, Journal G: "Tighten up the theoretical orientation in the introduction. It seems loose and filled with overgeneralizations (or, at least, undocumented conclusions) at the present"; Journal E: "Also, I don't know what it means to say that players had the ability to get different numbers of markers to the goal, since the game as described on page five was such that each player had only one marker. It is all very confusing. . . . I think the entire presentation of the results needs to be planned more carefully and reorganized"; Journal F: "Apparently, this is intended to be a summary. However, the style of writing leaves much to be desired in terms of communicating to the reader. It requires the reader to go from a positive result, to a double negative, to a qualification, to a negation of the results, and finally, to a couple of sentences (next to last in that paragraph) whose interpretations are just not clear."

Recognizing Previously Published Research

When we resubmitted articles to the journals that had originally published them, how many were detected or recognized? The answer can be found in table 2. The results are examined by (a) including all individuals representing each journal (editor, associate editors, and reviewers) who had some contact with the submitted manuscript, and thus could have detected the deception, and (b) including only the reviewers, since one could reasonably argue that it would be unfair to expect editors to be aware of the literature in every field covered by their journal. The results show that it makes very little difference which group is studied since the findings are essentially identical. To our surprise, the overwhelming majority of editors and reviewers (92 percent, or 35/38 of the editors and reviewers combined and 87 percent or 20/23 of the reviewers) failed to recognize the manuscripts as articles that had appeared in the mainstream literature appropriate for that research area during the past eighteen to thirty-two months. It should be noted that only two journals (C and I) had changed editors during this period.

Changes in Rejection Rates and Publication Criteria

Because changes in a journal's publication criteria or rejection rates could explain why the articles we resubmitted were not accepted the second time around, we examined the journals and other information sources to find out what changes, if any, had occurred. Our check of editorial statements and topic coverage in each journal revealed no shifts in research emphasis (with the one explicit exception of M, which was deleted from

Table 2. Detection of Resubmissions

	Editors and Reviewers		Reviewers Only	
Journal	Detected	Failed to Detect	Detected	Failed to Detect
A	0	3	0	2
B	0	5	0	3
C	0	1	0	1
D	0	2	0	2
E	0	4	0	2
F	0	3	0	2
G	0	4	0	2
H	0	4	0	2
I	0	4	0	2
J	1	2	1	1
K	1	2	1	1
L[a]	1	1	1	0
	3 (8%)	35 (92%)	3 (13%)	20 (87%)

Note: A thirteenth journal (M; see table 3) has been excluded from this analysis. The manuscript sent to the journal was rejected on the basis of not being appropriate. Following debriefing the editor informed us of a recent policy change that precluded publishing the type of article we had submitted.

a. We attempted to find out whether the editor, an associate editor, or a reviewer had recognized the manuscript. Unfortunately, the editor refused to disclose that information. We are therefore estimating that at least two individuals had seen the manuscript for this journal, since two names appeared in the correspondence we received.

Table 3. Stability of Rejection Rates

Journal	Original Rejection Rate Minus Rejection Rate at Time of Manuscript's Resubmission
A	16%
B	7%
C	-2%
D	-15%
E	-16%
F	0%
G	15%
H	3%
I	5%
J	5%
K	0%
L	7%
M[a]	-2%

Note: Information on rejection rates for APA journals was obtained by comparing figures listed in the June 1980 archival issue of the *American Psychologist* (American Psychological Association 1980) with those listed in earlier archival issues. Figures for non-APA journals were derived by comparing figures listed by Markle and Rinn (1977) with current figures reported by journal editors (personal communications).

Journals A–I failed to recognize the manuscripts and proceeded to review them.

a. Excluded from analysis because of change in journal's publication criteria.

all analyses, as mentioned earlier). Table 3 displays the net change in rejection rates for each journal from the time the original article appeared to the resubmission date for this study. It is clear that the overall rejection figure for the nine journals that reviewed the resubmitted articles had remained quite constant (and high, averaging around 80 percent) across the two review periods.

Discussion

The results show that out of the nine journals in question (A–H) only one repeated its earlier positive evaluation of the submitted paper and accepted it for publication. Since the articles we selected were from recognized and prestigious research journals and had originally passed a review system averaging 80 percent rejections, how does one explain their failure to be accepted a second time by the same journal? There are a number of hypotheses that should be considered in trying to answer this question.

A change in journal policy concerning the type of material considered appropriate or a substantial increase (of, say, 25–30 percent) in rejection rates, making it appreciably more difficult to get a paper accepted, might explain why the resubmitted articles were rejected. However, as just mentioned, we could find no evidence to suggest that either of these factors had in fact prevailed.

One might argue that the reviewers for the resubmitted papers did not remember the specific design or details of the original study, but could recall the points having been made experimentally. Since these articles had appeared in print some time after the work had been completed, it is possible that their results had already been incorporated into the reviewers' implicit sense of what was already known in the area. Thus, the reviewers might have felt that the work was redundant with what they could recall of the literature and rejected the manuscripts on that basis. We would agree with this account if the referees had indicated as much, and had raised this objection in their criticism, writing, for example, "This point is uninteresting and old," or "This work adds nothing new to the field," or "Similar findings have been reported by previous investigators." No such statements, or anything resembling them, were ever offered. As stated before, the manuscripts were rejected primarily for reasons of methodology and statistical treatment, not because reviewers judged that the work was not new.

Another hypothesis that might account for our results concerns regression effects. Since we selected only manuscripts that had been published, the only possible direction for change following a resubmission would be downward, that is, less than 100 percent acceptance, with some accepted articles being rejected. While regression to the mean was not controlled (rejected manuscripts were not resubmitted), it is still possible to ask how much regression would be probable. Even if the original acceptance figure of the article is taken to be a minimal 67 percent (i.e., with the editor and at least one of two reviewers recommending publication), and even if the correlation between pairs of reviewers were zero (the most extreme possibility), the expected regression could only be to the base rate, that is, the percentage of reviewers initially recommending acceptance—and this is obviously more than the 11 percent we see in table 1. In other words, one would have to hypothesize a large *negative* reliability for regression to account completely for the considerable shift in reviewers' judgments. We think that there are more reasonable ways to explain our findings.

Another way of addressing the regression issue would be to evaluate how probable the observed outcome was (eight out of nine manuscripts rejected) given varying levels of initial probability of being recommended for publication. In doing this one would have to conclude that *published* manuscripts in these journals have no more than a 43 percent conditional probability of acceptance because if the probable acceptance rate for any eventually published manuscript had been higher, the likelihood of our observed outcome of eight out of nine rejections would be less than 5 percent.

$$\text{probability} = 9(.43)^1 (.57)^8 + 1(.43)^0 (.57)^9$$
$$= .046 \text{ for } 43\% \text{ initial acceptance rate}$$

In practice, the more likely acceptance rate for "quality" manuscripts that one would have to hypothesize, given our data, would be much less than 43 percent, as this represents the extreme of the confidence interval for the binomial distribution.[5]

Since the most frequently mentioned grounds for rejecting the manuscripts were "serious methodological flaws," one might want to know whether these perceived flaws had been revealed by methodological or theoretical innovations that had appeared since the articles were first published. This seems not to have been the case. The criticisms were "old" and basic notions having to do with such matters as confounding, nonrandomization, use of ANOVA with dependent data, subject mortality, and the like. These points were considered flaws a year ago and will probably be considered flaws ten years from now.

Since we could detect no major shift in the qualifications or criteria used by the journals to select reviewers for the two periods, we concluded that perhaps one of the following two possibilities had prevailed:

Somehow, by chance, the initial reviewers were less competent than the average at that time, or less competent than the later reviewers. This possibility cannot be given too much credence, though, on purely statistical grounds. One would hardly expect such sizable systematic variation in reviewer competence to occur by chance from one to the other review period.

The second possibility is that systematic bias was operating to produce the discrepant reviews. The most obvious candidates as sources of bias in this case would be the authors' status and institutional affiliation. As mentioned earlier, these two variables have been cited (e.g., by Bowen et al. 1972; Cole and Cole 1972; Crane 1967; M. D. Gordon 1980; Merton 1968b; Tobach 1980; Zuckerman and Merton 1973) as sources of bias that can influence journal reviews in science. The authors of the articles used in our study were all from recognized, productive, and prestigious institutions with highly ranked psychology departments. For both sets of reviews, the authors' names and institutional affiliations were identified, except that fictitious names and institutions were substituted on the resubmitted manuscripts. The predominantly negative evaluations of the resubmissions may reflect some form of response bias in favor of the original authors as a function of their association with prestigious institutions. These individuals may have received a less critical, more benign evaluation than did our unknown authors from "no-name" institutions.

On the basis of his recent study of the reviewer bias in 619 physical sciences articles, M. D. Gordon (1980, p. 275) has concluded:

> It can therefore be argued that biases systematically operate within refereeing systems in such a way as to give advantage to those elements of a research community which supply the largest proportion of the referees used by editors of its journals. The papers of such authors may on occasion be less demandingly evaluated than those of authors outside the group. Hence, access to publication may sometimes be easier for them.

The mechanism underlying this form of bias may be something quite similar to Rosenthal's experimenter expectancy effect (see Rosenthal 1966; Rosenthal and Rubin 1978). Journal reviewers may expect manuscripts (and research) from persons at prestigious institutions to be superior in overall quality to those from individuals working in less distinguished settings; as a consequence, giving more variable evaluations to high-status individuals may serve as a self-fulfilling prophecy. (One might speculate that if reviewers were less rigorous toward prestige institutions and individuals, the publishing and publicizing of lower-quality work would have a negative feedback effect. Whether this would result in better papers or fewer submissions is not clear.) Another possibility is that when referees examine a manuscript submitted by researchers working at highly respected institutions, they may be more sensitive to making "false negative" evaluations, that is, rejecting papers of quality, whereas the major concern in reviewing papers of individuals from lesser known institutions may be that of avoiding "false positive" errors, that is, accepting flawed work. If reviewers base their evaluative criteria on experience or belief to the effect that papers of quality come mainly from prestigious individuals and institutions, then this could be viewed, in signal-detection terms, as criterion or response bias (as suggested in note 1). The cutoff point for publication acceptability may be lowered or raised as a function of status variables associated with an author. In fact, an institution's or an author's prestige could in principle prove to be a *valid* predictor—which would of course argue for the validity and continued exercise of such response biases. Unfortunately, little has been done to examine the validity of such a decision-making strategy empirically. Does this response bias maximize the ratio of "hits to misses" for a journal? At present this is just a matter of conjecture.

We do of course realize that a complete test of the bias hypothesis would call for resubmitting previously rejected articles with prestigious institutional affiliations. Such a procedure would obviously be much more complex and delicate, and unfortunately it was not possible for us to undertake such a project at the time we began.

The near perfect reviewer agreement regarding the unacceptability of the resubmitted manuscripts, coupled with the presumably near perfect agreement among the original reviewers in favor of publishing, provide additional convergent support for the response bias hypothesis. One might expect the initial manuscripts to elicit high positive consensus if the reviewers were impressed by or had high expectations for those with a Harvard or Stanford affiliation. But even the second time around, there are reasons—albeit different ones—to expect the reviewer consensus we found in our study. In the second case the reviewers may have been in agreement that there were serious *flaws* in the articles—perhaps the stereotypic muddled thinking of authors associated with a Tri-Valley Institute of Growth and Understanding. If this type of bias is actually operating to produce differential reviews and publication decisions, then one might predict that the highest levels of reviewer consensus should be found in journals with nonblind review, since an author's identity and affiliation are much more visible. While we do not have enough data to test this idea, the limited data on interrater agreement in the literature are in the predicted direction. Most reports of reviewer reliability showing good interreferee agreement (e.g., Crandall 1978a) have involved nonblind journals (Scarr and Weber 1978 is an exception). Viewed in this context, our finding of very high reviewer agreement with the resubmitted manuscripts is not so surprising; and considering the fate of the original manuscripts compared to the resubmissions, the response bias hypothesis seems to be a fair explanation for two sets of reviews showing near perfect, but *opposite* agreement.[6]

We did attempt to obtain the reviews from the *original* submissions to the nine journals in question. Unfortunately, we encountered some resistance to this idea, and the early lack of editorial cooperation indicated that a complete sample was not going to be possible. We therefore had to abandon this effort. We should add that not all editors were uncooperative: There were a few who were very gracious in supplying us with the requested information.

Although we had only three of the original reviews to examine and compare with our own set, we still contend that the reviews of the resubmissions represented a sizable and significant shift. Of the thirty new reviews twenty-six were clearly rejections [figure corrected in proof—see table 1], and if we accept the estimates given in the Scarr and Weber (1978) and Scott (1974) papers, then we would assume that the nine undetected resubmitted manuscripts that generated these thirty reviews had originally received eighteen favorable reviews; that is, at a minimum, the editor and one of the two referees were favorable. If we make these conservative figures (one reviewer recommending acceptance, the other rejection, instead of the more liberal unanimous acceptance) the expected frequencies for a chi-square test of the proposition that the resubmission reviews were not different from the original reviews, then the null hypothesis can be rejected (χ^2 (1) = 18.9 [21.8, corrected in proof—see table 1], $p < .001$). From this perspective it would seem that the outcome we observed was quite improbable.

Failing to Recognize Published Research

Often the cover letter an editor sends to a contributor following a review will contain some statement extolling the referees' knowledge and expertise. The findings in our study were no exception, as, for example, Journal H: "consultants who are very knowledgeable about theory and research in the area of concern to you"; Journal G: "both consultants who are experts in this area." Remarkably, though, almost 90 percent of the reviewers failed to recognize the resubmitted articles in our study. At the outset we thought that the major obstacle in collecting "real" journal reviews for our resubmissions would be the large number of detections by either the editors or the reviewers. This obviously did not happen—why not? No one could claim that the articles we selected were trivial reports that had appeared in minor, seldom read journals. We took articles from prestigious and widely circulated psychology journals having high "impact" ratings (Garfield 1979b). The articles themselves were above average in citations for the journals they appeared in, as well as for all social science articles in the first two years after publication (Garfield 1979b). Furthermore, these reports were resubmitted for review to the very journals and editors (excepting two cases, C and I) that had originally published them, and they had appeared recently (two to three years ago), not five or ten years in the past. Nor were these articles published too recently. Someone familiar with the literature would have had sufficient time to read and discuss them. Perhaps because of a large number of intervening reports, the articles had simply been forgotten by the reviewers (n = 20). It is also possible that those making the second set of reviews had nothing to remember. They may never have seen the original articles or heard them referred to or discussed by others working in the field. Under these circumstances, the failure to recognize the resubmissions, rather than being surprising, would be predictable. Although these explanations are certainly plausible, we suspect that few editors or contributors will find them encouraging, especially since the reviewers' reputed knowledge of an author's field can be such a sensitive issue in cases of negative reviews. Moreover, as mentioned, the articles we selected were above average in number of citations over the two-year period following publication.

Author-Reviewer Accountability

In addition to reliability and response bias, accountability has been an issue of concern in debates on the journal review system. Given that researchers in the behavioral and social sciences must often face rejection rates of 70 percent or higher from top journals in their field, and considering the large number of submitted manuscripts that editors and reviewers must evaluate each year, it is not surprising that much has been said, by both defenders and detractors of the journal review system, about the need for accountability. From one perspective, editors and referees, in light of the heavy time commitment called for by journal reviewing, might complain about the "bane of refereeing, the journal shopper" or "the repeated offender. Born of desperation, insensitivity, or stubbornness, a significant portion of a referee's efforts are repeat business—a succession of bad papers from the same individual" (Webb 1979, p. 60). It has been suggested that a central computer bank be created consisting of the titles and authors of rejected papers. "These would be categorized into two groups: (a) rejected, or (b) acceptable but not sufficient or appropriate for the journal. Minimally, these would be distributed to journal editors or ideally they would be placed on accessible tapes" (Webb 1979, p. 60). The assumption underlying this point of view is that the "journal shopper" is someone who basically knows that his manuscript is of questionable worth (perhaps a pilot study only appropriate for his private archives). The journal shopper, so this reasoning goes, hopes that with a lucky break, such as lenient reviewers, the manuscript might be accepted. Thus, repeated submissions occur until either the author "lucks out" (as perhaps most do, given the large number of existing publication outlets—see Garvey and Griffith 1971) or the list of journals is exhausted. The existence of a central computer bank supplying names of rejected authors to prospective editors is, of course, intended to deter "journal shopping." Certainly very few would want the potentially widespread notoriety of being identified as a "publication loser." The opportunity for a negative halo to develop should be obvious.

On the other side of this accountability issue one finds authors who believe that editors and referees should be more accountable and responsible for the quality of reviews they make in the course of reaching publication decisions (e.g., Coleman 1979; Jones 1974; McCutchen 1976; Stumpf 1980). It is not unusual to hear authors of rejected manuscripts argue that their papers were rejected, not because they did not have sufficient merit, but because of poor reviewer reliability (obviously most likely to be claimed in cases of split reviews), reviewer incompetence, or reviewer bias. One recent proposal that addressed the question of reviewer accountability suggested the creation of an "author review" of journal reviewers.

> The journal editor would send to the author, along with the letter of decision and reviews, a postcard questionnaire that would request the author to evaluate each review. I suggest that three dimensions are necessary: Fairness, carefulness, and constructiveness. There should also be a place on the card for comments. The editor would file the returned postcards under the reviewers' names, rating the editorial decision and final disposition of the manuscript. At intervals, perhaps once a year, the editor could examine these questionnaires. If a particular reviewer received repeated complaints, he or she could be terminated as a reviewer or could receive admonishment from the editor. (Hall 1979, p. 798).

It is argued that with such a reviewer evaluation procedure editors would have a basis for weeding out referees who were not current in their knowledge of the literature, consistently rejected articles on the basis of unreasonable or idiosyncratic criteria, or typically favored authors who were from their own institutions or shared similar research traditions. Journal reviewers faced with a record of accumulating author complaints might, one would hope, become more conscientious in their manuscript evaluations.

In our study none of the eighteen reviewers was identified to us either by the editors or on the manuscript reviews sent to the authors. We share the opinion of Hall (1979), Stumpf (1980), and others that anonymous peer reviews may be more costly than beneficial. A system that could allow a reviewer to say unreasonable, insulting, irrelevant, and misinformed things about you and your work without being accountable hardly seems equitable. To some degree the reviewer is indeed accountable—to the editor—but the potential for abuse is still too great to be ignored (see Ruderfer 1980, for an excellent example of this problem).

Suggestions for Improving the Journal Review System

However disquieting one finds evidence of reviewer bias, incompetence, or unreliability, it should not be ignored or dismissed as trivial. Scientists concerned about the quality of the review system should be encouraged to study this important area. We also hope that those choosing to do this will be guided by recent calls for hypothesis formation and discovery in naturalistic contexts (e.g., Bronfenbrenner 1977; Herrnstein 1977; McCall 1977;

McGuire 1973; Neisser 1976; cf. Gibbs 1979). However, those wishing to study the review process directly by using a procedure similar to the one employed in our investigation should be alerted to the possible costs. Be prepared for a lengthy time commitment (nearly two years for this study), practical difficulties (e.g., obtaining published materials or securing the cooperation of those in the journal hierarchy), and objections to your research approach.

In what is perhaps a sign of growing concern about the adequacy of our present journal review system, a number of different sources (editors and contributors) have recently offered suggestions for improvement (e.g., Crandall 1978a; Hall 1979; Harnad 1979; Hendrick 1977; McCartney 1973; Scott 1974; Stumpf 1980; Wolff 1973). Several writers have stressed the need to adopt a standard rating form in which an explicit set of evaluation criteria is listed. Some have called for the training of referees to increase the quality and reliability of their reviews. This might involve giving potential referees samples of actual editorial evaluations and subsequent publication decisions. Editors would have the responsibility of explaining the relationship between specified attributes of submitted manuscripts and their publishability. A collection of reviews and articles on which experts could agree (e.g., high quality, very publishable; low quality, reject) might be quite useful as a training or screening device for referees.

As mentioned above, another recommendation has been for a more accountable system of peer review, the basic idea being to establish some form of referee review, with referees formally evaluated by judges, authors, and editors. Systematically monitoring the quality of referee reports should have a corrective effect on journal review practices.

A further extension of author involvement and a move toward more openness and accountability in the review process can be seen in the recent suggestions for (and implementation of) an "open peer commentary" or its model, *Current Anthropology*). The basic idea is to complement the conventional closed peer review system by giving the authors of *accepted* (refereed) articles the opportunity to respond openly to criticism. With the article, commentaries (from first-round referees and others), and the author's formal response published together in their entirety, readers of the journal can have a chance to examine and appraise this process of "creative disagreement" and form their own opinions as to the merit of an individual's work.

If institutional affiliation or professional status can in fact bias peer review—and this bias proves to have no validity, or negative validity—then one possible solution to this problem (as several critics have recommended) would be to establish blind reviews as standard journal policy. We realize that this might not be totally effective in eliminating the problem (authors might, for example, be identified on the basis of several personal citations in the manuscript) and that blind reviewing may present additional problems (see American Psychological Association 1972; Rosenblatt and Kirk 1980), but it would certainly help minimize the influence of such biasing variable if done conscientiously. It is encouraging to note that there has been an increase in the number of psychology journals using blind reviews over the past decade (although the motive behind this move may be largely public relations, as was suggested by an APA editor involved in our study).

Given the professional importance placed on published research, and considering that science policymakers and funding agencies make practical decisions affecting the nature and future direction of scientific research on the basis of what gets reported in our journals, it is essential that we acquire a better understanding than we presently have of our journal review system. For years scientists have assumed that the review process is basically objective and reliable. Is it? Unfortunately, the peer review process has not received the experimental attention given other research topics—most of which have considerably less significance for and impact on scientists. We are sure that there are those who would not wish to see the somewhat delicate machinery of the review system tampered with by a wave of research projects. However, unless we subject the review process, and suggestions for improving it, to experimental analysis to learn more about the variables that do influence peer review, we are left with little to defend it other than faith.

Notes

The authors wish to thank Stevan Harnad, Jason Millman, David Palermo, Paul Ross, William Wilson, and several *anonymous* reviewers for helpful comments on earlier drafts of this paper.

1. By "response bias," we mean no more than the value-free signal-detection theoretic parameter usually called "c" or "η." This represents a referee's criterion or cutoff point in the trade-off in his "pay-off matrix" between "false positives" (overacceptance—analogous to "Type I errors" in decision theory) and "misses" (overrejection—"Type II errors"). The response bias may be based on various predictors (such as author's identity, reputation, institution) whose validity then also becomes an empirical question. The "signal" itself (acceptability) is usually assumed to have a certain independent "detectability," expressed as its distance (d') from noise.

2. The institutional affiliations of the original authors were: Harvard University, Stanford University, University of California at Berkeley, University of California at Los Angeles, University of Illinois at Urbana-Champaign, University of Minnesota

at Minneapolis, University of Texas at Austin, University of Wisconsin at Madison, and Yale University.

3. Other fictitious names used were Tri-Valley Institute of Growth and Understanding, Tri-Valley Institute of Human Learning, Northern Plains Center for Human Potential, and Northern Plains Research Station.

4. The following are the eight rejection statements made by the editors. Journal A: "Two consulting editors have examined your paper and I enclose copies of their reviews. I regret to conclude that the paper is not acceptable for publication, and judging from the reviews, I doubt that any revision would alter this decision." Journal B: "The considerable number of problems noted in the three reviews lead to a decision not to publish the paper." Journal C: "Your paper does not fall within priority areas having relevance to _____. Perhaps you might submit this work to some other journal in _____." Journal D: "The two reviews point to a number of serious methodological difficulties that would have to be overcome before a paper of this type could be considered publishable in _____. It is with regret that I must decline your paper." Journal E: "As you can see, the consultants are not enthusiastic about publishing your paper. Unfortunately, my own reading of your paper leads me to share this opinion." Journal F: "Unfortunately they all question its relevance for the _____ readers and suggest that it may be more appropriate for a more applied journal like _____. Therefore I have decided to reject the article." Journal G: "Both consultants, who are experts in this area, point out a number of methodological, conceptual, and stylistic problems with your paper. I agree with their judgments that these problems preclude publication of the paper in _____." Journal H: "Two individuals who provided reviews have raised a number of methodological and conceptual issues that militate against accepting the manuscript. Although we will be unable to publish your study in _____, it does seem that you are onto something good here, and I would encourage you to consider conducting another controlled study which addresses some of the reviewers' concerns."

5. In an unpublished manuscript, P. F. Ross (1981) has made a somewhat similar argument. On the basis of his analysis of interrater reliability (used to set validity intervals), citation index (used to determine quality of published articles), and acceptance rates of journals, he determined that the number of Type II errors (i.e., rejection of quality papers) is more than double the number of quality papers actually accepted for publication (and is also more than twice as large as the number of Type I errors). If his analysis is correct (cf. Garvey and Griffith 1971), it points to a large degree of error in peer reviewing.

Few would expect that the select 20 percent of submitted manuscripts actually accepted by our journals are completely flawless, and that they would without exception be reaccepted on a second review. However, in order to explain our own findings totally in terms of regression, one would have to accept the fact that the system is so flawed that it rejects quality papers far more often than it accepts them. While we do not deny that quality papers do get rejected, we feel that if there were no additional factors to explain our data other than regression, the implied level of Type II errors would be unreasonably high.

(Actually, the level of Type II errors is likely to be even greater than what we observed in our study, since the original manuscripts, when first accepted for publication, were probably not as polished as the printed versions serving as our resubmitted manuscripts. Thus, if anything, one would expect the resubmissions to have a *higher* acceptance rate than a typical manuscript of publishable quality being submitted for the first time.)

6. It is also possible that institutional prestige produced a criterion bias in the original reviewers toward being overgenerous, elevating marginal papers to the level of "publish if space permits." If this is taken to be the modal threshold for quality as perceived by the initial reviewers, then the later reviewers can be viewed as (validly) correcting this shift. It may be that the least variability among reviewers occurs in the region of outright rejection. This category is indeed reported to be the most reliable one among raters (Cicchetti 1980), and this could explain why our reviewers were in such high agreement—they may have been evaluating manuscripts of low quality despite their respectable citation count. (Now the question becomes: What if this was in fact a representative sample . . . ?)

References

American Psychological Association. "Eight APA Journals Initiate Controversial Blind Reviewing." APA *Monitor* 3, no. 5 (1972).

Bowen, D. D., R. Perloff, and J. Jacoby. "Improving Manuscript Evaluation Procedures." *American Psychologist* 27 (1972): 221–25.

Brackbill, Y., and F. Korton. "Journal Reviewing Practices: Author's and APA Members' Suggestions for Revision." *American Psychologist* 25 (1970): 937–40.

Bronfenbrenner, U. "Toward an Experimental Ecology of Human Development." *American Psychologist* 32 (1977): 513–31.

Cicchetti, D. V. "Reliability of Reviews for the *American Psychologist*: A Biostatistical Assessment of the Data." *American Psychologist* 35 (1980): 300–303.

Cicchetti, D. V., and H. O. Conn. "A Statistical Analysis of Reviewer Agreement and Bias in Evaluating Medical Abstracts." *Yale Journal of Biology and Medicine* 49 (1976): 373–83.

Cicchetti, D. V., and L. D. Eron. "The Reliability of Manuscript Reviewing for the *Journal of Abnormal Psychology*." 1979 Proceedings of the Social Statistics Section, pp. 596–600. Washington, D.C.: American Statistics Association.

Cole, J. R., and S. Cole. "The Ortega Hypothesis: Citation Analysis Suggests That Only a Few Scientists Contribute to Scientific Progress." *Science* 178 (1972): 368–74.

Colman, A. M. "Editorial Role in Author-Referee Disagreements." *Bulletin of the British Psychological Society* 32 (1979): 390–91.

Cox, W. M., and V. Catt. "Productivity Ratings of Graduate Programs in Psychology Based on Publication in the Journals of the American Psychological Association." *American Psychologist* 32 (1977): 793–813.

Crandall, R. "Interrater Agreement on Manuscripts Is Not So Bad!" *American Psychologist* 33 (1978): 623–24.

Crane, D. "The Gatekeepers of Science: Some Factors Affecting the Selection of Articles for Scientific Journals." *American Sociologist* 32 (1967): 195–201.

Endler, N. S., J. P. Rushton, and H. L. Roediger. "Productivity and Scholarly Impact (Citations) of British, Canadian, and U.S. Departments of Psychology." *American Psychologist* 33 (1978): 1064–82.

Garfield, E. *Citation Indexing: Its Theory and Application in Science, Technology, and Humanities.* New York: John Wiley & Sons, 1979a.

———. *Journal Citation Report: A Bibliometric Analysis of Social Science Journals in the ISI Data Base.* Philadelphia: Institute for Scientific Information, 1979b.

Garvey, W. D., and B. C. Griffith. "Scientific Communication: Its Role in the Conduct of Research and Creation of Knowledge." *American Psychologist* 26 (1971): 349–62.

Gibbs, J. C. "The Meaning of Ecologically Oriented Inquiry in Contemporary Psychology." *American Psychologist* 34 (1979): 127–40.

Goodstein, L. D., and K. L. Brazis. "Credibility of Psychologists: An Empirical Study." *Psychological Reports* 27 (1970): 835–38.

Gordon, M. D. "The Role of Referees in Scientific Communication." In *The Psychology of Written Communication*, edited by J. Hartley, pp. 263–75. London: Kogan Page, 1980.

Gottfredson, S. D. "Evaluating Psychological Research Reports: Dimensions, Reliability, and Correlates of Quality Judgments." *American Psychologist* 33 (1978): 920–34.

Gove, W. R. "The Review Process and Its Consequences in the Major Sociology Journals." *Contemporary Sociology* 8 (1979): 799–804.

Hall, J. "Author Review of Reviewers." *American Psychologist* 34 (1979): 798.

Harnad, S. "Creative Disagreement." *Sciences* 19 (1979): 18–20.

Hendrick, C. "Editorial Comment." *Personality and Social Psychology Bulletin* 3 (1977): 1–2.

Herrnstein, R. J. "Doing What Comes Naturally: A Reply to Professor Skinner." *American Psychologist* 32 (1977): 1013–16.

Ingelfinger, F. J. "Peer Review in Biomedical Publication." *American Journal of Medicine* 56 (1974): 686–92.

Jones, R. "Rights, Wrongs, and Referees." *New Scientist* 61 (1974): 758–59.

Koulack, D., and H. J. Keselman. "Ratings of Psychology Journals by Members of the American Psychological Association." *American Psychologist* 30 (1975): 1049–53.

McCall, R. B. "Challenges to a Science of Developmental Psychology." *Child Development* 48 (1977): 333–44.

McCartney, J. L. "Manuscript Reviewing." *Sociological Quarterly* 14 (1973): 444–46.

McCutchen, C. "An Evolved Conspiracy." *New Scientist* 70 (1976): 225.

McGuire, W. J. "The Yin and Yang of Social Psychology: Seven Koan." *Journal of Personality and Social Psychology* 26 (1973): 446–56.

McReynolds, P. "Reliability of Ratings of Research Papers." *American Psychologist* 26 (1971): 400–401.

Mahoney, M. J. *Scientist as Subject: The Psychological Imperative*. Cambridge, Mass.: Ballinger, 1976.

———. "Publication Prejudices: An Experimental Study of Confirmatory Bias in the Peer Review System." *Cognitive Therapy and Research* 1 (1977): 161–75.

Markle, A., and R. C. Rinn. *Author's Guide to Journals in Psychology, Psychiatry, & Social Work*. New York: Haworth Press, 1977.

Merton, R. K. *Social Theory and Social Structure*. New York: Free Press, 1968.

Neisser, U. *Cognition and Reality: Principles and Implications of Cognitive Psychology*. San Francisco: Freeman, 1976.

Oromaner, M. "Professional Age and the Reception of Sociological Publications: A Test of the Zuckerman-Merton Hypothesis." *Social Studies of Science* 7 (1977): 381–88.

Revusky, S. "Interference with Progress by the Scientific Establishment: Examples from Flavor Aversion Learning." In *Food Aversion Learning*, edited by N. W. Milgram, L. Knames, and T. M. Alloway. London: Plenum, 1977.

Roose, K. D., and C. J. Anderson. *A Rating of Graduate Programs*. Washington, D.C.: American Council on Education, 1970.

Rosenblatt, A., and S. A. Kirk. "Recognition of Authors in Blind Review of Manuscripts." *Journal of Social Service Research* 3 (1980): 383–94.

Rosenthal, R. *Experimenter Effects in Behavioral Research*. New York: Appleton-Century-Crofts; rev. ed., New York: Irvington, 1976.

Rosenthal, R., and D. B. Rubin. "Interpersonal Expectancy Effects: The First 345 Studies." *Behavioral and Brain Sciences* 3 (1978): 377–86.

Ross, P. F. "The Sciences' Self-Management: Manuscript Refereeing, Peer Review, and Goals in Science." Unpublished manuscript, 1981.

Ruderfer, M. "The Fallacy of Peer Review—Judgment without Science and a Case History." *Speculations in Science and Technology* 3 (1980): 533–62.

Scarr, S., and B. L. R. Weber. "The Reliability of Reviews for the *American Psychologist*." *American Psychologist* 33 (1978): 935.

Scott, W. A. "Interreferee Agreement on Some Characteristics of Manuscripts Submitted to the *Journal of Personality and Social Psychology*." *American Psychologist* 29 (1974): 698–702.

Stumpf, W. E. "'Peer' Review." *Science* 207 (1980): 822–23.

Tobach, E. " . . . That Ye Be Judged." In *An Evaluation of the Peer Review System in Psychological Research*. Open forum presented at the American Psychological Convention (chairman J. Demarest), Montreal, 1980.

Walster, G. W., and T. A. Cleary. "A Proposal for a New Editorial Policy in the Social Sciences." *American Statistician* 24 (1970): 16–19.

Watkins, M. W. "Chance and Interrater Agreement on Manuscripts." *American Psychologist* 34 (1979): 796–97.

Webb, W. B. "Continuing Education: Refereeing Journal Articles." *Teaching Psychology* 6 (1979): 59–60.

White, M. J., and K. G. White. "Citation Analysis of Psychology Journals." *American Psychologist* 32 (1977): 301–5.

Wolff, W. M. "Publication Problems in Psychology and an Explicit Evaluation Schema for Manuscripts." *American Psychologist* 28 (1973): 257–61.

Yotopoulos, P. A. "Institutional Affiliation of the Contributors to Three Professional Journals." *American Economic Review* 51 (1961): 665–70.

Zuckerman, H. "Stratification in American Science." *Sociological Inquiry* 40 (1970): 235–57.

Zuckerman, H., and R. Merton. "Patterns of Evaluation in Science: Institutionalization, Structure, and Functions of the Referee System." In *The Sociology of Science*, edited by N. Storer. Chicago: University of Chicago Press, 1973.

~~~

No Bias, No Merit:
The Case against Blind Submission
Stanley Fish

When members of an institution debate, it may seem that they are arguing about fundamental principles, but it is more often the case that the truly fundamental principle is the one that makes possible the terms of the disagreement and is therefore not in dispute at all. I am thinking in particular of the arguments recently marshaled for and against blind submission to the journal of the Modern Language Association. Blind submission is the practice whereby an author's name is not revealed to the reviewer who evaluates his or her work. It is an attempt, as William Schaefer explained in the *MLA Newsletter*, "to ensure that in making their evaluations readers are not influenced by factors other than the intrinsic merits of the article" (4). In his report to the members, Schaefer, then executive director of the association, declared that he himself was opposed to blind submission because the impersonality of the practice would erode the humanistic values that are supposedly at the heart of our enterprise. Predictably, Schaefer's statement provoked a lively exchange in which the lines of battle were firmly, and, as I will argue, narrowly, drawn. On the one hand those who agreed with Schaefer feared that a policy of anonymous review would involve a surrender "to the spurious notions about objectivity and absolute value that . . . scientists and social scientists banter about"; on the other hand those whose primary concern was with the fairness of the procedure believed that "[j]ustice should be blind" ("Correspondence" 4). Each side concedes the force of the opposing argument—the proponents of anonymous review admit that impersonality brings its dangers, and the defenders of the status quo acknowledge that it is important to prevent "extraneous considerations" from interfering with the identification of true merit (5).

It is in phrases like "true merit" and "extraneous considerations" that one finds the assumptions to which all parties subscribe. The respondent who declares that "the point at issue is how to avoid the bias of a reviewer upon grounds other than those intrinsic to the article under review" (5) is making an unexceptional statement. Everyone agrees that intrinsic merit should be protected; it is just a question of whether or not the price of protection—the possible erosion of the humanistic community—is too high. In what follows I would like not so much to enter the debate as to challenge its terms by arguing that merit is not in fact identifiable apart from the "extraneous considerations" that blind submission would supposedly eliminate. I want to argue, in short, that there is no such thing as intrinsic merit, and indeed, if I may paraphrase James I, "no bias, no merit."

We might begin by noting that while in the course of this debate everyone talks about intrinsic merit, no one bothers to define it, except negatively as everything apart from the distractions of rank, affiliation, professional status, past achievements, ideological identification, sex, "or anything that might be known about the author" (Schaefer 5). Now this is a list so inclusive that one might wonder what was left once the considerations it enumerates were eliminated. The answer would seem to be that what is left is the disinterested judgment as to whether or not an article does justice to the work or works it purports to characterize. But that answer will be satisfactory only if the notion "does justice to" can be related to a standard or set of standards that operates independently of the institutional circumstances that have been labeled extraneous. My thesis is, first of all, that there is no such standard (which is not the same thing as saying there is no standard) and, second, that while we may, as a point of piety, invoke it as an ideal, in fact we violate it all the time by practices that are at once routine and obligatory. Consider, for example, the practice of referring, at the beginning of an essay, or in the course of its unfolding, or in a succession of footnotes (the conditions under which it would be proper to do it one way rather than another could themselves be profitably studied) to the body of previous scholarship. This is a convention of the profession, and a failure to respect it will sometimes be grounds for rejecting an article. The reason is obvious. The convention is a way of acknowledging that we are engaged in a community activity in which the value of one's work is directly related to the work that had been done by others; that is, in this profession you earn the right to say something because it has not been said by anyone else, or because it is a reversal of what is usually said, or because while it has been said, its implications have not yet been spelled out. You do not offer something as the report of a communion between the individual critical sensibility and a work or its author; and if you did, if your articles were all written as if they were titled "What I think about *Middlemarch*" or "*The Waste Land* and Me" they would not be given a hearing. (The fact that this is not true of some people does not disprove but makes my point.) Instead they would be dismissed as being a waste of a colleague's time, or as beside the point, or as uninformed, or simply as unprofessional. This last judgment would not be a casual one; to be unprofessional is not simply to have violated some external rule or piece of decorum. It is to have ignored (and by ignoring flouted) the process by which the institution determines the conditions under which its rewards will be given or withheld. These conditions are nowhere written down, but they are understood by everyone who works in the field and, indeed, any understanding one might have of the field is inseparable from (because it will have been produced by) an awareness, often tacit, of these conditions.

What are they? A full answer to the question would be out of place here, but a partial enumeration would include a canon of greater and lesser works and hence a stipulation as to what is or is not a major project, a set of authorized methodologies along with a recognized procedure by which members of one set can be moved into another, a list of the tasks that particularly need doing and of those that have already been well done, a specification of the arguments that are properly literary and of the kinds of evidence that will be heard as telling and/or conclusive (authorial statements, letters, manuscript revisions, etc.). Of course these conditions can and do change and the process by which they change is one of the things they themselves regulate—but they always have some shape or other, and one cannot, without risk, operate independently of them.

Everyone is aware of that risk, although it is usually not acknowledged with the explicitness that one finds in the opening sentence of Raymond Waddington's essay on books 11 and 12 of *Paradise Lost*. "Few of us today," Waddington writes, "could risk echoing C. S. Lewis's condemnation of the concluding books of *Paradise Lost* as an 'untransmuted lump of futurity'" (9). The nature of the risk that Waddington is about *not* to take is made clear in the very next sentence, where we learn that a generation of critics has been busily demonstrating the subtlety and complexity of these books and establishing the fact that they are the product of a controlled poetic design. What this means is that the kind of thing that one can now say about them is constrained in advance, for, given the present state of the art, the critic who is concerned with maintaining his or her professional credentials is obliged to say something that makes them better. Indeed, the safest thing the critic can say (and Waddington proceeds in this essay to say it) is that, while there is now a general recognition of the excellence of these books, it is still the case that they are faulted for some deficiency that is in fact, if properly understood, a virtue. Of course, this rule (actually a rule of thumb) does not hold across the board. When Waddington observes that "few of us today could risk," he is acknowledging, ever so obliquely, that there are some of us who could. Who are they, and how did they achieve their special status? Well, obviously C. S. Lewis was once one (although it may not have been a risk for him, and if it wasn't why wasn't it?), and if he had not already died in 1972, when Waddington was writing, presumably he could have been one again. That is, Lewis's status as an authority on Renaissance literature was such that he could offer readings without courting the risk facing others who might go against the professional grain, the risk of not being listened to, of remaining unpublished, of being unattended to, the risk of producing something that was by definition—a definition derived from prevailing institutional conditions—without merit.

With this observation, we return to the notion of "intrinsic merit" as it relates to the issue of blind submission; for what the Waddington-Lewis example shows (among other things) is that merit, rather than being a quality that can be identified independently of professional or institutional conditions, is a product of those conditions; and, moreover, since those conditions are not stable but change continually, the shape of what will be recognized as meritorious is always in the process of changing too. So that while it is true that as critics we write with the goal of living up to a standard (of worth, illumination, etc.) it is a standard that had been made not in eternity by God or by Aristotle but in the profession by the men and women who have preceded us; and in the act of trying to live up to it, we are also and necessarily, refashioning it. My use of "we" might suggest a communal effort in which everyone pulls an equal weight and exerts an equal influence. But of course this is not the case. Ours is a hierarchical profession in which some are more responsible for its products than others; and since one of those products is the standard of merit by which our labors will, for a time, be judged, there will always be those whose words are meritorious (that is, important, worth listening to, authoritative, illuminating) simply by virtue of the position they occupy in the institution. It is precisely this situation, of course, that the policy of blind submission is designed to remedy; the idea is to prevent a reviewer from being influenced in his or her judgment of merit by the professional status of the author; but on the analysis offered in this essay, merit is inseparable from the structure of the profession and therefore the fact that someone occupies a certain position in that structure cannot be irrelevant to the assessment of what he or she produces.

The point is made in passing by a respondent (anonymous, I am afraid) to the Executive Council's survey who asserts that "[I]f Northrop Frye should write an essay attacking archetypal criticism, the article would by definition be of much greater significance than an article by another scholar attacking the same approach" (Schaefer 5). The reason, of course, is that the approach is not something independent of what Northrop Frye has previously said about it; indeed, in large part archetypal criticism *is* what Northrop Frye has said about it, and therefore anything he now says about it is not so much to be measured against an independent truth as it is to be regarded, at least potentially, as a new pronouncement of what the truth will hereafter be said to be. Similarly, an article by Fredson Bowers on the principles of textual editing would automatically be of "general interest to the membership" because the sense the membership has of what the principles of textual editing could possibly be is inseparable from what Fredson Bowers has already written. Of course it is not necessary to search for a hypothetical example. The fact that the judgment on *Paradise Lost* 11 and 12 was made by C. S. Lewis in a book that was immediately recognized as authoritative—a recognition that was itself produced in no small part by the prior authority of *The Allegory of Love*—was sufficient to ensure that it would be over fifteen years before a group of scholars could begin the rehabilitation of those books and another fifteen before Waddington could pronounce their effort successful by declaring that few of us today could risk echoing C. S. Lewis.

It could be argued that these are special cases, but they are special only in that Frye, Bowers, and Lewis are (or were) in the position of exerting a general authority over the entire discipline; but in the smaller precincts of subdisciplines and subsubdisciplines, there are words that matter more than other words spoken by those who address a field that they themselves have in large part constituted. These are men and women who are identified with a subject (Frances Yates on arts of memory), with a period (M. H. Abrams on Romanticism), with a genre (Angus Fletcher on allegory), with a poet (Hugh Kenner on Pound), with a work (Stephen Booth on Shakespeare's *Sonnets*). When Geoffrey Hartman speaks on Wordsworth, is his just another voice, or is it the voice of someone who is in great measure responsible for the Wordsworth we now have, insofar as by that name we understand an array of concerns, formal properties, sources, influences, and so on? Of course Geoffrey Hartman's Wordsworth is not everyone's, but everyone's Wordsworth is someone's; that is everyone's Wordsworth is the product of some characterization of him that has been put forward (within constraints that are already in place) and has been found to be persuasive by a significant number of workers in the profession. The point is that whatever Wordsworth we have he will not be available independently of the institution's procedures; rather he will be the product of these procedures, and of the work of certain men and women, and therefore the identity of the men and women who propose to speak about him cannot be irrelevant to a judgment of the merit of what they have to say.

I make the point in order to anticipate an obvious objection to the preceding paragraphs: it may be the case that the merit of pieces of literary criticism is a function of conditions prevailing in the profession, but surely the merit of literary works themselves is another matter, for they precede the profession and are the occasion of its efforts and the justification of its machinery. This is a powerful objection because it is rooted in the most basic myth the profession tells itself, the myth that it is secondary in relation to literary works that are produced independently of its processes; but it is precisely my contention that literary works have the shape they do because of the questions that have been put to them, questions that emerge from the work of the profession and are understood by members of the profession to be the proper ones to ask. We often think of our task as the *description* of literary works, but description requires categories of description and those categories, in the form of the questions we think to ask, will limit in advance the kinds of things that can be described, which in turn will limit the shapes that can even be seen. That is to say, the objects of our professional attention—texts, authors, genres, and so on—are as much the products of the institution as are the acceptable forms that attention can take. It follows then that the machinery of the institution does not grow up to accommodate needs that are independently perceived but that, rather, the institutional machinery comes first and the needs then follow, as do the ways of meeting them.

In short, the work to be done is not what the institution responds to but what it *creates*, and it was not long ago that this truth was brought home to me when I received the first of many mailings from the then fledging Spenser Society of America. So fledgling was that society in 1977 that I hadn't yet heard of it, and I was therefore somewhat surprised to open a letter from its treasurer thanking me for my support. What became clear as the letter proceeded was that my ignorance of the society in no way exempted me from its operations. "We are almost two hundred strong," read the second sentence of the letter, and the suggestion of a military organization into which I had been conscripted was unmistakable. Moreover, that organization was already fully articulated. I was informed of the identity of "my" officers, who had arranged "our luncheon," for which I was urged to make an immediate reservation because my fellow members had already spoken for thirty of the fifty available seats. By the end of the second paragraph I was not only firmly placed in the rank and file of a marching army but informed that I was already behind in my dues. It was not until the third and final paragraph, however, that the true significance of the society's operation was revealed in the announcement of an annual volume to be called *Spenser Studies*, the first number of which was already scheduled by an editorial board that had already signed an agreement, in my name, I suppose, with a prominent university press. We would be happy, wrote my treasurer, "if you would inform colleagues and students that we Spenserians now have another possibility for publication." Here is the real message of the letter and the real rationale of the Spenser Society of America: to multiply the institutional contexts in which writing on Spenser will at once be demanded and published. It so happens that the letter was written before the society's first meeting, but as this sentence shows, the society need never have met at all, since its most important goal—the creation of a Spenser industry with all its attendant machinery—had already been achieved.

In later communications that machinery was further elaborated, first of all by the calling of an International Conference on Cooperation in the Study of Edmund Spenser. The scheduled panels indicate the directions the cooperative studies will take: "Cooperation in the Study of Spenser's Medieval English Backgrounds," "Cooperation in the Study of Spenser's Continental Backgrounds." What is emerging here is not simply the shape of an organization but the shape of Edmund Spenser. Nor will that shape be allowed to grow like Topsy. The topic of the first panel is the *limits* of cooperative study; the same document at once calls into being an activity and begins to regulate it. It is not long before both cooperation and regulation take on a more substantial form in the promised production of a Spenser *Encyclopedia* (if a category or subject is not in the encyclopedia, it will not be in Spenser), plans for which, I was informed, were already "well advanced." It is a feature of this correspondence that the world it declares is provided with a past and a future that tend to obscure its purely documentary origin. Things are always "well advanced" or "previously discussed" in a way that suggests events are being reported rather than made. But it takes only a moment's reflection to see that in a paragraph like this one every event is brought into being by a piece of paper that is underwritten by a bureaucracy that is itself created and sustained by other pieces of paper:

Plans are now all advanced for the projected *Spenser Encyclopedia*, which was discussed at conferences last October and December. (See reports on these conferences in the latest issue of *Spenser Newsletter*, 10, no. 1.) An official announcement of the *Encyclopedia* will be made on 4th May 1979 at Kalamazoo, Michigan, where we hope to continue the cooperative spirit of the International Conference at Duquesne.

It may seem that I am overestimating the power of a series of letters, even if the first in the series was written on the 4th of July; and it is true that this letter and subsequent ones did not create the society's machinery and the possibilities attendant upon it in a vacuum or ex nihilo: there is, it turns out, an authority that legitimizes these documents and accounts for their immediate force. The identity of that authority was revealed in the reporting of a lack. The Spencer Society, it seems, was at the time of its birth, without constitution, and therefore the framing of a constitution was declared to be the first order of business at the first meeting. Before that meeting was held, however, a second letter arrived, written this time by "my" president, informing me that the constitution was in fact already available in the form of the constitution, ready-made as it were, of the Milton Society, which also, the letter went on to say, was to provide the model for a banquet, a reception, an after-dinner speaker, an honored scholar, and the publication of a membership booklet, the chief function of which was to be the listing of the publications, recent and forthcoming, of the members. The manner in which work on Spenser is to be recognized and honored will have its source not in a direct confrontation with the poet or his poem but in the apparatus of an organization devoted to another poet. Spenser studies will be imitative of Milton studies; the anxiety of influence, it would seem, can work backwards. Moreover, it continues to work. The recent mail has brought me, and some of you, an announcement of a new publication, the *Sidney Newsletter*, to be organized, we are told, "along the lines of the well-established and highly successful *Spenser Newsletter*," which was organized along the lines of the well-established and highly successful *Milton Newsletter*.

Now I wouldn't want to be understood as criticizing the Spenser Society for its colonizing activities or for having been colonized, in its turn, by the Milton Society. My account of these matters is offered with affection and, indeed, with gratitude, for were it not for the opportunities made available by these organizations there would be nothing for us to do. As I have already said, the work to be done is not what the institution responds to but what it *creates*, and it is the business of these societies first to create the work and second to make sure that it will never get done. I say this from a position of authority, as a past president of the Milton Society, an office whose only duty is to reside over an annual meeting. At the meeting over which I presided the members of the society heard reports on the *Milton Encyclopedia*, the *Var-*

iorum Commentary, The Complete Prose, the friends of Milton's cottage, the Milton Society Archive and Library, the Milton Society awards, and "upcoming panels and conferences at which members of the society might speak." These were labeled as "progress reports," and to some extent the label was accurate; but the rate of progress was reassuringly slow and there were signs that mechanisms were already in motion to ensure that it would never get too far. *The Complete Prose* was threatening to become, in fact, complete; but there was an announcement that the seventh volume would soon be reissued in a revised and improved version, and if the seventh volume, could the first, second, third, fourth, fifth, and sixth be far behind? The volumes of the *Variorum* have hardly begun to appear, but already there is talk that the *Paradise Regained* is inadequate and will have to be redone. I myself was aghast to discover that antinomianism was not even an entry in the *Milton Encyclopedia* and began to think that similar omissions might necessitate the issuing of a new and improved edition. In so thinking I was not being cynical or opportunistic; I was responding with an honest act of judgment to a project that was called into being by the needs of the field. The fact that those needs corresponded to the need of the workers in the field to have something to do is worth noting; to note it, however, is not to call into question the sincerity of their efforts but to point out that those efforts are first and foremost professional and that therefore the motives one might have for engaging in them are professional too. To say this is to say what should go without saying: we do not write articles in order to report to no one in particular in no context in particular our unmediated experience of a literary work; articles are written by men and women who have something to contribute as "contribution" is defined by the conditions prevailing in the institution, an institution that provides both the questions and acceptable ways of answering them and provides too the canon of works to which the questions can be put. Indeed, the very writing of an article only makes sense within an institutional framework, and when an article gets published, it is not because some independent agency has validated its merit but because in the machinery of a *political* agency—the Milton Society, the Spencer Society, the MLA—there is already a place for it.

With the word *political* we come to the heart of the matter, for that word names everything that so many in the profession would like to deny. It is the mark of a profession to claim that its activities are not tied to any one set of economic or social circumstances but constitute a response to needs and values that transcend particular times and places. (For the topic of professionalism, see Bledstein; Haskell; Larson.) The profession of literary criticism carries this claim to an extreme that is finally self-destructive by declaring that

its activities finally have very little value at all. The explanation for this cu-
rious maneuver lies in the relationship between what literary critics do and
the commodity that occupies the center of the enterprise—literature. It is an
article of faith in the profession that this commodity precedes the profession's
efforts, which are seen as merely exegetical; and that means that from the
very first the profession has a sense of itself as something secondary and su-
perfluous. If the work itself is all-sufficient (a cardinal principle of twentieth-
century aesthetics) the work of the critic is ultimately unnecessary, and criticism would seem to have compromised its claim to be a profession, even
before that claim has been made.

One sees this clearly, for example, in John Crowe Ransom's "Criticism
Inc.," a manifesto in which the literary community is urged to become more
self-consciously professional. "Criticism," Ransom declares, "must become
more scientific, or precise and systematic, and this means that it must be developed by the collective and sustained effort of learned persons—which
means that its proper seat is in the universities" (World Body 329). This is the
very language of professionalism and it is accompanied by a disdain for ama-
teurs (327) and by a rejection of the notion that criticism "is something
which anyone can do" (335). But when it comes time to describe this new
profession, its principles turn out to be unlike any other in that they are directed *away* from the public. To the question "What is criticism?" Ransom
answers with what it is not, and what it is not is anything that might recommend it to the community at large; it does not report on the "moral content"
of literature; it is not concerned with the lives of authors, or with literature's
relationship to science, politics, the law, or geography; it must not make
claims that its commodity is "moving" or "exciting" or "entertaining" or
"great"; and above all it must not suggest that "art comes into being because
the artist . . . has designs upon the public, whether high moral designs or box
office ones" (3B). In this last phrase, high moral designs (which might include the design to enlighten one's readers, or to make them better, or to en-
list them in some social or religious cause) are tarred, by association, with the
brush of vulgarity; they are just another version of box-office designs because
the intention of those who have them is to move others to this or that action in relation to this or that quotidian concern. Poetry, by contrast, is an
effort deliberately abstracted from such concerns; the poet, Ransom writes,
"perpetuates in his poem an order of existence which in actual life is con-
stantly crumbling beneath his touch" (348); and the critic must attend only
to that order and avoid attending to anything that would deny or compromise "the autonomy of the work itself as existing for its own sake" (343). In
practice this means an exclusive focus on technique as it exists apart from

any social or moral end (346), a focus that promotes rapt contemplation as the only attitude that can properly belong to an activity defined in opposition to the business of everyday life, or to the everyday life of business.

The result is a professionalism that is divided against itself. It claims for itself the exclusive possession of a certain skill (the skill of attending properly to poems), but then it defines that skill in such a way as to remove its exercise from the activities of the marketplace where professions compete for the public's support. Indeed, it is a skill that can be exercised only if the conditions of the marketplace are resolutely ignored in favor of the *eternal* conditions that obtain, or should obtain, between poem and reader. So long as it is a first principle that poetry must be studied "for its own sake," the profession of literary criticism will exist in a shamefaced relationship with professional machinery, which will be regarded as a temporary and regrettable excrescence.

That is why the literary community teaches its members a contradictory lesson: literary criticism is a profession—it is not something that anyone can do—but it is not professional—it is not done in response to marketplace or political pressures. A policy of blind submission is an extension of that lesson and is also the extension of a general practice by which the profession hides from itself the true (political) nature of its own activities. As we have seen, the case for blind submission is that it protects the intrinsic from the extraneous; but what I have been trying to show, from a variety of perspectives, is that everything labeled extraneous—considerations of rank, professional status, previous achievement, ideology, and so on—is essential to the process by which intrinsic considerations are identified and put into place. I said at the beginning of this essay that there is no such thing as intrinsic, and I would say it again if by "intrinsic" was meant a category of value that was in place for all time; but if we think of the intrinsic as something that profession determines, then there is always a category of the intrinsic but isn't always the same one. It therefore cannot be defined in opposition to the profession, because it is a part of the profession's work to produce it, and then, in the course of discussion and debate, to produce it again.

The intrinsic, in short, is a political rather than an essential category, and as such it will always reflect the interests—wholly legitimate because without interest there would be no value—of those who have had a hand in fashioning it. In the process the interests of the others will have been excluded or slighted and those groups will, more often than not, protest their exclusion in the name of intrinsic merit; but what they will really be doing is attempting to replace someone else's notion of intrinsic merit with their own; that is, they will be playing politics. This is precisely what the proponents of blind submission are doing, whether they know it or not, and therefore the one claim they cannot legitimately maintain, although they make it all the time, is that they are doing away with politics. These are certainly arguments that can be made for blind submissions, but they are frankly political arguments and if they were presented as such they might even receive a more sympathetic hearing. As things stand now, for example, I am against blind submission because the fact that my name is attached to an article greatly increases its chances of getting accepted. But that is just the condition we wish to change, someone might object, and to this I might reply that I have paid my dues and earned the benefit of the doubt I now enjoy and don't see why others shouldn't labor in the vineyards as I did. I would, that is, be responding in terms of my own self-interest, by which I don't mean *selfish* interests but interests that appear to me to be compelling given a sense of myself as a professional with a history and with a stake in the future of the profession.

A similar point is made by some of the participants in a discussion of peer review published in the *Behavioral and Brain Sciences: An International Journal of Current Research and Theory with Open Peer Commentary* (5 [1982]: 187–255). The occasion was the report of research conducted by D. P. Peters and S. J. Ceci. Peters and Ceci had taken twelve articles published in twelve different journals, altered the titles, substituted for the names of the authors fictitious names identified as researchers at institutions no one had ever heard of (because they were made up), and resubmitted the articles to the journals that had originally accepted them. Three of the articles were recognized as resubmissions, and of the remaining nine eight were rejected. The response to these results ranges from horror ("It puts at risk the whole conceptual framework within which we are accustomed to make observations and construct theories" [245]) to "so what else is new." Almost all respondents, however, agreed with the researchers' call for the development of "fair" procedures, "fair . . . defined here as being judged on the merit of one's ideas, and not on the basis of academic rank, sex, place of work, publication record, and so on" (253). Nevertheless, there were a few who questioned that definition of fairness and challenged the assumption that it was wrong for reviewers to take institutional affiliation and history into consideration. "We consider a result from a scientist who has never before been wrong much more seriously than a similar report from a scientist who has never before been right. . . . It is neither unnatural nor wrong that the work of scientists who have achieved eminence through a long record of important and successful research is accepted with fewer reservations than the work of less eminent scientists" (196). "A reviewer may be justified in assuming at the outset that [well-known] people know what they are doing" (211). "Those of us who publish establish some kind of track record. If our papers stand the test of time . . . it can be expected that we have acquired expertise in scientific methodology" (244). (This last respondent is a woman and a Nobel laureate.) What this minority is saying is that a paper identified with a distinguished record is a better bet than a paper not so identified. I would go even further and say that a paper so identified will be a *different paper*. In a footnote to his *Structure of Scientific Revolutions* Thomas Kuhn reports that when Lord Rayleigh submitted a paper to the British Association, his name was "inadvertently omitted" and the paper was rejected "as the work of some 'paradoxer'" (153). But when his name was subsequently restored the paper was accepted immediately. On its face this might seem to be a realization of the worst fears of those who argue for blind submission, but I would read the result differently: shorn of its institutional lineage the paper presented itself as without direction, and whimsical; but once the reviewers were informed of its source they were able to see it as the continuation of work—of lines of direction, routes of inquiry—they already knew, and all at once the paper made a different kind of sense than it did when they were considering it "blindly."

Of course they were not considering it blindly at all. Reviewers who receive a paper from which the identifying marks have been removed will immediately put in place an (imagined) set of circumstances of exactly the kind they are supposedly ignoring. Indeed, in the absence of such an imaginative and projective act, the paper could not be read as a paper situated in a particular discipline. Strictly speaking, there is no such thing as blind submission. The choice is not between a reading influenced by "extraneous" information and a reading uninflected by "extraneous" information but between readings differently inflected. The pure case of a reading without bias is never available, not because we can never remove all our biases but because without them there would be nothing either to see or to say. A law school colleague told me the other day of a judge who was asked to disqualify himself from a case involving a black plaintiff and a white defendant on the grounds that since he himself was black he would be biased. The judge refused, pointing out that "after all, he had to be one color or the other." The moral is clear and it is my moral: bias is just another word for seeing from a particular perspective as opposed to seeing from no perspective at all, and since seeing from no perspective at all is not a possibility, bias is a condition of consciousness and therefore of action. Of course perspectives differ, as do the actions that follow from them, and one can predict that *PMLA* after blind submission will not be the same journal; but to the extent that it is different, that difference will be the result not of a process that has been depoliticized but of the passage from one political agenda to another.

⌐

I wrote the preceding pages in 1979 and revised them slightly in 1982, and by one of those accidents that attend professional life the collection for which the piece was intended was never published. It is of course now out-of-date, but its out-of-dateness can be seen as an extension of my point, that it is the conditions currently obtaining in the profession rather than any set of independent and abiding criteria that determine what is significant and meritorious. The point still holds, although many of the examples used to illustrate it will now strike readers as either obvious (and hence not worth elaborating) or simply wrong. The examples that are obvious will be so in part because of work subsequently done by me and by others. The reference to the status of books 11 and 12 of *Paradise Lost* has been expanded into a study of the critical history of that poem. The "professional antiprofessionalism" of literary studies has been explored in a series of essays that show it to be a constituent of professional ideology. (To be a professional is to think of oneself as motivated by something larger than marketplace conditions—by, for instance, a regard for justice or for the sanctity of human life or for the best that has been thought and said—even as that larger something is itself given shape and being by the very market conditions it supposedly transcends.) These essays have been vigorously criticized by James Fanto, Drucilla Cornell, Bruce Robbins, Steven Mailloux, Samuel Weber, Martha Nussbaum, David Luban, Gerald Graff, Walter Davis, and others, and the resulting dialogue has done its part (along with the work of Michel Foucault, Pierre Bourdieu, Michel de Certeau, Terry Eagleton, Robert Scholes, Paul Bové, William Cain, John Fekete, Jonathan Arac, and Russell Jacoby) in making the question of professionalism a more familiar and respectable one than it was in 1979.

Other things have changed since 1979. Antinomianism is no longer absent from the *Milton Encyclopedia*, having been added as an entry in a special supplement to the final volume. The Spenser Society is fully established and its activities are ritualized no less than are the activities of the Milton Society, which of course goes on as it always has. (Some things never change.) Romanticism is no longer firmly identified with M. H. Abrams or with anyone else. The canon of greater and lesser works is no longer firmly in place; indeed, it never was except as an assumption continually belied by history. Now the fact of the canon is no longer ever assumed; new challenges emerge every day and have become as orthodox as the orthodoxy they indict.

But perhaps the greatest change is the one that renders the key opposition of the essay—between the timeless realm of literature and the pressures and exigencies of politics—inaccurate as a description of the assumptions prevailing in the profession. There are of course those who still believe that literature is defined by its independence of social and political contexts (a "concrete universal" in Wimsatt's terms), but today the most influential and up-to-date voices are those that proclaim exactly the reverse and argue that the thesis of literary autonomy is itself a political one, part and parcel of an effort by the conservative forces in society to protect traditional values from oppositional discourse. Rather than reflecting, as Ransom would have it, an "order of existence" purer than that which one finds in "actual life," literature in this new (historicist) vision directly and vigorously "participates in historical processes and in the political management of reality" (Howard 25). Moreover, as Louis Montrose observes, if literature is reconceived as a social rather than a merely aesthetic practice, literary criticism, in order to be true to its object, must be rearticulated as a social practice too and no longer be regarded as a merely academic or professional exercise (11–12).

It is with this turn in the argument that one begins to see something strange (or perhaps not so strange): in at least one of its aspects, the new historicism is the old high formalism writ political. I say "in one of its aspects" because the kind of work produced by the two visions is markedly different in many important ways, in the questions asked, in the materials interrogated, in the structures revealed, and in the claims made for the revelation—on one hand the claim to have reaffirmed a distinct and abiding aesthetic realm, on the other the claim to have laid bare the contradictions and fissures that an ideology can never quite manage. Within these differences, however, one thing remains the same: the true and proper view of literature and literary studies defines itself against academic politics, which are seen by the aestheticians as being too much like the politics of "actual life" and by the new historicists as being not enough like the politics of "actual life." The complaint is different, but its target—the procedures and urgencies of professional activity—is the same, and so is the opposition underlying the different complaints, the opposition between an activity in touch with higher values and an activity that has abandoned those values for something base and philistine. Whether the values are generality, detachment, disembodied vision, and moral unity on the one hand or discontinuity, rupture, disintegration, and engagement on the other, the fear is that they will be compromised by the demands that issue from the pressures of careerism, the pressure to publish, to say something new, to get a job, to get promoted, to get recognized, to get famous, and so on. In the context of the aesthetic vision, these pressures are destructive of everything that is truly intellectual; in the context of the historicist vision, they are destructive of everything that is truly (as opposed to merely institutionally) political. Not only do the two visions share an enemy, they share a vocabulary, the vocabulary of transcendence, for in the discourses of both we are urged to free ourselves from parochial imperatives, to realize the true nature of our calling, to participate in that which is *really* and abidingly important. It is just that in one case the important thing is the life of the poetic mind, while in the other it is the struggle against repression and totalization; but that is finally only the difference between two differently pure acts, both of which are pure (or so is the claim) by *not* being the acts of an embedded professional. In 1979 (and in the years before) I was arguing for politics and against transcendence; now I am arguing for politics and against Politics (the new transcendence). As Donne might have said, small change when we are to (materialist) bodies gone.

It would seem then that there is some point to publishing this essay even nine years later (I have heeded, involuntarily, Horace's advice), since its argument is still being resisted, although from another direction. That argument, to rehearse it one last time, is that professional concerns and urgencies, rather than being impediments to responsible (meritorious) action, are determinative of the shape responsible action can take. One does not perform acts of criticism by breaking free of the profession's norms and constraints whether in the service of timeless masterpieces or in the name of political liberation, and whenever the claim to have broken free is made you can be sure that it is underwritten, authorized, and rendered intelligible by the very disciplinary boundaries it purports to have left behind.

Works Cited

Bledstein, B. J. *The Culture of Professionalism.* New York: Norton, 1977.

"Correspondence." *MLA Newsletter* 10, no. 3 (1978): 4–6.

Haskell, Thomas L. *The Emergence of Professional Social Science.* Urbana: University of Illinois Press, 1977.

Howard, Jean. "The New Historicism in Renaissance Studies." *English Literary Renaissance* 16 (1986): 13–43.

Kuhn, Thomas. *The Structure of Scientific Revolutions.* Chicago: University of Chicago Press, 1962.

Larson, M. S. *The Rise of Professionalism.* Berkeley: University of California Press, 1977.

Montrose, Louis. "Renaissance Literary Studies and the Subject of History." *English Literary Renaissance* 16 (1986): 5–12.

Ransom, John Crowe. *The World's Body.* Baton Rouge: Louisiana State University Press, 1938.

Schaefer, William D. "Anonymous Review: A Report from the Executive Director." *MLA Newsletter* 10, no. 2 (1978): 4–6.

Waddington, Raymond. "The Death of Adam: Vision and Voice in Books XI and XII of *Paradise Lost.*" *Modern Philology* 70 (1972): 9–21.

Fish on Blind Submission

Jeffrey Skoblow

To the Editor:

Reading Stanley Fish's guest column in the October *PMLA*, I felt like I was back in the class I took with Fish in graduate school—willing to grant him the premise of his argument but unwilling to grant the conclusion he preferred to draw from that premise.

I agree with him that the notion of intrinsic merit is a myth and that criticism does not operate in a political vacuum. I agree too that the presence of scholarly luminaries in a discussion enhances the status of that discussion and propels it toward deepening insight—both by providing their own luminous insights and by drawing other minds into the discussion. But I don't see that this is an argument against blind submission, at least not a compelling argument. And of course my understanding of the matter rests on my own political agenda. It seems to me that what Fish is trying to do, in his argument, is to extend tenure into the realm of publishing—and that the forces behind such a move are precisely the forces that don't need further support.

I think back on the little composition discussion group Fish organized at Hopkins—weekly gatherings of grad students in his office to knock around strategies for teaching writing. He was just becoming interested in the field of composition pedagogy; it seemed to me (I had been interested in the field for several years and was working in it) that it seemed to him (who apparently had not) to be the next hot issue on the horizon. And reading his *PMLA* piece, I couldn't help but think that the reason he had become interested (more or less suddenly) in these matters—he and other powerful types—was that a growing body of work in the field had begun to come to his attention. But this body of work was being done initially not by scholars like Stanley Fish but by folks like me, and if we had discarded the policy of blind submission, this body of work would have been less likely to see the light of day.

The fact is that as much as Fish may enjoy publishing—even need to publish—and as much as our profession may enjoy and need his work to be published, I need my work published more. The vineyard that he toiled in and that he suggests I toil in is the vineyard of blind submission; if the rules are changed, then my toil becomes less freely rewarded. I lose, and (according to my example in the previous paragraph) he loses, and the profession loses.

Again, I'm not suggesting that there's anything wrong with institutionalized power. Our profession depends on it and grows within it. But our profession depends on and grows by challenges to that power as well—as Fish's own recent interest in canon reformation should make plain to him—and there is something wrong, to my mind, with enhancing the power of those already far more powerful at the expense of those aspiring to join them. His piece strikes me as a bit of scholarly Reaganomics.

The myth of intrinsic merit is only one of the arguments in support of the practice of blind submission. But Fish makes a specious, even cynical leap. To dispense with the myth, as he does, is not therefore fully to undermine the basis for the practice. A stronger argument, which he doesn't address, is the political need of poor laborers like myself. And not only our political need but our indispensable value to the profession.

Just because intrinsic merit is a myth, and just because scholarly luminaries are in *some* sense more important than scholarly novices, is no reason to make the efforts of the lesser known more arduous. Debunking a myth is one thing—bravo!—but weakening the lower rungs of the academic ladder is another. Stanley Fish will get published, the profession will grow, and the examples he cites of important critics rejected under blind submission will be rare in any case.

Reply to Skoblow

Stanley Fish

Jeffrey Skoblow discovers a politics of repression: I argue against blind submission in order to protect my privileged position from the hungry generations that will tread me down were I to let them. The trouble with this point is that I don't (despite my title) argue against blind submission; I argue against a certain *characterization* of blind submission as a policy that will eliminate politics from the process of selection and point out that inevitably that policy will have its own politics. Whether that is a politics I can support depends on the arguments its proponents might make; it is just that one argument *I* won't listen to (although to the ears of others it may be immediately persuasive) is one that claims moral and intellectual purity for a practice that is informed no less than any other by the interests and hopes of particular groups. When Skoblow observes that "to dispense with the myth . . . is not therefore . . . to undermine the basis of the practice" and that to think otherwise would be to make a "specious, even cynical leap," he is right, but that is a leap I precisely do not make, and indeed I would say that it is a leap no one could make since one's account of a practice has no necessary relationship to one's commitment to it. And when Skoblow complains that I do not address the "political needs of poor laborers" like himself, my response is, "But that's *your* job, Jeffrey, since they're your needs." Of course if one of those needs is to be published, it is being met even now, courtesy of the piece that occasioned the response Skoblow has been able to place in the profession's leading journal. (You're welcome, Jeffrey.)

This last point may seem to be made fliply, but I don't intend it that way. It is a response to an assumption informing both Skoblow's letter and James Holstun's,[1] the assumption that the accumulation of "professional capital" is the work of a hoarder who wishes to dine alone at his own table while millions starve. In this age of Foucault, Bourdieu, de Certeau, and company, it is somewhat surprising to meet with such an unsophisticated view of the dynamics of an economy. The truth is that professional capital, like any other, can only grow by being expended; professional critics must put their funds into circulation if they are to see them increase. In the case of this profession, circulation means (among other things) reading for journals and presses, writing recommendations, refereeing for presses and foundations, merchandising one's graduate students, recruiting for one's department, organizing conferences, and appearing at conferences. Each of these activities has its part in the formation of a network of opportunities and obligations that can only grow thicker with each passing year, until finally there is scarcely anything the veteran professional can do that is not of benefit, direct and indirect, to many others.

Note

1. In the same issue of PMLA.

~~~

The Invisible Hand of Peer Review

Stevan J. Harnad

The refereed journal literature needs to be freed from both paper and its costs, but not from peer review, whose "invisible hand" is what maintains its quality. The residual cost of online-only peer review is low enough to be recovered from author-institution-end page charges, covered from institutional subscription savings, thereby vouchsafing a toll-free literature for everyone, everywhere, forever.

Introduction

Human nature being what it is, it cannot be altogether relied upon to police itself. Individual exceptions there may be, but to treat them as the rule would be to underestimate the degree to which our potential unruliness is vetted by collective constraints, implemented formally.

So it is in civic matters, and it is no different in the world of Learned Inquiry. The *"quis costodiet"* problem among scholars has traditionally been solved by means of a quality-control and certification (QC/C) system called "peer review"[1]: The work of specialists is submitted to a qualified adjudicator, an editor, who in turn sends it to fellow-specialists, referees, to seek their advice about whether the paper is potentially publishable, and if so, what further work is required to make it acceptable. The paper is not published until and unless the requisite revision can be and is done to the satisfaction of the editor and referees.

Pitfalls of Peer Policing

Neither the editor nor the referees is infallible. Editors can err in the choice of specialists (indeed, it is well-known among editors that a deliberate bad choice of referees can always ensure that a paper is either accepted or rejected, as preferred); or editors can misinterpret or misapply referees' advice. The referees themselves can fail to be sufficiently expert, informed, conscientious or fair.

Nor are authors always conscientious in accepting the dictates of peer review. (It is likewise well-known among editors that virtually every paper is eventually published, somewhere[2]: There is a quality hierarchy among journals, based on the rigor of their peer review, all the way down to an unrefereed vanity press at the bottom. Persistent authors can work their way down until their paper finds it own level, not without considerable wasting of time and resources along the way, including the editorial office budgets of the journals and the freely given time of the referees, who might find themselves called upon more than once to review the same paper, sometimes unchanged, for several different journals.)

The system is not perfect, but it is what has vouchsafed us our refereed journal literature to date, such as it is, and so far no one has demonstrated any viable alternative to having experts judge the work of their peers, let alone one that is at least as effective in maintaining the quality of the literature as the present imperfect one is.[3]

Self-Policing?

Alternatives have of course been proposed, but to propose is not to demonstrate viability. Most proposals have envisioned weakening the constraints of classical peer review in one way or other. The most radical way being to do away with it altogether: Let authors police themselves; let every submission be published, and let the reader decide what is to be taken seriously. This would amount to discarding the current hierarchical filter—both its active influence, in directing revision, and its ranking of quality and reliability to guide the reader trying to navigate the ever-swelling literature.[4]

There is a way to test our intuitions about the merits of this sort of proposal a priori, using a specialist domain that is somewhat more urgent and immediate than abstract "learned inquiry"; if we are not prepared to generalize this intuitive test's verdict to scholarly/scientific research in general, we really need to ask ourselves how seriously we take the acquisition of knowledge: If someone near and dear to you were ill with a serious but potentially treatable disease, would you prefer to have them treated on the basis of the refereed medical literature or on the basis of an unfiltered free-for-all where the distinction between reliable expertise and ignorance, competence or charlatanism is left entirely to the reader, on a paper by paper basis?

A variant on this scenario is currently being tested by the *British Medical Journal*,[5] but instead of entrusting entirely to the reader the quality control function performed by the referee in classical peer review, this variant, taking a cue from some of the developments and goings-on on both the Internet and Network TV chat-shows, plans to publicly post submitted papers unrefereed on the Web and to invite any reader to submit a commentary; these commentaries will then be used in lieu of referee reports as a basis for deciding on formal publication.

Expert Opinion or Opinion Poll?

Is this peer review? Well, it is not clear whether the self-appointed commentators will be qualified specialists (or how that is to be ascertained). The expert population in any given specialty is a scarce resource, already overharvested by classical peer review, so one wonders who would have the time or inclination to add journeyman commentary services to this load on their own initiative, particularly once it is no longer a rare novelty, and the entire raw, unpoliced literature is routinely appearing in this form first. Are those who have nothing more pressing to do with their time than this really the ones we want to trust to perform such a critical QC/C function for us all?

And is the remedy for the possibility of bias or incompetence in referee-selection on the part of editors really to throw selectivity to the winds, and let referees pick themselves? Considering all that hangs on being published in refereed journals, it does not take much imagination to think of ways authors could manipulate such a public-polling system to their own advantage, human nature being what it is.

Peer Commentary vs. Peer Review

And is peer commentary (even if we can settle the vexed "peer" question) really peer review? Will I say publicly about someone who might be refereeing my next grant application or tenure review what I really think are the flaws of his latest raw manuscript? (Should we then be publishing our names alongside our votes in civic elections too, without fear or favor?) Will I put into a public commentary—alongside who knows how many other such commentaries, to be put to who knows what use by who knows whom—the time and effort that I would put into a referee report for an editor I know to be turning specifically to me and a few other specialists for our expertise on a specific paper?

If there is anyone on this planet who is in a position to attest to the functional difference between peer review and peer commentary,[6] it is surely the author of the present article, who has been umpiring a peer reviewed paper journal of Open Peer Commentary, *Behavioral and Brain Sciences* (BBS)[7] published by Cambridge University Press[8] for over two decades,[9] as well as a brave new online-only journal of Open Peer Commentary, likewise peer reviewed (*Psycoloquy*,[10] sponsored by the American Psychological Association),[11] which entered its second decade with the millennium.

Both journals are rigorously refereed; only those papers that have successfully passed through the peer review filter go on to run the gauntlet of open peer commentary, an extremely powerful and important *supplement* to peer review, but certainly no *substitute* for it. Indeed, no one but the editor sees [or should have to see] the population of raw, unrefereed submissions, consisting of some manuscripts that are eventually destined to be revised and accepted after peer review, but also (with a journal like BBS, having a 75 percent rejection rate) many manuscripts not destined to appear in that particular journal at all. Referee reports, some written for my eyes only, all written for at most the author and fellow referees, are nothing like public commentaries for the eyes of the entire learned community, and vice versa. Nor do 75 percent of the submissions justify soliciting public commentary, or at least not commentary at the BBS level of the hierarchy.

It has been suggested that in fields such as physics, where the rejection rate is lower (perhaps in part because the authors are more disciplined and realistic in their initial choice of target journal, rather than trying their luck from the top down), the difference between the unrefereed preprint literature and the refereed reprint literature may not be that great; hence one is fairly safe using the unrefereed drafts, and perhaps the refereeing could be jettisoned altogether.

Successful Test-Site in Los Alamos

Support for this possibility has been adduced from the remarkable success of the NSF/DOE-supported Los Alamos Physics Archive,[12] a free, public repository for a growing proportion of the current physics literature, with over 25,000 new papers annually and 35,000 users daily. Most papers are initially deposited as unrefereed preprints, and for some (no one knows how many), their authors never bother replacing them with the final revised draft that is accepted for publication.[13] Yet Los Alamos is actively used and cited by the physics community.[14]

Is this really evidence that peer review is not indispensable after all? Hardly, for the "Invisible Hand" of peer review is still there, exerting its civilizing influence: Just about every paper deposited in Los Alamos is also destined for a peer reviewed journal; the author knows it will be answerable to the editors and referees. That certainly constrains how it is written in the first place. Remove that invisible constraint—let the authors be answerable to no one but the general users of the Archive (or even its self-appointed "commentators")—and watch human nature take its natural course, standards eroding as the Archive devolves toward the canonical state of unconstrained postings: the free-for-all chat-groups of Usenet,[15] that Global Graffiti Board for Trivial Pursuit—until someone reinvents peer review and quality control.

A Subversive Proposal

Now it is no secret that I am a strong advocate of a free literature along the lines of Los Alamos.[16] How are we to reconcile the conservative things I've said about QC/C here with the radical things I've advocated elsewhere about public author archiving?[17]

The answer is very simple. The current cost of the refereed paper journal literature is paid for by Subscription, Site License, and Pay-Per-View (S/L/P). Both the medium (paper) and the method of cost-recovery (S/L/P) share the feature that they block access to the refereed literature, whereas the authors, who contribute their papers for free, would infinitely prefer free, universal access to their work.

The optimal (and inevitable) solution is an online-only refereed journal literature, which will be much less costly (less than $\frac{1}{3}$ of the current price per page) once it is paper-free[18] and resides in open archives[19] but still not entirely cost-free, because the peer review (and editing) still needs to be paid for.[20] If those residual QC/C costs are paid at the author-institution-end (not out of the author's pocket, of course, but out of institutional publication funds redirected from $\frac{1}{3}$ of the $\frac{2}{3}$ annual institutional savings from serial S/L/P cancellations), the dividend will be that the papers are all accessible for free for all (via interoperable open archives such as CogPrints[21]—integrated seamlessly into a single global "virtual" archive, mirrored worldwide, which will then have an unrefereed preprint sector and a refereed, published, reprint sector, tagged by journal name). Journal publisher will continue to provide and be paid for their QC/C while the public archive will serve as the "front end" for both journal submissions (tagged "unrefereed preprints") and published articles (tagged "refereed reprints [plus journal name, etc.]").[22]

Streamlining Peer Review for the Airwaves

Peer review is medium-independent, but the online-only medium will make it possible for journals to implement not only more cheaply and efficiently, but also more equitably and effectively than was possible in paper, through subtle variants of the very means I have criticized[23]: Papers will be submitted in electronic form, and archived on the Web (in hidden referee-only sites, or publicly, in open-archive preprint sectors, depending on the author's preferences). Referees need no longer be mailed hard copies; they will access the submissions from the Web.[24]

To distribute the load among referees more equitably (and perhaps also to protect editors from themselves), the journal editor can formally approach a much larger population of selected, qualified experts about relevant papers they are invited to referee if they have the time and inclination. Referee reports can be e-mailed or deposited directly through a password-controlled Web interface. Accepted final drafts can be edited and marked up online, and the final draft can then be deposited in the public Archive for all, superseding the preprint.

Galactic Hitch-hiking, PostGutenberg

Referee reports can be revised, published, and linked to the published article as commentaries if the referee wishes; so can author rebuttals. And further commentaries, both refereed and unrefereed, can be archived and linked to the published article, along with author responses. Nor is there any reason to rule out postpublication author updates and revisions of the original article—2nd and 3rd editions, both unrefereed and refereed. Learned Inquiry, as I have had occasion to write before[25] is a continuum; reports of its findings—informal and formal, unrefereed and refereed—are milestones, not gravestones; as such, they need only be reliably sign-posted. The discerning hitch-hiker in the PostGutenberg Galaxy can take care of the rest.[26]

Overall, the dissemination of learned research, once we have attained the optimal and inevitable state described here, will be substantially accelerated, universally accessible, and incomparably more interactive in the age of Scholarly Skywriting than it was in our own pedestrian, papyrocentric one; Learned Inquiry itself—and hence all of society—will be the chief beneficiary.

Notes

1. Stevan J. Harnad, "Rational Disagreement in Peer Review," *Science, Technology and Human Values* 10 (1985): 55–62.

2. Stephen Lock, *A Difficult Balance: Editorial Peer Review in Medicine* (Philadelphia: ISI Press, 1986) and Stevan J. Harnad, "Policing the Paper Chase," *Nature* 322 (1986): 24–25, a review of Stephen Lock, *A Difficult Balance.*

3. Stevan J. Harnad, ed., *Peer Commentary on Peer Review: A Case Study in Scientific Quality Control* (New York: Cambridge University Press, 1982).

4. S. Hitchcock, L. Carr, Z. Jiao, D. Bergmark, W. Hall, C. Lagoze, and S. Harnad, "Developing Services for Open Eprint Archives: Globalisation, Integration and the Impact of Links" (Proceedings of the 5th ACM Conference on Digital Libraries, San Antonio, Texas, June 2000). URL: <http://www.cogsci.soton.ac.uk/~harnad/Papers/Harnad/harnad00.acm.htm>

5. *British Medical Journal.* URL: <http://www.bmj.com/cgi/shtml/misc/peer/index.shtml>

6. See Harnad, ed., *Peer Commentary on Peer Review* and Stevan J. Harnad, "Commentaries, Opinions and the Growth of Scientific Knowledge," *American Psychologist* 39 (1984): 1497–98.

7. *Behavioral and Brain Sciences* (BBS). URL: <http://www.cogsci.soton.ac.uk/bbs/>

8. *Cambridge University Press.* URL: <http://www.journals.cup.org/>

9. Stevan J. Harnad, "Creative Disagreement," *Sciences* 19 (1979): 18–20.

10. *Psyoloquy.* URL: <http://www.cogsci.soton.ac.uk/cgi/psyc/newpsy>

11. *American Psychological Association.* URL: <http://www.apa.org/>

12. *Los Alamos Physics Archive.* URL: <http://xxx.lanl.gov/>

13. S. Hitchcock et al., "Developing Services for Open Eprint Archives," and L. Carr, S. Hitchcock, W. Hall, and S. Harnad, "A Usage Based Analysis of CoRR," *ACM SIGDOC Journal of Computer Documentation* (May 2000), a commentary on Joseph Y. Halpern, "CoRR: a Computing Research Repository." URL: <http://www.cogsci.soton.ac.uk/~harnad/Papers/harnad/harnad00.halpern.htm>

14. Paul Ginsparg, "First Steps Towards Electronic Research Communication," *Computers in Physics* 8, no. 4 (August 1994): 390–96. URL: <http://xxx.lanl.gov/blurb.>; Paul Ginsparg, "Winners and Losers in the Global Research Village" (invited contribution, UNESCO Conference HQ, Paris, February 19–23, 1996). URL: <http://xxx.lanl.gov/blurb/pg96unesco.html>; and G. K. Youngen, "Citation Patterns to Traditional and Electronic Preprints in the Published Literature," *College and Research Libraries* 59, no. 5 (1998): 448–56. URL: <http://www.physics.uiuc.edu/library/preprint.html>

15. *The Complete Reference to Usenet Newsgroups,* TILE.NET/NEWS. URL: <http://tile.net/news/listed.html>

16. Ann Okerson and James J. O'Donnell, eds., *Scholarly Journals at the Crossroads: A Subversive Proposal for Electronic Publishing* (Washington, D.C.: Office of Scientific and Academic Publishing, Association of Research Libraries, 1995). URL: <http://www.arl.org/scomm/subversive/>

17. Stevan J. Harnad, "For Whom the Gate Tolls? Free the Online-Only Refereed Literature," *American Scientist Forum* (1998). URL: <http://www.cogsci.soton .ac.uk/~harnad/amlet.html>; Stevan J. Harnad, "On-Line Journals and Financial Fire-Walls," *Nature* 395, no. 6698 (1998): 127–28. URL: <http://www.cogsci.soton .ac.uk/~harnad/nature.html>; and Stevan J. Harnad, "Free at Last: The Future of Peer-Reviewed Journals," *D-Lib Magazine* 5, no. 12 (December 1999). URL: <http://www.dlib.org/dlib/december99/12harnad.html>

18. *Archives of SEPTEMBER98-FORUM@LISTSERVER.SIGMAXI*, American Scientist Forum (September 1998). URL: <http://amsci-forum.amsci.org/archives/ september98-forum.html>

19. *The Open Archives Initiative*. URL: <http://www.openarchives.org/>

20. A. M. Odlyzko, "The Economics of Electronic Journals," in *Technology and Scholarly Communication*, ed. Richard Ekman and Richard E. Quandt (Berkeley: University of California Press, 1999). URL: <http://www.research.att.com/~amo/doc/ economics.journals.txt>

21. *CogPrints*. URL: <http://cogprints.soton.ac.uk/>

22. *Eprints.org*. URL: <http://www.eprints.org/>

23. Stevan J. Harnad, "Implementing Peer Review on the Net: Scientific Quality Control in Scholarly Electronic Journals," in *Scholarly Publishing: The Electronic Frontier*, ed. Robin P. Peek and Gregory B. Newby (Cambridge, Mass.: MIT Press, 1996), 103–18. URL: <http://www.cogsci,soton.ac.uk/~harnad/Papers/Harnad/harnad96 .peer.review.html> and Stevan J. Harnad, "Learned Inquiry and the Net: The Role of Peer Review, Peer Commentary and Copyright," *Learned Publishing* 11, no. 4 (1997): 283–92. URL: <http://www.cogsci.soton.ac.uk/~harnad/Papers/Harnad/harnad98 .toronto.learnedpub.html>. A short version of this paper appeared in *Antiquity* 71 (1997): 1042–48. Excerpts also appeared in the University of Toronto Bulletin: 51 (6) P. 12. URL: <http://citd.scar.utoronto.a/Epub/talks/Hardad_Snider.html>

24. *Using the Web for Peer Review and Publication of Scientific Journals*. URL: <http://www.consecol.org/Journal/consortium.html>

25. Stevan J. Harnad, "Scholarly Skywriting and the Prepublication Continuum of Scientific Inquiry," *Psychological Science* 1 (1990): 342–43. URL: <http://www. cogsci.soton.ac.uk/~harnad/Papers/Harnad/harnad90.skywriting.html>

26. Stevan J. Harnad, "Post-Gutenberg Galaxy: The Fourth Revolution in the Means of Production of Knowledge," *Public-Access Computer Systems Review* 2, no. 1 (1991): 39–53. URL: <http://www.cogsci.soton.ac.uk/~harnad/Papers/ Harnad/harnad91.postgutenberg.html>

Index

203, 225–27; media demand for quick information, 3–4; no intrinsic merit, 53–55, 69, 225, 231–34; no objective values, 113; spotting duplication, 61; star authors, 55, 56; ubiquity of bias, 51–53, 69; values besides impartiality, 166, 170

book reviews: affected by personal factors, 113; differ from reviews of restaurants, films, concerts, 115; exception to peer review: generally accepted as submitted, 11, 110–11; no justifications included for judgments on style and organization, 111–12; no rewards for, 119; and prestige publishers, 116–17; suggestions for improving, 118–19; supporting evidence not required, 112; three purposes of, 115–16

Booth, Stephen, 219

Bowers, Fredson, 219

British Medical Journal, 237

Byrne, Edward, 48, 49

Cahn, Steven M., 113

Campanario, Juan-Miguel, 90–92

Castaneda, Hector-Neri, 112

Ceci, Stephen J., 39–41, 42, 126, 226

certification, peer review as system of, 1, 165, 180–81, 183, 192

Chichilnisky, Graciella, 83

Citation Classics, 90, 91

CogPrints, 239

conservatism: affects political structure of profession, 84; belief perseverance studies, 42; as characteristic of peer reviewing, 85; evidential asymmetry of new and old theories, 88–89; and falsifiability, 84–85; hampers growth of knowledge, 83. *See also* epistemic conservatism, principle of

Crane, Dana, 39

Damrosch, David, 49

Davidoff, Frank, 90

De George, Richard T., 58–59

Donellan, Keith, 94

double jeopardy refereeing, 11, 33n22, 172

Douglas-Wilson, Ian, 92

Dworkin, Gerald, 110, 116, 118

Eble, Kenneth, 18

editor's responsibility, 58–59; may choose reviewers whose positions are known, 169; must indicate whether blind review was used, 171; to presses, 174–75

electronic publishing, advantages of: cost, 140–41; distribution, 142; improves content, 142–43; overcomes problems of proliferation, 142; research tools, 143; searchability, 143; speed, 141; varies length of works, 143

electronic publishing, disadvantages of: archiving, 143; inundation, 143; keeping track of versions, 143; lack of discipline, 139–40, 189n9

electronic publishing, peer review in, 27, 235–40; closed review, open commentary, 151–52; open peer review, 149–51; Paul Ginsparg's system, 146; public peer review, 152–53

electronic work and tenure cases, 11, 121–23, 132–34, 154–55

employment-at-will, 58, 166

epistemic conservatism (EC), principle of: formulation of, 86, 100–101; justification for, 87; Millian arguments for rejecting, 98–100

epistemic paternalism, 29

error, false positive versus false negative, 203

Ethics (journal), 109, 110

About the Author

David Shatz is professor of philosophy at Yeshiva University. He has published articles and reviews in the fields of epistemology, free will, philosophy of religion, medical ethics, medieval Jewish philosophy, and contemporary Jewish philosophy. Besides authoring the present volume, he has edited or coedited nine other books, including *Contemporary Philosophy of Religion*; *Definitions and Definability*; *Philosophy and Faith*; and *Mind, Body, and Judaism*. He is also the editor of *The Torah u-Madda Journal*, a journal devoted to the interaction between Judaism and general culture. He received his B.A. from Yeshiva University, graduating as valedictorian, and earned his Ph.D. with distinction from Columbia University.